The Science Fiction of
H.G. WELLS

Science-Fiction Writers

ROBERT SCHOLES, GENERAL EDITOR

The Science Fiction of
H.G. WELLS
Frank McConnell

OXFORD UNIVERSITY PRESS
Oxford New York Toronto Melbourne
1981

OXFORD UNIVERSITY PRESS

Oxford   London   Glasgow
New York   Toronto   Melbourne   Wellington
Nairobi   Dar es Salaam   Cape Town
Kuala Lumpur   Singapore   Jakarta   Hong Kong   Tokyo
Delhi   Bombay   Calcutta   Madras   Karachi

Library of Congress Cataloging in Publication Data

McConnell, Frank D   1942–
    The science fiction of H. G. Wells.

    (Science fiction writers series)
        1. Wells, Herbert George, 1866–1946
—Criticism and interpretation.
I. Title. II. Series.
PR5777.M3   1981   823'.912   80-19675
ISBN 0-19-502811-2
ISBN 0-19-502812-0 pbk.

Grateful acknowledgment is given to Jupiter Books for
permission to reprint two photographs of Wells from
H. G. Wells: A Pictorial Biography, by Frank Wells,
1977. Both pictures are from a private collection.

Printed in the United States of America

For
Carolyn,
Christopher,
and Kathryn

EDITOR'S FOREWORD

For the first eight decades of this century critics of fiction have reserved their highest praises for novels and stories that emphasize individual psychology in characterization, unique stylistic nuances in language, and plausibility in the events presented. It is an interesting feature of literary history that during this same period of time a body of fiction has flourished which privileges the type over the individual, the idea over the word, and the unexpected over the plausible event. This body of work, which has come to be called—with only partial appropriateness—"science" fiction, has had some recognition from serious critics but still hovers between genuine acceptance and total dismissal in literary circles.

Schools now offer courses in science fiction—either because one zealous teacher insists upon it, or because "the kids read that stuff." But it is rare to hear of works of science fiction integrated into "regular" courses in modern literature. The major reason for this is that as long as the dominant criteria are believed to hold for *all* fiction, science fiction will be found inferior: deficient in psychological depth, in verbal nuance, and in plausibility of event. What is needed is a criticism serious in its standards and its concern for literary value but willing to take seriously a literature based on ideas, types, and events beyond ordinary experience.

The *Science-Fiction Writers* series of critical volumes is an attempt to provide that sort of criticism. In designing the series we have selected a number of authors whose body of work has proved substantial, durable, and influential, and we have asked an appropriate critic to make a book-length study of the work of each author selected, taking that author seriously enough to be critical and critically enough to be serious.

In each volume we will include a general view of the author's life and work, critical interpretations of his or her major contributions to the field of science fiction, and a biographical apparatus that will make these volumes useful as a reference tool. The format of each book will thus be similar. But because the writers to be considered have had careers of different shapes, and because our critics are all individuals who have earned the right to their own interpretive emphases, each book will take its own shape within the limits of the general format. Above all, each volume will express the critical views of its author rather than some predetermined party line.

In the present volume Frank D. McConnell presents an introduction to the writer whose work has done more to shape the whole field of science fiction than that of any other person. H. G. Wells is a very special case as a science-fiction writer. First of all, he wrote before the field of fiction had been clearly divided into "serious" and "popular" works, with science fiction relegated to the "popular" sphere. And then Wells worked both sides of the division between the realistic novel and the speculative romance. His "scientific romances," as he called them, were different from his novels of contemporary life in that they assumed possibilities (time travel, invisibility) contrary to the facts of ordinary existence, but they used science to make these impossibilities plausible, and they described the romance world in the same realistic manner Wells had developed for his ordinary novels. The result was a series of short novels that have remained steadily in print for nearly a century while much of Wells's more realistic work has disappeared from the publishers' lists.

These works were indeed popular and have remained so, but they were more than that. They attracted the attention and the praise of writers like Yevgeny Zayatin in Russia and Jorge Luis Borges in Argentina, as well as that of the American impresario of pulp science fiction, Hugo Gernsbach. However, the literary critics, with a few honorable exceptions like Bernard Bergonzi, have remained reluctant to take Wells's scientific romances seriously as literature.

This, of course, is precisely what Frank D. McConnell has done in this book. Himself an expert in British literature of the nineteenth century (and the author of books on romantic poetry, and mythmaking) McConnell locates Wells in the intellectual life of his time and argues the case for the importance of the scientific romances *as literature*. This is perhaps not a case one would wish to make for all good science fiction; some of it may be good as something other than literature. But it is a case that can be made for Wells, as McConnell demonstrates.

It is, however, not exactly the case Wells would have made for himself. In his celebrated dispute with Henry James, Wells argued in favor of a fiction of ideas and social commitment, while James made the Art of the novel (with a capital A) his cause. The triumph of modernism in fiction made James the apparent victor in this dispute. In the work of James Joyce, Virginia Woolf, and others, a fiction of formal elegance and psychological depth established its dominance, relegating Wells's fiction of ideas and social commitment to the status of a secondary or "popular" literature.

Meanwhile, Wells's own admittedly popular and entertaining scientific romances have triumphed over the works Wells himself considered serious literature. Perhaps everyone was wrong in some way that is only becoming apparent to us now, as science fiction is breaking out of the ghetto of "popularity." McConnell's study of the literary quality of Wells's science fiction should help us to answer that question. Meanwhile, it will also serve—as it is meant to serve—as an introduction to the work of a science-fiction writer whose contribution to the field, because it was so early, will never be equaled.

August 1980   R.S.

ACKNOWLEDGMENTS

The research for this book was begun during my stay at the Woodrow Wilson International Center for Scholars in Washington, D.C. It is a pleasure again to express my gratitude to that extraordinary institution, and to its administrators. I am also grateful to the Northwestern University Office of Research and Sponsored Programs for a grant that aided in the completion of the manuscript.

Robert Scholes made some important suggestions that, I think, have improved the quality of the book. John Wright, as always, has been infallible in his support. And Kim Lewis of Oxford Press did a splendid job of editing. The students in my Science Fiction class at Northwestern have been an ideal, perceptive, and responsive audience for much of what is written here. And the people to whom the book is dedicated have, as always, made the whole enterprise worthwhile.

Evanston, Illinois   F.M.
August 1980

CONTENTS

The Science Fiction of
H.G. WELLS

1

"A VERY ORDINARY BRAIN"

H. G. Wells has been called the father, the one authentic genius, even the Shakespeare of science fiction. All these judgments can be called into question. But even today, when science fiction is attracting more first-rate writers than ever and is taken more seriously by "official" literary critics than ever, the burden of proof is still on the person who wants to question such judgments, not the one who affirms them. Wells's first novel, *The Time Machine* (1895), was an immediate success. Between 1895 and 1914 he produced, among many other works, a series of "scientific romances" that, by the outbreak of the First World War, had helped to make him one of the best-selling and most controversial writers of his time. And the influence of those novels and stories on what came to be called "science fiction" continues to be nothing less than gigantic.

If science fiction is, as some defenders argue, mainly important as technological prophecy, Wells's record is impressive. *The Time Machine* can be read, as we shall see, as a prophecy of the effects of rampant industrialization on that class conflict which was already, in the nineteenth century, a social powder keg. Disraeli had warned—and Marx had demonstrated—that the industrialized state was in danger of becoming two nations, the rich and the poor; but the real horror, Wells warns, is that they might become two races, mutually uncomprehending and murderously divided. In *The War of*

3

the Worlds (1898) he hinted at, and in later stories fully anticipated, the disastrous innovations the discovery of flight could
bring to the business of warfare. In When the Sleeper Wakes
(1899) he predicted a future society in which devices very like
video cassettes have replaced printed books, and an ignorant
populace is force-fed censored news through things he calls
"Babble Machines." In "The Land Ironclads" (1903) he predicted the use of armored tanks in war (he later got involved
in a long and futile lawsuit, claiming royalties for the "invention" of the tank). Long before "ecology" became a fashionable phrase and concern, Wells was using it as one of the common concepts of his utopias. And in The World Set Free
(1914)—perhaps his most celebrated anticipation—he invented the phrase "atomic bomb," and detailed with some accuracy the apocalyptic power of chain reaction weapons or, in
his phrase, "continuing explosives."

But there are other ideas of science fiction beyond the
weatherman's standard of accurate forecasting. Some very
good science-fiction writers never do manage a prophecy that
later history ratifies. And the rest, Wells included, guess
wrong at least as often as they guess right. We can say that
science fiction matters not just because of the occasional random prediction of technological innovation, but because it
seriously examines the implications of scientific and technological development as a whole for our lives, and our sense of
the nature and goals of our lives. "The history of science,"
write Robert Scholes and Eric S. Rabkin in their book, Science
Fiction, "is also the history of humanity's changing attitudes
toward space and time. It is the history of our growing understanding of the universe and the position of our species in that
universe." Science fiction, then, like science itself, is a facet of
the history of the human spirit. It is an authentic fiction for
our time, whose visionary tales are not so much visions of
"things to come" as versions of things as they are right now,
though seen against the immense backdrops of geological
time and sidereal space (which are, after all, the true stage on
which the human drama is played).

This is a more or less sociological definition of the genre,
and under its terms too, Wells is not only primary but preemi-

nent. *The Island of Doctor Moreau* (1896) and *The Invisible Man* (1897) are versions, respectively horrible and tragicomic, of the conflict between knowledge and goodness, what less perceptive minds than Wells's have cheapened into the "mad scientist" theme. With penetrating insight into the problems besetting technology not only in his own time but in ours, Wells asks: though we demonstrably can do almost anything we want to do, may we do anything we want or is there still, in some deep sense, such a thing as Forbidden Knowledge? This is, of course, the theme of Mary Shelley's *Frankenstein* (1818), which also has claims to being the "first" novel of science fiction. But Wells's treatment, though no subtler or "greater" than Mary Shelley's, takes on added force simply by being embedded in the giant fabric of his lifelong discussion of human science, human morality, and their conflict. Once again in *The War of the Worlds* and *The First Men in the Moon* (1901) he imagined extraterrestrial aliens who are not just the picturesque bug-eyed bogeymen of later science fiction at its simplest, but projections of the possible deformity of the human species if present trends toward bloodless intellectualism, the fissure of heart and head, were to continue. And beginning with *The Food of the Gods* (1904) and *A Modern Utopia* (1905), and continuing nearly to the end of his life, he gave us a series of novels of more and more homiletic, more and more strenuous and urgent social analysis and prophecy whose explicit aim was to change the course of history, bringing human science into congruity with human moral development and thereby saving the world from a second, total, perhaps final world war.

These later utopias are not, by any means, his best books. Most of them are long out of print, and they are not often discussed in histories of science fiction. But that may be a mistake. Flawed though they are, they are flawed honorably. Wells's passion for social reform could overweigh his instincts as a storyteller; his desire to convince the reader could get in the way of his ability to keep the reader reading. But if all these later books in part (and some of them throughout) are muscle-bound, it is because they are strong. And if we wish to regard science fiction seriously as a sociological form, we have to remember that Wells, more than any other writer in the genre, tried to harness the powers of narrative to the great tasks of social change and man's salvation.

There is a third way of describing science fiction. It is the most obvious way, and includes within itself the possibilities of technological forecasting and social analysis, though it is the last way critics have come to regard the form. This is the view of science fiction as, simply, literary art. It is prophecy, it is portent, and more. But above all it is *fiction*, and it satisfies our elementary, permanent human need to be told a story no less and no differently than other kinds of fiction.

There are dangers to taking this view. The science-fiction fan, with his guilty, gleeful secret passion for E. E. Smith's *The Skylark of Space* and his copy of the latest *Galaxy* or *Analog* clutched under his arm, may fear to confront the chilly scorn of the literary intellectual who will overwhelm him with comparisons of his treasures to Henry James or James Joyce and leave him groveling in the admission that what he loves so much is shoddy and second-rate. And the literary intellectual—for he, too, has his fears—may worry that if he admits, even grudgingly, the brilliance of some works of science fiction he will throw open the Temple of Art to desecration by the barbarians, betray its holy things into the hands of the irresponsible.

I don't think I exaggerate. There are still people, on both sides of the great divide, who actually think this way; though, thankfully, their number diminishes every year; the only "great divide" there is between science fiction and "serious" literature is in the heads of the people who *think* it is there. A genre that can boast of writers like Jules Verne, Olaf Stapledon, John Wyndham, Robert Heinlein, Arthur C. Clarke, Isaac Asimov, Walter Miller, and Ursula K. Le Guin need not fear comparison with any but the most austere and, therefore, irrelevant standards of greatness. (No science-fiction writer has produced a work to equal Joyce's *Ulysses:* nor has anyone else.)

My main concern in this book is with the art of Wells's science fiction. And, when he was writing at the top of his form, that is great art indeed. Through a combination of historical moment and personal strategy, he transformed the scientific and social controversy of his time into an extended fable of apocalypse and terror that is sometimes grim and sometimes ennobling in its vision of the human condition, but always compelling and crafted with immense skill. And it is in terms of this artistry that he looms largest over the later development of science fiction. Olaf Stapledon, the central figure of British science fiction after Wells, said of his debt to Wells, "A man does not record his debt to the air he breathes." James Gunn, in his recent and admirable history of the form, *Alternate Worlds,* makes a list of fourteen classic themes, with references to the major books or stories employing that theme. All but two major themes include a citation from a work of Wells's and that usually the earliest. (The omission of Wells from those two is debatable.)

Nevertheless, there are some preliminary qualifications to be made about Wells and science fiction. The first, to which I have already alluded, is that Wells didn't really *write* "science fiction." The term was invented by Hugo Gernsback, who founded *Amazing Stories* in 1926. By that time Wells's output of "scientific romances" had dwindled to an occasional heavily sociological utopian novel every few years. (Of course, this was "dwindling" only for a man like Wells, who between 1895 and 1946 wrote an average of three books a year.)

This qualification is a version, perhaps, of the old cliché that Plato was no Platonist, Marx no Marxist. But it makes a difference. Because the form had not been named yet, it was freer to associate itself with the great mainstream tradition of storytelling. After Gernsback named science fiction, making it both a suburb and a ghetto of fiction itself, it would be many years before a writer in the field would unblushingly admit a sense of his own continuity with the works of Lucan, Rabelais, Swift, and Voltaire. Wells could, and often did, avow this debt.

The second qualification is implicit in the first. Those works of Wells that exercise the greatest influence on later science fiction were all written during the first twenty years of his fifty-year career as a writer and make up only a small percentage of his total output. Indeed, if you had asked the average English reader during the period of Wells's most unalloyed success and fame, who H. G. Wells was, the answer would probably have been that he was the author of the massive, two-volume *Outline of History* (1920), the lengthy novel of ideas *The World of William Clissold* (1926), or the compendium *The Science of Life: A Summary of Contemporary Knowledge about Life and Its Possibilities* (1930).

The titles alone of the first and third of these books indicate how ambitious, or arrogant, they and their author are. The H. G. Wells who was a constant and noisy presence throughout the twenties and thirties, and whom many men who grew up during those years remembered as a formative influence on their lives, was not primarily the author of the early scientific romances. He was a self-appointed prophet, a scrappy, self-assertive, pudgy little Londoner who claimed no less a mission than that of interpreting the human race to itself. What is the relation between this later and the earlier Wells? For an answer, let us look to Wells near the last.

In 1939 things were out of control, falling the way we fall in nightmares into a war that, everyone knew, would be even more ferocious, even more cataclysmic, even more *total* than the First World War. The thirties—called by poet W. H. Auden a "low dishonest decade"—had begun in worldwide economic collapse and with the hope of social revolution. The decade was ending in worldwide conflagration and despair. And Wells, seventy-three years old, was ill and tired. Sir Ernest Barker records seeing him sitting alone at a reception and asking how he was.

> "Poorly, Barker, poorly," he said. I asked him what he was doing. "Writing my epitaph." I asked him what it was. "Quite short," he said, "just this—God damn you all: I told you so."

To understand how bitter, how funny, and how arrogant that epitaph really is, is to understand Wells. He *was* a bitter, funny, arrogant man. But he was something else too: a writer of genius who took it upon himself, early in his long career, to represent the interest of the human race before the tribunal of science; a self-taught, ferocious intellectual who dedicated giant energy to waking up men and women to their perilous position, and their chances for survival, in a hostile, uncaring universe. And if his prescriptions for world health could be ludicrous and impractical as often as they were cogent and prophetic, he was admirably brave even at his silliest—and admirably honest in admitting that he had been silly.

In *The Fate of Homo Sapiens* (1939—the same year he composed his "epitaph") he describes himself: "Put favorably, mine is a very direct mind; put unfavorably, it is unsubtle," he says. And again, "I *hammer* at my main ideas, and this is an offense to delicate-minded people. If a door is not open I say it is shut, and I am impatient with the suggestion of worldly wisdom that it may be possible to wangle a way round." This is the same kind of insistent self-effacement that produced the subtitle of his 1934 *Experiment in Autobiography: Discoveries and Conclusions of a Very Ordinary Brain—Since 1866.* And it is disingenuous. Any man who argues so strenuously that he is unsubtle is being subtler, perhaps, than he wants to admit. Wells was a complicated and troubled man who held (as most complicated and trouble people do) that simplicity and resolute cheerfulness are supreme virtues.

In this he was a true son of his age. The Victorian Era, we learn more and more, was a period of murderous psychological and political tensions kept just below the surface of consciousness by an energetic (and, at best, ironic) assertion of the will. Through an act of will, the hero of Alfred, Lord Tennyson's "Locksley Hall" (1842) overcomes his romantic melancholy in order to commit himself to the infinite promise of a new industrial and technological age:

> Not in vain the distance beacons. Forward, forward let us
> range,
> Let the great world spin for ever down the ringing grooves
> of change.

That was written twenty-four years before Wells was born. But Wells throughout his life was a great believer in Will (the capital was put there by the Victorian Era). The word and the concept appear in his fiction and his nonfiction from nearly the beginning to nearly the end of his career. But the "ringing grooves of change" led in directions Tennyson could not have imagined in 1842. Twenty years *after* Wells was born the poet revised that optimistic vision, in terms that have much to do with Wells's and his century's intellectual development. The promise of an eternally improving human lot has disappeared, and what is left in its place is a grim new idea of the chanciness, the immitigable pain of human life. In "Locksley Hall Sixty Years Later," Tennyson asks,

> Is there evil but on earth? or pain in every peopled sphere?
> Well, be grateful for the sounding watchword "Evolution"
>   here,
>
> Evolution ever climbing after some ideal good,
> And Reversion ever dragging Evolution in the mud.

The "sounding watchword 'Evolution,' " was a watchword indeed during the second half of the nineteenth century. In 1859 a quiet, almost pathologically shy naturalist named Charles Darwin published a book with the daunting title *On the Origin of Species by Means of Natural Selection*, and the world was never the same. If Darwin was right (and even in the earliest, most violent attacks upon him, the sense is strong that he probably was), then humankind was demoted. No longer lord of the world, a special creation with a special mission in history, it was simply a random and temporarily successful adaptation of the primal world-stuff in its ceaseless blind struggle to survive. And it was, on the cosmic scale of things, a temporary and perishable commodity.

Wells, then, was the heir to not only the Victorian apotheosis of the Will, but its Darwinian negation. In his brief encounter with formal education, he studied at the newly formed Normal School of Science (now the Royal College of Science) under Thomas Henry Huxley, Darwin's defender and popularizer. It was an experience he never forgot. Those doubts, despairs, and depressions that the official, liberal myth of Victorianism had managed to suppress were openly admitted, in the wake of science after Darwin, to be the central and inescapable condition of human life. Defeat was man's lot, man's fate, and, if he was strong enough to face it, man's supreme test. So that if Wells was a true Victorian in his faith in the power of Will, he was also a true Edwardian in his open doubt about the final usefulness of that faith when weighed against the inexorable processes of uncaring nature. The narrator of *The Time Machine* says of the Time Traveller that he "thought but cheerlessly of the Advancement of Mankind, and saw in the growing pile of civilisation only a foolish heaping that must inevitably fall back upon and destroy its makers in the end." There speaks the evolutionary theorist, the connoisseur of futility. But, the narrator himself continues, "If that is so, it remains for us to live as though it were not so." And there speaks the romantic, the exponent of Will, the man who never stopped hoping that there might after all be some final appeal against entropy, against fate, against the Second Law of Thermodynamics.

Those two voices continue their debate in Wells's work to the very end of his life, and their uncertain contest is one of the great dramas of his writing. One of Wells's favorite and most frequently cited authors is Shelley—another impetuous, revolutionary spirit drawn simultaneously to romantic willfulness and scientific objectivity. And what one critic has observed of Shelley we can observe with equal justice of Wells, that he was infinite in hope yet sober in expectation.

Think again of his projected epitaph; "God damn you all: I told you so." It is not just an epitaph, it is an open letter to the world. And what, after all, *did* he tell us? Well, just this: that the major disease of modern man is that his scientific and technological expertise has outstripped his moral and emotional development; that the human race, thanks to its inherited prejudices and superstitions and its innate pigheadedness, is an endangered species; and that mankind must learn—soon—to establish a state of worldwide cooperation by burying its old hatreds and its ancient selfishness, or face extinction.

Today, these assertions are not shocking. They might appear in a presidential campaign speech or an address to the United Nations. (They would probably not be taken seriously, of course, but they have entered the realm of consoling pieties, buzzwords that do not raise eyebrows.) And even when Wells first uttered them, they were not being uttered for the first time. Wells was a brilliant man, but he was not an original thinker. His gift was for *imagining*, for realizing firmly, almost visually, the implications of his age's philosophy and science and for communicating those implications to his readers with the urgency of myth. The same may be said of Shakespeare.

If there was something permanently Victorian in Wells's optimism and permanently Edwardian in his qualifications of that optimism, there is nevertheless something distinctively modern about the whole man. It used to be fashionable to speak of him, if at all, as a historical curio of English letters, the author of a few interesting realistic novels and a few more vastly entertaining tales that "fathered" the minor genre of science fiction; but, ran the conventional appraisal, the young author of those interesting stories turned, by the second decade of the twentieth century, into a windy and pompous bore, a shrill controversialist whose dismal themes were the glory of technology, the irrelevance of the fine arts, and the coming wonders of the Age of the Scientific Man.

Anyone who reads Wells seriously will feel how grossly unfair this caricature is. But it was a widely accepted one, beginning well before the last years of his life. No less a writer and apologist for Christianity than C. S. Lewis, in his celebrated "Space Trilogy" of the thirties and forties, *Out of the Silent Planet, Perelandra,* and *That Hideous Strength,* bitterly and crudely satirized Wells's (and Olaf Stapledon's) ideas while at the same time imitating the narrative technique of Wells's early scientific romances. Indeed, Wells at the end of his life had much to be bitter about: the Second World War, which seemed the fulfillment of all his worst prophecies, as well as the waning of his once immense popularity and influence upon the reading public in general and the intellectual world in particular. He couldn't have known that within twenty years of his death that eminence would again be on the rise.

Who, then, was H. G. Wells? There is always, inevitably, a strong connection between the inmost details of a writer's life and the kinds of books he writes. But someone who could say—and mean it—"God damn you all: I told you so" obviously *feels* this connection more than do most writers. At about the time of Wells's greatest fame, T. S. Eliot described the cardinal sin of romantic and modern writing as the "dissociation of sensibility," the separation of intellect from emotion until we can no longer, as, say, Dante did, feel the force of a theorem as immediately as the odor of a rose—or, conversely, experience passion while retaining the analytic intelligence of the experimenter. It was a formula that fascinated and convinced literary critics for decades. But if it was ever really true of literature, it was certainly not true of Wells, whose passion for ideas and whose elaborate ideas about the passions were the talk and often the scandal of his (and Eliot's) time. In fact, his most vituperative and prissiest critics liked to argue, though not in these precise terms, that Wells's problem was that his sensibility wasn't dissociated enough. He seemed incapable of assimilating an idea—and he assimilated many ideas—without immediately exploring its implications for everyday life and behavior. And he seemed incapable of feeling a passion—and he felt many passions—without erecting it into a standard or a program of conduct.

For Wells there was no real distinction between the life of the mind and the life of the body, between theory and behavior. This is one way of understanding his description of himself as "a very ordinary brain." For all his energy and brilliance, he was an ordinary brain because he never stopped believing in the importance, the tragedy, and the salvageability of ordinary life. He grasped this "ordinariness" ferociously, and held on to it throughout a career that brought him as much fame, eminence, and wealth as a man could want. His fondest hope for the new age of science he forecast was that it would dignify and enrich the ordinary life of the middle classes. And in his fiction, both his science fiction and his "realistic" novels, he gives us as convincing and valuable a representation of that middle class as we have. The reason why is plain: Wells was of that class, and made it a point of honor never to forget that he was. This does not mean that he ignored its shortsightedness, vulgarity, or squalor. But all these things, he kept insisting, could be changed, and something of real human value could be retained. It was his world.

It was the world to which he was born. Herbert George Wells, "Bertie" to his family, was born September 21, 1866, the youngest child of Joseph and Sarah Wells, in Bromley, Kent, on the fringes of London. Since the boy was destined to be an aggressive, powerful, stubborn writer—a literary bull, in other words—it is appropriate that he was born in a china shop. Joseph Wells was a part-time gardener, a semiprofessional cricketer, and, at the time Bertie arrived, a half-successful importer of chinaware. He was, by all accounts, a fulltime, charming loafer and good companion. Unfortunately, none of his talents were the kind that got bills paid. Sarah Wells, before her marriage, had been maid to Lady Fetherstonhaugh (Mary Ann Bullock) of Uppark in Sussex. When the china shop finally failed in 1880, she returned to that position and became virtually the sole breadwinner for her family. She was a valiant, untiring woman, after the good Victorian model. She was also, after the same model (at least for women), grimly, gloomily religious, obsessed with belief in the natural sinfulness of mankind and the sure, swift chastisements of an implacable God. Wells's biographers, Norman and Jeanne MacKenzie, rightly describe Sarah's marriage to easygoing, irresponsible Joe Wells as "no more than a lingering disaster."

It is important to understand Wells's family and class because they marked his life more than is usually the case. His was a *lower*-middle-class background, just a notch or two above the feared level of "laboring class." And that implied some rather urgent things in the Victorian age. First, the chances of dying young were very good—most likely of something easily enough treated if only you had the money to buy competent medical care (but you didn't). Second, you would probably spend your life uneducated—and knowing it. "Universal education" was being talked about, mainly by radicals, but it was still decades away from being seriously considered. Illiteracy was uncommon in Wells's class (among men, anyway)—but so was anything beyond a rudimentary training in the skills needed to be an efficient shopkeeper or maid. And finally (as is implied by the first two conditions) your odds were poor ever to rise out of the class you were born to and quite good to fall below it. Once you fell—into insuperable debt, bankruptcy, or to the level of common laborers—you never came back. Darwin shocked the intellectual world by describing life as a "struggle for existence." But people of Wells's background, if they had been invited to join the debate over The Origin of Species, would have been confused over the controversy: they had known the struggle for existence, in its ferocity, all along.

When Sarah returned to service at Uppark, she arranged for Bertie, then fourteen, to begin a career as a draper's assistant. His mother's faith in God, Wells was later to say, was almost equaled by her faith in drapers.

He failed at it miserably. Dreamy and disorganized, he couldn't (or didn't care to) keep accounts straight and was sent back to Uppark, to Sarah's consternation and his own unconcern. While he stayed there, until Sarah could think of another position for him, he was coddled as a darling below stairs and indulged as a mascot above. And he gorged himself on the Uppark library, reading feverishly and at random but—as he later remembered—treasuring especially the fantasies, satires, and histories of writers like Plato, Swift, Voltaire, Gibbon, and Shelley—doubters and revolutionaries, to a man.

This was as much of a liberal education as Wells would ever receive, and probably better than most. Returns to Uppark became something of a custom over the next few years. Young Bertie would be sent into apprenticeship (first to a druggist, then to another draper), return to Uppark in disgrace, and enjoy a period of spoiling and reading. Finally he went to work as an assistant teacher at the Midhurst Grammar School run by a Mr. Horace Byatt, where he had studied briefly while trying to become an apprentice druggist. As he was later to realize, this was the turning point in his life.

Teaching in Byatt's school gave him the leisure he had needed to indulge his appetite for learning. And it gave him something else, a way up and out of the dismal life of a shopkeeper. The Normal School of Science in South Kensington offered a number of annual scholarships to potential science teachers who scored well on their national examinations. Wells entered the competition and in 1884 won a scholarship.

Darwin's ideas were still causing aftershocks throughout the philosophical and theological world and had already revolutionized the world of science. And one of Wells's teachers in his first year at the Normal School was "Darwin's bulldog," T. H. Huxley. His essays on evolution are among the masterpieces of English prose. Under the influence of the brilliant, articulate, and skeptical Huxley, Wells flourished in that first year.

But, as he had failed at more menial occupations, he was to fail at this one too. During his second year he began to lose interest in his classes. He helped found the *Science Schools Journal*, a student paper he edited briefly and to which he contributed a number of stories and essays—among them a curious tale called "The Chronic Argonauts," about a man who could journey through time. By the end of his third year it was obvious he would not take a degree, would not become a scientist or a distinguished teacher of science. But little Bertie was now a grown man, with a man's responsibilities: he had wasted a once-in-a-lifetime opportunity. He was sick, discouraged, a self-pitying bore even to his close friends. He was also dying.

He had hemorrhaged a number of times. And though we shall never know for certain what his illness was, we can be fairly sure it was not altogether psychosomatic. But one afternoon in 1889, he walked into the woods behind the house of some friends he was visiting. He met a girl (he never learned her name), talked with her for a while, and went on, feeling strangely lightened by this encounter with youth and hope. "I have been dying for nearly two-thirds of a year, and I have died enough," he told himself. It was his first, though not his most massive, exercise of that Will so dear to the Victorian myth of the Real Man. He resolved to be healthy, to live, and to find a teaching position in London.

He did find a teaching position and also began writing articles for the London papers, both humorous essays and interpretations of that new science which was still so frightening to so many people. These two enterprises made him, by 1891, feel secure enough to marry his cousin, Isabel.

That was the latest in what was becoming a lengthy series of disastrous choices. Wells possessed, or was possessed by, a voracious and athletic sexual appetite; and Isabel, in whom he had invested all his hopes and fantasies, was simply not up to it. It is hard to see how she could have been, since she had been raised in a culture that taught its "nice" young women to feel shame and fear at the possibilities of their bodies. Wells came to understand this, though not in time to spare Isabel or himself much anguish.

There was a conventionally cozy home, and by 1893, another woman. He had fallen in love with one of his students, a brilliant girl named Amy Catherine Robbins whom he pet-named "Jane." He divorced Isabel, eloped with Jane, and by early 1894 was living with her in London, supporting her, her mother, and Isabel.

It was a hopeless situation. Wells's newspaper articles had attracted attention and even enthusiasm but, as with his father, not enough to pay the bills. In 1893, though, William Ernest Henley, editor of the *National Observer*, asked him to do something of an extended length for the paper. He reworked, and serialized in 1894, his old story from the *Science Schools Journal*, "The Chronic Argonauts." In 1895 Henley founded another paper, *The New Review*, and asked Wells again to rework the articles for stronger continuity between the installments. Wells complied, and the serialized story was a great success, published in book form the same year. It was called *The Time Machine*.

The book did not make Wells instantly wealthy, but it went far toward doing so. He also published three other books in the same year. Suddenly, Wells was everywhere, one of that indefatigable set of late Victorian writers (including Shaw and Chesterton) who seemed always to have something to say and was always able to say it cleverly. During the ten years following publication of *The Time Machine* he wrote twenty-four books, including nearly all of his important science-fiction novels and tales, and won the respect and delighted admiration of the most prominent authors of his time. Of *The Invisible Man* (1897), Joseph Conrad wrote to Wells, "Impressed is *the* word, O Realist of the Fantastic!" Henry James, the most self-conscious of novelists, praised his stories.

He was courted by political parties as a promising propagandist, especially by the Fabian Society. This curious collection of gentle, intellectual revolutionaries had been established by Sidney and Beatrice Webb and had found one of its staunchest supporters in Wells's friend, George Bernard Shaw. Its principles included a strong commitment to social-

H. G. Wells at about the time of writing *The Time Machine*.

ism as the only workable form of government, and an equally strong belief that the change to socialism should and would be a gradual one, effected by reasoned argument rather than by armed class warfare. Wells joined the Fabian Society in 1903.

Like his other love affairs, it didn't last. If he had been born a bull in a china shop, then the polite and antiseptic world of Beatrice and Sidney Webb was only a wider, more temptingly fragile scene for his thrashing. By 1905, only two years after he had joined the Society, he was challenging the Webbs for its leadership. It was a challenge he finally lost, and it ruptured some of his closest friendships for years.

By the time he began to drift away from the Fabians, they were not entirely unhappy to see him go. Jane had turned out to be as unsatisfactory an object of his passion as Isabel. So, as was natural for a man of his time and training, Wells rather than looking closely at his own expectations and desires looked elsewhere for someone to satisfy them. Quite a few someones, as it happened, were interested. He was a famous man, a great, energetic talker with large, alert, expressive eyes; and he genuinely *liked* women, not at all a usual thing among adventurers. But, then, Wells was not an adventurer. He had a habit that the true seducer never acquires: he loved the women he slept with.

Rumors of his sexual misconduct grew rife, even threatening to affect the sales of his books. And to make matters worse, Wells began writing fiction that argued strenuously, and with obvious autobiographical implications, for free love. *In the Days of the Comet* (1906), one of his earliest utopian stories, tells how a mysterious comet passes over Earth, releasing a gas that kills all the enzymes that make people selfish and violent, and thereby establishing a new Golden Age of peace and love. But by "love," Wells meant free love. The hero, who has been on the point of murdering the man his girlfriend has married, discovers after the great Change that the girl and her husband are perfectly willing to let him share her favors, out of sheer good nature and friendship. But that was carrying socialism a little too far. The Fabians were deeply embarrassed, and many less gentle readers thought Wells should be thrashed.

Wells's response to attacks on his "immorality" was, naturally, to raise his voice. *In the Days of the Comet*, shocking as it was, had at least a flimsy veil of make-believe thrown, though thrown indecorously, over its naked assertions. But in *Ann Veronica* (1909) the veil was drawn aside. Ann Veronica Stanley is a brilliant, independent young girl being stultified, strangled by the pieties and sexual snobberies of her society. "She wanted to live," Wells says of her in one of the most famous lines from the book. And for her, living includes flaunting all the cherished moral conventions of her stuffy father, and eloping with her dashing chemistry professor, Mr. Capes—even though Capes is already married. The allusions to Wells's early years with Jane are obvious; but that story was ten years old. What bothered people was Wells's obvious point that this sort of thing is both a natural and a *continual* possibility of human behavior. And what also bothered people was that the book was transparently "about" his latest scandalous love affair: with the young, beautiful, and intellectual Amber Reeves, daughter of one of the leading members of the Fabian Society. Wells was even to elope to France with Amber, before a virtual delegation of Fabians and friends talked him back, briefly, to reason. And *Ann Veronica* became the most scandalous book of its time. For its poisonous author, thundered the influential *Spectator*, "Self-sacrifice is a dream and self-restraint a delusion. Such things have no place in the muddy world of Mr. Wells's imaginings. His is a community of scuffling stoats and ferrets, unenlightened by a ray of duty or abnegation."

He had been, for almost a decade, one of England's most sought-after, admired writers. Suddenly, he was losing friends fast. In fact, he was fighting a war on multiple fronts. His Fabian friends were embarrassed by his novels and hurt by his bullying bid for leadership of the society; many of his readers were scandalized and angered by his sexual revolutionism and the rumors about his private life; and, what may have stung most, his fellow novelists were beginning to express grave doubts about his talents as a storyteller.

It was Henry James more than anyone else who expressed these doubts, precipitating a quarrel that is one of the most curious, painful, and significant literary disagreements of the twentieth century. James was already an established, master novelist when Wells published his first books, and he generously praised the younger writer's work. Wells, of course, was immensely flattered, and they became good friends (one of the best photographs of James in his later years was taken by Wells—an ardent amateur photographer—on a visit by James to Wells's home).

The two could not have been more unlike one another. James, who had been born into an already distinguished family of New England intellectuals, was a mandarin, an obsessively polite, restrained man who dreaded excess and vulgarity as most people fear death or mortal sin. He seems to have had almost no private, passional life. Or rather, he sublimated whatever libidinal drive he may have felt into the one clear, overwhelming, irresistible love of his life, the art of fiction. No man ever devoted more precision or intelligence to the business of telling stories, of analyzing and realizing on the page the reactions and interchanges of people in society. And if it cost James a lifetime of labor and anxiety, it bore abundant fruit. His novels—especially *The Portrait of a Lady, The Ambassadors, The Golden Bowl,* and *The Wings of the Dove*—are among the greatest achievements of his age, masterpieces of fiction that defy analysis or imitation.

The friendship between James and Wells was obviously a relationship of mutual support. James's ponderous respectability, his deep and assured culture, satisfied a need the scruffy, impetuous young man from Bromley must have felt very much as he entered the literary world. And Wells's energy and ebullience, his insatiable appetite for life must have meant even more to the lonely old man who had spent his life in the monastic service of art.

But for James, "art" was a sacred term, the highest and most exacting reach of human possibility. For Wells, it was always, even from the beginning, a means to an end—to making a living, supporting a family, changing men's minds, or saving the human race: a noble means, to be sure, perhaps an indispensable one, but still a means. As Wells's fiction became more explicitly argumentative, more and more a blueprint for social change, James's letters to Wells became more alarmed, more troubled with the fear that the younger man had abandoned the holy craft of the novel for the easy but lowly trade of propaganda.

And maybe, at least in part, he had. It is certainly true that, after 1911, the year of *The New Machiavelli*, Wells never again wrote a novel, either realistic or science-fiction, equal to his best work before that date.

The MacKenzies in their biography suggest that what happened around this time was that Wells, frustrated in his political ambitions and angered at the general clucking over his personal life, turned from the imagination to the will as the driving force of his writing. If the world would not accept his vision of things, he would *make* them listen, he would turn the novel into a forensic tool to confound his adversaries.

To James, this was sacrilege. He wrote Wells expressing, with agonizing diffidence, his disappointment at the direction the younger man's fiction was taking. Wells answered dutifully and apologetically. But he had made his choice, and the friendship began to cool perceptibly. The next year, 1912, James was instrumental in having Wells invited to the distinguished Royal Society of Literature. Wells declined, rather huffily, saying that "literature" in that exalted, polite sense was not really his concern: "better the wild rush of . . . the Quack than the cold politeness of the established thing." And James, regretfully, had to agree with Wells's refusal.

It has been said that in every friendship one member grows stronger and the other grows weaker; and the one who grows weaker is the one who loves more. Certainly, Wells loved less. In 1915 he ruptured the friendship decisively in his novel, *Boon*, which includes a cruel and bitter attack upon James and the mandarin, irresponsibly aesthetic pretensions of the Jamesian novel.

What is so important about the quarrel between James and Wells is that it is perfectly symbolic of what was happening to the English novel at the same moment. Throughout the Victorian period and into the first decades of the twentieth century, the novel had enjoyed an exalted position and at the same time had been a truly popular art—popular not merely in terms of its sales, though those were considerable, but also in the most profound sense of the word, an accurate reflection of the aspirations and fears of a wide range of its reading public.

But by the early years of this century, a fissure was becoming evident between novels that were "artistic" and those that were "popular."

James himself was the most exemplary victim of this split. His later novels are among the glories of civilized discourse, profound and moving examinations of the moral choices of men and women in society. But they are also as intricate, as difficult as any stories ever written and therefore read only by a select audience—though James to the end of his life wanted desperately to be a popular writer in the special sense I have described of Victorian fiction's popularity. The later James was crucified by his own intelligence and by his ferocious dedication to the idea of art. He *could not* simplify what was the complexity of human life, and out of that agonized honesty the modern tradition of the art novel, at least in English, arises.

Wells, on the other hand, who hammered away at his ideas, seemed to be turning the novel into a mere vehicle for propaganda. His style became more brusque, his action more schematically violent and allegorical, his ideas more unrelentingly clear. He was, for a long time, very popular—but not in the full Victorian sense, for his popularity was won at the expense of the respect and the attention, even, of the artistic community.

But this is an oversimplification. It used to be thought, in conventional literary wisdom, that Wells lost the quarrel with James—at least before the bar of history. Lately, however, the final returns seem less clear. Granted, Wells never again wrote anything as fine as *The Time Machine* or *The First Men in the Moon,* but he did write fine things, even in the longest and dreariest of his later books. And if his books suffered as "art," they also kept alive an important tradition: the tradition of fiction as public forum, as a clearinghouse of ideas.

But by the time of *Boon* Wells had other things to think about besides his position as an artist. "Early in the twentieth century came the great disillusionment." That ringing sentence, from the first page of *The War of the Worlds,* refers to the Martian invasion of Earth. But by 1914, or any year thereafter, it was difficult not to read this as the most uncannily accurate of Wells's many prophecies. For the great disillusionment did come, not as war machines from another planet but as war machines from every advanced nation on Earth, in a conflict of unprecedented ferocity and futility that was called, by general consent and with a very Wellsian inflection, the World War.

Wells reacted to the war, at first, with a chauvinism that ever afterward embarrassed him. The war, he thought, would be a splendid crusade of the enlightened nations against the barbaric Germans, and victory would usher in a new age of peaceful and rational international government. He argued as much in a book of 1914 that, as it happened, gave its most famous and, later, most grimly ironic name to World War I: *The War That Will End War.*

As the conflict dragged on year after year, with an obscene and pointless waste of life on both sides, he came to see the foolishness of his first, nationalistic fervor—and even to see the wisdom of the absolute, "traitorous" pacifism of his friend, George Bernard Shaw. The war left permanent marks on his fiction. It strengthened his conviction, which had already been apparent in *The War in the Air* (1908) and *The World Set Free* (1914), that the next great change in human society would have to come by bloodshed and disaster; that humans were too stupid or too conservative to pay attention to any message—even the necessity for world peace—unless they had put their fingers into the fire. And it also led him to the passionate faith of his later years that nationalism and nationalistic prejudice were the rotten core of mankind's disease, and that this disease could only be effectively cured by a worldwide dictatorship of benign intellectuals—what he came to refer to as the World Brain. This vision, of a world-shaking conflict that would lead to a new society of the just, he owed perhaps not only to the First World War but also to the apocalyptic religion of his mother. It remained his vision to the end and in 1933 found its fullest expression in his massive, strange book *The Shape of Things To Come.*

The war, though, was not his only concern. A brilliant, beautiful young woman had written a witty, biting review of one of his more fatuous novels, *Marriage,* in 1912. Her name was Cicely Fairfield, but she had changed it to Rebecca West after the liberated heroine of Henrik Ibsen's play *Ros-*

mersholm. Wells wrote her, complimenting the intelligence of her review. They met and soon were lovers. So they remained until 1923, when Rebecca West broke off the relationship, mainly to preserve her own intellectual independence. But it was the most satisfying love of his life (except, perhaps, for the immensely tolerant Jane, who remained his wife until her death in 1927). Their son, novelist and essayist Anthony West, later wrote a touching and revealing memoir of his father.

By the time the World War ended in 1919, Wells had gone through some momentous changes. He had dissociated himself from the world of literary artists, he had discovered a new theory of internationalism as the salvation of the race, and he had found a new lover, one who was his intellectual equal. What better time for new beginnings—indeed, for a whole new direction to his career as a writer? In 1918 he had developed—and sold—the prospectus for a large, ambitious, astonishing book. It was to be nothing less than a history of the human race, from Paleolithic origin to aerodynamic present—with, as if that weren't enough, a consistent overview of the evolution of the species and speculations about its probable, or possible, future development.

Perhaps no one who has not written a book can imagine the flamboyance, the arrogance, the breathtaking courage in what Wells wanted to do. "It was a mark of his emotional commitment," say the MacKenzies, "that H. G. was willing to face both the labour involved and the risk that would be torn to pieces by his critics." That is an understatement: the labor and the risk were both, literally, enormous. For two years Wells worked on his project, which appeared in 1920 as *The Outline of History,* in two volumes. It is flawed, and it is brilliant. Near the end of Volume One, in the midst of a discussion of the origins of Christianity, he announces the overriding and consistent theme of his study—and, indeed, of his lifework:

> The history of our race and personal religious experience run so closely parallel as to seem to a modern observer almost the same thing; both tell of a being at first scattered and blind and utterly confused, feeling its way slowly to the serenity and salvation of an ordered and coherent purpose. That, in the simplest, is the outline of history; whether one have a re-

ligious purpose or disavow a religious purpose altogether, the lines of the outline remain the same.

"That . . . is the outline of history": the emergence, out of a scattered, barbaric, quarrelsome collection of particularly specialized apes, of a rational and just human community. We can ask whether that is the outline Wells saw in history, or whether it was the outline he *wanted* to see. But we cannot blame him for wanting to see it. And we cannot deny that others have tried to see the same shape in the fire. Jesuit theologian and anthropologist Pierre Teilhard de Chardin argues in *The Phenomenon of Man* that the Darwinian theory of evolution through natural selection is not only true, but is God's handiwork: that nature's ultimate tendency is toward a unification of the whole human race in what he calls the "noosphere," the realm of pure mind, the New Jerusalem of the brotherhood of man. Chardin's book has had a massive influence on religious thought since its publication in 1955. But its publication is posthumous. It was written in 1938, but suppressed by both the Jesuit Order and the Roman Catholic Church Curia, and for good reason: it is Wellsian. It is, in fact, a version of the argument of *The Outline of History*. We will have more to say of Teilhard and Darwinian thought in the next chapter.

The *Outline* received the predictable nitpicking reviews from the academic community and also a witty though bitter series of attacks by Catholic apologist Hilaire Belloc. (Wells responded to these in a clumsily angry book.) But it sold. It sold better than either Wells or his publishers had expected, in both England and America. Wells had been a successful writer for twenty-five years, but the *Outline* went beyond mere success: it was a phenomenon.

The tubercular, impulsive little man from Bromley had come a long way. He had been widely read, he had been famous, he had been notorious; now he was an international figure. Intellectuals from the Continent solicited his opinions, and he numbered among his acquaintances some of the leaders of the recent Communist revolution in Russia. Indeed, he later (in the thirties) became a lover of Moura Budberg, former mistress of his friend, Russian writer Maxim Gorki.

There were, however, other books to be written, other cures to be proposed for the disease of human life. In 1928 he gave a permanent name to his hopes for the future in a book called *The Open Conspiracy: Blue Prints for a World Revolution*. The "Open Conspiracy" was to be a worldwide union of intellectuals, an aristocracy of the mind dedicated to redirecting the course of history, turning mankind away from its predestined journey to extinction and, for once, overcoming the cold mathematics of natural selection by an effort of intellect and will. The equations of natural selection are heartless and immutable: when a species becomes too overspecialized to survive in its environment, it begins to die. But, Wells hoped, man would not have to go the way of the dinosaur because he could *choose* not to.

Now he had fully become the H. G. Wells whom his enemies loathed most, and who influenced, for better and worse, nearly every English or American writer educated during the period. This era of urgent prophecy and propaganda for the world state culminated, as I have said, in 1933 with *The Shape of Things To Come: The Ultimate Revolution*, Wells's last major utopian book. Here, in what was partly a novel, partly a tract on economics and international relations, and altogether a singular act of imagination, he projects what must be the future of the race if it is to survive. A second and massively barbaric World War reduces the population of the world to a handful of scattered near-savages, who are saved from spiraling down the evolutionary vortex by the puritanical, benevolent but cold dictatorship of engineers and scientists. They are the airmen, the men who have mastered the sky—always, for Wells, an image of the highest reach of human possibility—and they reorganize the planet along sane, peaceful, and clean lines of command. And though their dictatorship is temporary, it forms the basis for the new world order that succeeds it, an era of unprecedented freedom, beauty, and domination over nature. Of this last revolution, Wells writes at the end of the book, "It has been an adaptation, none too soon, of our species to changing conditions that must otherwise have destroyed it." At first this seems to be Darwinian theory at its purest. But it is an inversion, or a reversal, of Darwin's idea of "natural selection." Man survives the changes in his environment not because he spontaneously adapts to its variations, but because he *decides* to do so—and does. Wells throughout his life believed in two mutually contradictory ideas, the immutability of history and the omnipotence of will. And now for the last, fullest and richest time, he asserts the indomitable power of intelligence to forestall the inevitable.

But by now, also, it was an old story. Wells had sounded its themes in most of his major books since *A Modern Utopia* in 1905. And while *The Shape of Things To Come* is a powerful restatement of those themes, by 1933 people were getting tired of hearing them: especially since, at that time, arguments for a puritanical dictatorship of social engineers sounded uncomfortably like a defense of that ugliest of human growths, fascism, now established in half of Europe. Wells was not a fascist. He understood, and wrote about, the stupidity and brutality of fascism in its German, Italian, and even its Soviet forms. But the charge was raised against him, and it was a charge he did not bother, after a while, to refute.

Like some of his readers, Wells was tired. After finishing *The Shape of Things To Come* he turned to writing *Experiment in Autobiography*, and that is a significant fact. He had thirteen years of life left: thirteen years during which he worked as incessantly and inexhaustibly as ever. But there is something special, something final, about the moment you decide to write your autobiography. Perhaps it is simply an admission that the major part of your life is over. Or perhaps it is more serious, a kind of pact with death, an agreement that it can come if it wishes now. Wells had finished his last, massive, most explicit and urgent plan for the future of the race. And as he was finishing that, his last major love affair, with a Frenchwoman named Odette Keun, was also coming to a bitter and fractious end. He had lived with Odette for some years in France, but he was now thinking of returning to England, leaving his expensive house and, he hoped, all his troubles abroad. It was time to take stock, to add up accounts (something he had never been good at, from his first apprenticeship in the draper's shop); and in 1934 he published *Experiment in Autobiography*.

The last twelve years of his life were spent in a battle

against age, illness, and public neglect that is not without its brilliant accomplishments, and not without touches of (very Wellsian) comedy. He may have lost much of his popularity, but he had certainly lost little of his wealth. He was, as the middle class to which he was born would have put it, comfortable. Comfort, though, was not a condition Wells could be comfortable with. In 1936 he produced, among other books, *The Idea of a World Encyclopedia*, a self-advertising prospectus for yet one more compendium of science, history, and social theory designed to illumine and save the world from itself. But he could not interest any publishers in more than the prospectus. The age of the ambitious and expansive *Outline* had passed. Europe and the world, intellectually as well as politically, were taking short views, were more interested in designing efficient bomb shelters than in planning a world state.

Of course, Wells still had disciples, and some dauntingly intelligent ones, especially the young Olaf Stapledon, whose book of scientific and sociological prophecy *Last and First Men* (1930), Wells praised in his novel of 1937, *Star Begotten*. But the crowds had turned away. And to a writer like Wells, nurtured in the 1890s, that golden era of British journalism when the interchange and expression of serious ideas were the stuff of popular writing, this loss of audience must have been especially poignant. The worst thing that can happen to a populist intellectual, probably, is that he should live long enough to see himself the founder of a sect. His last books, from *The Fate of Homo Sapiens* (1939) to the despairing *Mind at the End of Its Tether* (1945) are increasingly tinged with a bitter sense of isolation from that audience he wanted most to address, wanted most to save.

Wells died on August 13, 1946, a year almost to the day after the first use of atomic bombs in warfare. He had begun planning a film, with Sir Alexander Korda, on the implications of the atomic bomb for the future of mankind (he had worked with Korda previously, in 1935, on his one complete filmscript, *Things To Come*). A few days later his sons G. P. Wells and Anthony West scattered his ashes over the sea off the Isle of Wight.

But the century whose birth he saw, and in whose life he

took such a passionate interest, has not been able to forget him. Thirty years ago, just after his death, it might have been acceptable to say that H. G. Wells was an important but minor literary figure, the inventor of a new kind of storytelling that evolved into a prolific if mildly disreputable subgenre of literature, and for a while a journalist of wide influence and strong if limited talents. But we cannot say that any more. With each passing year and with each new study of his work, Wells seems increasingly one of the strong, essential writers of our era. He was an artist of major gifts who questioned the morality of "art" divorced from social usefulness. He was an intellectual who insisted, to the end, that intellect must be put to the service of mankind or must wither into an inhuman caricature of itself. And he was, above all, a storyteller who came to believe that storytelling makes sense only if it is also prophecy: that fairy tales are important and necessary to the race, but only if the fairy tales make reality more livable. In all of these aspects, Wells seems more and more a writer for our times—a writer whose real time has not yet come, but is coming.

For the nineteenth-century middle class in which Wells was raised, one of the most important authors was an English clergyman named Samuel Smiles, an ardent believer in the power of positive thinking, in the will, and in man's ability to raise himself above his bestial origin by sheer effort and spunk. Smiles's best-selling book (which was translated into almost every civilized language in the nineteenth century) was called *Self-Help*. Its American fruits include the rags-to-riches stories of Horatio Alger. And without trivializing Wells, we can say that his career is in its way a version of Samuel Smiles's formula for success. It is a historical accident of some irony that *Self-Help* appeared in 1859, the year also of *The Origin of Species*. The two books almost define the two voices of Wells's imagination, the scientific analysis of cosmic futility, and the middle-class, absurd but admirable insistence on the possibility of hope, the power of Will. A large part of Wells's genius is that he remained faithful, in his way, to both voices.

By effort, and effort alone, Wells raised himself from a hopeless situation to become one of the most influential writers of his time. And by effort alone he managed to over-come a despair so cosmic and so well informed that it would have crushed many a lesser man. Wells believed in the power of Will; and he understood, as well as anyone ever has, how deceptive that faith might be. We value him, now, both for the energy of that faith and for the dark power of the doubt that underlies it.

2
THE AGE OF UNEASE:
The Background of Wells

Wells's major science fiction appeared between 1895 and the outbreak of World War I in 1914. It is with the Wells of these two decades that we will be mainly concerned for the rest of this book, as it is *this* Wells who seems, as years go by, to have the surest claim to permanence. But if the Wells of these years matters to us as much as he does, if he seems more and more one of us, it is because at the beginning of his career, he was so brilliantly and completely one of *them*—"they" being our ideological and spiritual ancestors around the turn of the century.

In the utopian novels he wrote after this period, he liked to refer to the origins of the modern era as the "Age of Confusion" (in *Men Like Gods*) or the "Age of Frustration" (in *The Shape of Things To Come*). And confusing, frustrating, upsetting the intellectual life of the years 1895–1914 certainly was. In an important study of *The Early H. G. Wells*, Bernard Bergonzi indicates the relationship between the scientific romances and that set of attitudes, emotions, and opinions tagged, by the people who held them, *fin de siècle*. A popular expression during the 1890s, it simply means "century's end." But, as Bergonzi writes, it meant much more:

> In its widest sense *fin de siecle* was simply the expression of a prevalent mood: the feeling that the nineteenth century . . . had gone on too long, and that sensitive souls were growing weary of it. In England this mood was heightened by the feel-

ing that Queen Victoria's reign had also lasted excessively long. But at the same time, no one knew what the coming twentieth century was going to bring, though there was no lack of speculation. The result could be described as a certain loss of nerve, weariness with the past combined with foreboding about the future.

"Confusion," "frustration," "weariness," "foreboding": the words used to describe the beginning of the twentieth century all have a common tone: one of excited, fascinated fear of what lies just around the corner. Wells caught this tone in his first scientific romances. *The Time Machine, When the Sleeper Wakes,* and *The First Men in the Moon* show us, through the eyes of eccentric, nervous, *fin de siècle* men, future human civilizations where technology has obliterated all struggle (for the rich at least), and yet where the beneficiaries of that gift have declined below the horizon of the really human. As Graham, the "sleeper" of *When the Sleeper Wakes,* dies he pronounces a single grim judgment on the men of the future struggling for their freedom: "Weak men." *The Island of Doctor Moreau, The Invisible Man,* and *The War of the Worlds* show us not a future de-evolving toward weakness and mass suicide, but rather the explosion of the technological future into the present. The eruption of science's cold equations and bitter wisdom into the world of the everyday corrodes the comfortingly "normal" through the sheer power of its murderous efficiency. "Cities, nations, civilisations, progress—it's all over," shrieks the artilleryman to the narrator of *The War of the Worlds* as the Martians rampage toward London. "That game's up. We're beat."

In *The Food of the Gods, In the Days of the Comet,* and *The World Set Free,* Wells was to give these elementary situations a more positive, hopeful turn. And later still he was to make situations like these the vehicles for a full-scale attempt to save mankind from itself. But it is nevertheless true that his science fiction, always, remained an elaboration of one of these two central themes: a man of the present is cast or voyages into a possible future organization of mankind, or the future of mankind somehow invades or possesses—and tests—the resilience and vitality of men of the present. It is a sign of Wells's genius that these two archetypal situations are also, with very few exceptions, the two elementary forms of all science fiction written after him. It is also a sign of his genius that these archetypes are ones he inherited, and creatively transformed, from the anxious, self-doubting, apocalyptic *fin de siècle* world of his youth.

But Bergonzi's discussion of this end-of-the-century, end-of-the-world sensibility explains only part of the early Wells's science fiction. Queen Victoria died in 1901—she could hardly have chosen a more symbolic date—and was succeeded by her portly, self-indulgent, and (at least at first) liberal son, Edward VII. Wells himself described the transition from the late Victorian to the Edwardian spirit: "Queen Victoria was like a great paper-weight that for half a century sat upon men's minds, and when she was removed their ideas began to blow about all over the place haphazardly." Of course, there had been forward-looking, enthusiastic architects of social change before 1900, and there remained many celebrants of degeneration and decay after that date. But the total effect of the transition was largely of the sort Wells describes. William Bellamy, an important critic of Edwardian fiction, sees the transition as one from a culture-bound to a culture-free or "post-cultural" mental environment. While late Victorians had lived with the claustrophobic sense of a cultural inheritance too rich and too consolidated to allow for personal freedom, Edwardians—having survived the reign of the old Queen and lived past the magic year 1900—enjoyed a sense of new beginnings and of individual self-realization that often implied a possiblility of personal fulfillment outside the conventional sanctions of society.

There is much justice in this description of the Edwardian mood, particularly since it allows us to see the close connection between the passions, enthusiasms, and warring ideologies of the Edwardian period and later twentieth-century movements of the same "post-cultural" sort. As Samuel Hynes observes in *The Edwardian Turn of Mind*, "virtually everything that is thought of as characteristically modern already existed in England by 1914: aircraft, radiotelegraphy, psychoanalysis, Post-Impressionism, motion picture palaces. . . ." The late Victorians, we can say, lived through and acted out all the modes of anxiety and despair that were to characterize the coming century; and the Edwardians—who were by and large the same people—felt and articulated that century's greatest expectations.

Here, too, Wells managed to be quintessentially a man of his time. We have already seen that his personal revolution, his lifelong sexual adventurism, became full-fledged in the years just after the turn of the century. And parallel to this private transformation is a transformation in the tone of his speculative fiction. He begins to think not just in terms of the disasters awaiting technological man in his quest for survival, but of the chances available to him for transcendence, for final victory over the stern dictates of history and the struggle for existence. It is no accident then, following this argument, that to this period also belong the best of Wells's "realistic" novels: *Kipps* in 1905, *Tono-Bungay* and *Ann Veronica* in 1909, and *The History of Mr. Polly* in 1910. In these books he takes the common stuff of existence in an industrial society as his theme, without the apocalyptic trappings of voyages through time or invasions from beyond the atmosphere, and manages to demonstrate convincingly that the apocalyptic spirit, regardless of the trappings, is still there—that the life of the middle classes in England is *already*, as he writes, moving toward a future which must be either radically liberating or radically destructive for the individual psyche.

His "realistic" novels of this period, in other words, should be read along with his more explicitly scientific romances, since they explore many of the same themes with only a slight change of tone. Stylistically, Wells was a shape-shifter. He seldom wrote the same sort of book twice, and if he did, the second one was usually a parody or inversion of the first. But ideologically, he was a remarkably consistent man. From his first books to his last, in despair or in optimism, his theme was obsessively that of middle-class man's chances for survival in a world which through the accumulated weight of technology and the inexorable pressures of evolutionary history threatens his life. If there is a single question to which all Wells's books are addressed, it might be phrased as this one: How shall Man live through his own coming of age?

But to understand the special urgency of that question for Wells, it is necessary to understand how the question came to be asked not only by him but by his time, the time of the late Victorian and Edwardian period. And to understand that, we have to look more closely at the bundle of ideas called *fin de siècle*. People felt apocalyptic toward the end of the nineteenth century, we have said. But why? Why did they feel so *very* apocalyptic? For the beginning of an answer, it is convenient and appropriate to look to a single year: 1895, the year of Wells's first novel, *The Time Machine*.

In 1895 the first motion pictures were shown to a mass audience, in Paris, by the brothers Louis Jean and Auguste Lumière. The first international trade union, the French General Confederation of Labor, was formed under the guidance of the radical socialist Georges Sorel. In Vienna a young physician, Sigmund Freud, published his first book, *Studies in Hysteria* (with his older colleague, Josef Breuer). The German physicist Wilhelm Roentgen discovered an anomalous wavelength of light which he called the X-Ray. And, in England, Oscar Wilde began the first of the trials that would lead to his public humiliation and imprisonment for homosexuality. On the whole, it was an auspicious year.

Many of its events were both ends and beginnings, culminations of nineteenth-century trends of thought and auguries of things to come. And the event which may have had the most immediate effect upon Wells's popularity, and perhaps also on his developing ideas about art, was the one that was most definitely the end of something: the trial of Oscar Wilde.

A COMMUNITY OF ARTISTS

Born in 1854, Wilde was only twelve years Wells's senior. But by the time Wells was just beginning his career as a writer, Wilde was the most famous and feared literary figure of his day: famous because he wedded to a real genius for language an unerring gift for public relations, advertising himself as a scandalously immoral poseur and an aesthete whose sense of the beautiful embraced a large fascination with the beauty of sin and depravity; and feared for the same reasons. Wells owed an important boost in his career to Wilde. In 1891 Wells had published an essay, "The Rediscovery of the Unique," in the *Fortnightly Review*. Wilde read it and enthusiastically praised it to William Ernest Henley, who, as we have seen, commissioned *The Time Machine*. Wilde's good opinion of a writer, in other words, could—before the trial—make that writer's future.

Wilde was wellborn, handsome, and undeniably brilliant. His best writing still sparkles with unforgettable and sinister paradoxes, and his conversation was reputedly even more dazzling than his writing. As he wrote in 1894, in "Phrases and Philosophies for the Use of the Young," "One should either be a work of art, or wear a work of art." And as he said later to André Gide, "Would you like to know the great drama of my life? It is that I have put my genius into my life—I have put only my talent into my works."

Wilde died in 1900 (another well-chosen date), and in his last years he bitterly regretted having squandered his very real genius on being a great personality instead of a great artist. But the regrets did not come soon enough. Some of his plays, including *Lady Windermere's Fan* and *The Importance of Being Earnest*, are among the glories of comic drama, and his 1890 novel *The Picture of Dorian Gray* is a masterpiece of a very special kind of overheated, plastic-plant horror. But for all his continuing fascination, and for all his immense attractiveness as a tragicomic figure, the enduring sense one has about Oscar Wilde is a sense of great, foolish, and pointless waste.

The man was suicidal, and bent on advertising his suicide for the highest reasons, with the best examples. Wilde was famous as the most extreme, and extremely public, of the "aesthetes" who seemed to populate English letters almost exclusively in the last decade of the nineteenth century. Among the names most frequently associated with him were illustrator and writer Aubrey Beardsley, essayist Max Beerbohm, poet Lionel Johnson, American painter James McNeill Whistler, and young Irish poet and folklorist W. B. Yeats. These men did not form a "movement" with specific principles and aims—as did, for example, the roughly parallel and contemporary French Symbolists—nor did they, generally, produce the same sorts of works. And yet for England in the late 1880s and early 1890s they seemed to constitute a school. And to many, the lesson of that school was poisonous.

Poetry and physics, art and science, had for most of the nineteenth century been drawing farther and farther away from each other, despite the best efforts of poets and physicists. In 1800, in the *Preface* to the second edition of *Lyrical Ballads*, William Wordsworth had expressed the hope that with the advancement of knowledge, the language of the natural sciences would soon become as immediate a subject of lyric poetry as the languages of nature had been in the past. It was not a hope soon realized. As science came increasingly to mean "technology" for the British public and to manifest its accomplishments as an industrial complex incapable of taking account of individual aspirations or identity, poetry began to fight more and more a rearguard action, retreating to a smaller and smaller audience of those willing or capable of appreciating it. Wordsworth had written for the people; Browning wrote for the salons; and Wilde (and Yeats and their contemporaries) were forced to write more or less for one another. As we have seen in the last chapter, Tennyson at midcentury was probably the last poet of real genius capable of celebrating both the lyric impulse and the advance of industry—and even he had his problems doing it. The Victorian novel, of course, was a brief if splendid exception to the isolation of the artist. William Thackeray and Charles Dickens, and for a time George Eliot and Henry James, created a world in which industrial man (from the lowest classes, in Dickens, to the highest, in James) could still be expected to find his freedom, his salvation, his fate in things as they most demonstrably were.

But this was not to last. Contemporary with Tennyson's celebrations of the progress of knowledge and civilization were the stern warnings of John Ruskin that industrial culture, in its headlong race toward mass production, was crushing all that individual handicraft, that private initiative which had in the ages of faith made every craftsman a potential poet and every poet a dedicated craftsman. And, after Ruskin, writer, painter, and graphic artist William Morris constituted almost a one-man movement dedicated to returning craftsmanship to the realm of art and art to the realm of craftsmanship. Morris's Kelmscott Press, where the "technologies" of design, printing, and bookbinding were performed by the same men who produced the artistic works printed, was an important influence on the aesthetes of Wilde's generation.

But an influence is not necessarily an inspiration. It was also possible to argue, following the lead of Ruskin and Morris, that *any* product of technology was inartistic, and that the only "true" art was one that dissociated itself absolutely from the productions of mass industry—one, in fact, that set out deliberately to shock and offend those who were still in thrall to the machinery of industrial culture. Enter Wilde and the aesthetes, who—at least in the mind of the reading public—stood for an "art" so special, so delicate, and so dangerously immoral that to appreciate it fully one had to be (or claim to be) a member of a special, delicate, immoral—and anti-technological, anti-scientific—class.

It was dead-end Romanticism. Since Wordsworth's hope of the union of the language of poetry and the language of science had not come true, poetry tried to exile science and all its pomp from the realm of human experience. One must either be a work of art, or wear a work of art: what is missing in Wilde's epigram is any sense that the "work of art" is ever *made* with hard labor and muscular effort. For making, at least with a purpose, smacked too much of the soul-killing methods of industry and commercialism. In 1891 Wilde added his famous "Preface" to *The Picture of Dorian Gray* (the novel had been first published the previous year). It is a series of defiant, and defiantly amoral, paradoxes about the nature of art and its dissociation from conventional, middle-class morality, concluding with this passage:

> We can forgive a man for making a useful thing as long as he does not admire it. The only excuse for making a useless thing is that one admires it intensely.
> All art is quite useless.

Out of such coy defiance was constructed the legend of Oscar Wilde, and therefore the greater part of the legend of the "art for art's sake" movement in the early 1890s. In 1894 *The Yellow Book* began publication, a magazine of poetry, fiction, essays, and art devoted exclusively to the productions of the aesthetes and (as they were also called) "decadents" whose artistic standards were a deliberate affront to the values of the solemn, late-Victorian middle class.

And this, as much as the scruffling world of journalism, was the literary atmosphere into which the young, undereducated, hungry H. G. Wells entered. It made an impression. Not only was Wilde an early and generous admirer of his work, but Wells himself in his early work showed definite tendencies toward the aesthetic for its own sake. The Eloi of *The Time Machine*, those fragile, pale, consumptive children of 802,701 A.D., are partly a satirical vision of the aesthetes and decadents of the nineties (they could only be drawn, one feels, by Beardsley), but they are more than simply satire. They are sad, innocent, and doomed. Continually preyed upon by the monstrous, cannibalistic, machine-tending Morlocks, they are, in a way, a melancholy and unironic extension of the languid claims to beautiful uselessness of some of *The Yellow Book*'s contributors. And in *The Wonderful Visit*, a little read but fascinating novel published in the same year as *The Time Machine*, Wells came as close as he ever would to writing a full-scale aesthete's fantasy.

The Wonderful Visit is the story of an Angel who accidentally finds himself on Earth. Flying over rural England, he is shot down by a Vicar with a passion for hunting, who mistakes the Angel for a flamingo. Taking the wounded Angel home, the well-meaning Vicar tries to accustom his otherworldly guest to the conventions of English social life, but to no avail. The Angel is too innocent, too beautiful, too unconventionally brilliant for the tawdry, boring people among whom he is thrown, and his wings keep shrinking throughout the book. At last he dies, while heroically trying to save a servant girl from a burning house, leaving the townspeople to sink back into their humdrum lives—all except the Vicar who, having briefly known a glory beyond the everyday, dies soon after of a broken heart.

It is the kind of bittersweet fairy tale *The Yellow Book* set was enamored of, with its contrast between the experience of pure, "useless" beauty and the shabby hypocrisies of those who cannot appreciate such beauty. Wells is even careful, in introducing the Angel, to strike the proper aesthetic tone. "Let us be plain," he writes. "The Angel of this story is the Angel

of Art, not the Angel that one must be irreverent to touch . . .
the Angel of Italian art, polychromatic and gay. He comes
from the land of beautiful dreams and not from any holier
place."

But *The Wonderful Visit* also helps us see how constitu-
tionally incapable Wells was of writing a deliberately "artistic" story—in the sense of course, the aesthetes meant by "artistic." Partly because of his class and partly because of his
own inclinations, he could never subscribe to an opinion that
"all art is quite useless." Nor could he, even at this early
stage, refrain from a vision of middle-class mediocrity that has
less to do with the aesthete's easy contempt than with the re-
former's angry zeal. Near the middle of the novel the Angel
asks the Vicar to explain the quality and course of human life.
The Vicar begins by describing the happiness and innocence
of childhood—a time very like that which the Angel inhabits
permanently. But what then? asks the Angel.

> "Then," said the Vicar, "the glamour fades and life begins
> in earnest. The young men and young women pair off—most
> of them. They come to me shy and bashful, in smart ugly
> dresses, and I marry them. And then little pink babies come to
> them, and some of the youths and maidens that were, grow fat
> and vulgar, and some grow thin and shrewish, and their pretty
> complexions go, and they get a queer delusion of superiority
> over the younger people, and all the delight and glory goes
> out of their lives. So they call the delight and glory of the
> younger ones, Illusion. And then they begin to drop to
> pieces."

This is a *fin de siècle* vision, indeed. But it is a vision from
within the middle class, from the midst of that ugly, pointless,
crushing life that to many in the nineties seemed to represent
the dead end of civilization. Something ought to be done
about all this, one feels; and one is meant to think so. It is easy
to recognize here, more so than anywhere in *The Time Machine*, the tone Wells later used to describe the "Age of Confusion" in his utopias: perhaps the tone is so striking because it
contrasts so jarringly with the coy fairy-tale surface of the
story.

The aesthetic "movement," in England at least, did not
long outlive the trial and humiliation of Wilde. The public

uproar against him was so great, and so gleefully vicious, that most of the members of this non-school found it healthy to dissociate themselves from its non-tenets, and from one another. *The Yellow Book*'s subscriptions fell, and the magazine closed in 1897. For the next two decades, at least, literature in England would try to dissociate itself from the stigma of aestheticism and demonstrate its connections, revolutionary or conservative, with the cause of the ordinary, urban, literate middle class. The world-weary and effete sensibility of *fin de siècle* was slowly supplanted by the Edwardian sensibility, which critic P. N. Furbank has characterized as the urge *"to redeem the suburban."*

For Wells it was a perfect transition, as it was for his great Edwardian friends and sometime adversaries George Bernard Shaw and G. K. Chesterton. The opposition of art and industrialism, poetry and the suburb, gave way to the necessity of obliterating that opposition, of interpreting the modern developments of science and philosophy to the solid, earnest—and very confused—members of the middle class who ought best to profit from those developments if only they could be made to understand them. In Shaw's dramas, Chesterton's stories and essays, and Wells's fiction after the end of the century, art was pressed into the service not simply of shocking the bourgeois but of educating them. In this respect it is appropriate that the year of Wilde's trial was also the year that saw the birth of the commercial cinema and the radio, two technologies that were to become the most powerful and deeply influential popular art forms of the century to come, outstripping even the newspaper and the Victorian novel in their power to reach and direct the imagination of millions.

Nevertheless, Wilde left his mark on the age that succeeded him. Shaw's drama of ideas owes a large debt to the darting, lighthanded metaphysics of Wilde's plays; Chesterton's gift for paradox is Wilde's, chastened; and Wells most of all remembered what aestheticism, at its best, had represented. His utopias, his versions of what life at its richest and fullest might look like, always include the assertion that, in the truly happy society, all men and women will be at once artisans and artists, capable of and dedicated to making beautiful things whose "use" is precisely that they are admired and loved for their beauty alone. The aesthetes had insisted that the appreciation of art for its own sake was a kind of test that only the civilized man would pass. Wells's point was that a *real* civilization would make sure everybody could pass.

A CENTURY OF REVOLUTION

Wells's fiction, from its beginning, was also intimately related to the currents of social theory and reform which characterized the waning years of the century. We have mentioned as significant the formation of the French General Confederation of Labor in 1895. Georges Sorel, the socialist whose call for a massive, international strike gave rise to the founding of the Confederation, was only one of the most radical thinkers who, during the 1880s and 1890s, served clear notice to Europe that the century to come would be characterized by social experiment and popular unrest on a scale that would rival the seismic effects of the French Revolution.

Of course, from a broad point of view the revolutions and revolutionary social theories of the nineteenth and twentieth centuries can be seen as a continual development and expansion of the American Revolution of 1776 and the French Revolution of 1789: much as modern physics teaches us to regard the history of the universe, the birth and death of stars and the vagrancies of planetary systems, as the expansion of an original, massive explosion. Like many others, Wells inclined to this "big bang" theory of modern European history. He wrote of the French Revolution in *The Outline of History*, "It is as if something had thrust up from beneath the surface of human affairs, made a gigantic effort, and for a time spent itself." The people's revolution rapidly degenerated into the Reign of Terror and, finally, the Napoleonic Empire and the return of the Bourbon monarchy in 1814. But even this failure Wells interpreted in favorable—and characteristic—terms. "After all," he wrote, "this wave of revolution had realized nearly everything that had been clearly thought out before it came. It was not failing now for want of impetus, but for want of finished ideas. Many things that had oppressed mankind were swept away for ever. Now that they were swept away it became apparent how unprepared men were for the creative opportunities this clearance gave them."

The revolution failed, or rather, momentarily spent its force, "for want of finished ideas." Here, as in his thinking about the art of fiction, Wells emphasizes the importance of education, the crucial necessity of finished, clear ideas as a guide to action. This most impetuous and restless of men insisted, to the end of his life, that a fully evolved human should act only for the most deliberate and explicit reasons (remember his self-definition, "I hammer at my main ideas").

But Wells's observations about the French Revolution also indicate his indebtedness to the social thought of the nineteenth century. The Revolution of 1789, indeed, had been anticipated and to some degree inspired by the great French rationalists of the eighteenth century: especially by the scathing wit of Voltaire (whom Wells venerated) and the passionate, romantic social theory of Jean Jacques Rousseau (whom Wells disliked intensely). But it was not, really, an ideological movement, with clear goals and "finished ideas." Its aftershocks throughout the next century, culminating in the Russian Revolution of 1917, were.

It has been a cliché for some time now to say that the nineteenth century "discovered" history as a science. And like many clichés, this one is fundamentally true. Historians of the late eighteenth and early nineteenth century, partly because of the upheavals in European society and culture taking place around them, began to regard the study of history as more than simply the preservation of the past or even the understanding of the present through the past. History, it came to be believed, might be approached with the same analytical rigor and, perhaps, predictive efficiency that had been so brilliantly employed in the physical sciences since Sir Isaac Newton. Underneath the surface of time past might be perceived patterns, vectors of force, that properly understood would yield elementary formulas for the rise and fall of civilizations, allowing us to see also the shape of things to come. In the 1960s and 1970s the profession of "futurist" gained increasing academic recognition and respect: the business of analyzing past and contemporary society with the deliberate aim of forecasting specific short- and long-term developments. It has always been, of course, the unofficial profession of many science-fiction writers, and was very nearly the lifework of Wells himself. But it is important to realize that "futurism" is really not new; its roots are firmly in the nineteenth-century discovery of history-writing as science.

Besides its far-reaching effects on Western man's whole sense of time, the growth of scientific historiography had an immediate and decisive effect upon social analysis and revolutionary theory. If the future could be extrapolated from the structures of the past, it could also be planned, and planned in accordance with the "true," "natural," or "ideal" shape of a human society as discerned beneath the failed experiments of previous cultures. G. W. F. Hegel, the most influential and controversial philosopher of the age, presented, in the first decades of the century, a vision of history—or History, as we must now call it—as something very like the progressive self-manifestation of the absolute will of God. In *The Philosophy of History* (published posthumously in 1832) he writes:

> The only Thought which Philosophy brings with it to the contemplation of History, is the simple conception of *Reason;* that Reason is the Sovereign of the World; that the history of the world, therefore, presents us with a rational process.

For Hegel, history is the incarnation of reason, order, truth. And the chaotic surface of history, its contradictory and warring systems, beliefs, and cultures, is simply the dialectical process through which the truth, the *Zeitgeist* or "Spirit of the Age" inevitably manifests itself: the *Zeitgeist*'s "struggle for existence," as it could be imagined after Darwin.

But why just discern the evolving shape of the *Zeitgeist;* why not also help it manifest itself? In 1845, the twenty-seven-year-old Karl Marx had already set himself the task of purging Hegel's philosophy of its mystical, spiritualist elements and transforming it into an efficient tool for the analysis and governance of the "real," i.e., material, world. In his *Theses on Feuerbach*, written that year, Marx sounded the note for all subsequent revolutionary theory:

VIII. Social life is essentially *practical*. All mysteries which mislead theory to mysticism find their rational solution in human practice and in the comprehension of this practice.

* * *

XI. The philosophers have only *interpreted* the world in various ways; the point however is to *change* it.

Three years after this was written, Marx and his collaborator Friedrich Engels published the *Communist Manifesto*. Almost simultaneously, a massive workers' revolution erupted in Paris, threatening the precarious order of the restored monarchy and put down only through brutal police action. Henceforth the theory of history (at least among social revolutionaries) would be not only theoretical, but at least potentially violent; and violence would be theoretically, as well as practically, motivated.

It is important to understand this development of nineteenth-century thought, for it produced, finally, a figure who haunts many of the age's dreams and nightmares: the anarchist, socialist, or communist whose high intelligence masks a deep and frightening commitment to chaos, destruction, or whatever terrible means are necessary to the overthrow and transformation of society. Terrorism becomes possible precisely *as* an "ism," a reasoned plan of action rather than a random overflow of emotion; and the terrorist enters fiction as he enters history. V. I. Lenin, whom Wells met in 1920 when he visited Russia (they did not like one another), was not only the culmination of a century's worth of philosophy, but the incarnation of a half-century-old myth.

Wells, as we have seen, was by both class and temperament a revolutionary soul. He was also a true nineteenth-century ideologue, at least to the extent of insisting on "finished ideas" as the only possible basis for social action or social planning. But he was also—as Lenin is reported to have called him—a petty bourgeois. He mistrusted the brute force and inarticulate aspirations of the laboring class—that "mass man" whose existence Marx had discovered and whose destiny he had hymned as world dominion. He mistrusted the figure of the bomb-toting, metaphysically inclined terrorist (or "anarchist" or "nihilist," to use the age's catchphrases), the man willing to commit the unspeakable for the sake of a theory.

And, perhaps most of all, he mistrusted theory itself. A voracious assimilator of systems and abstractions, he was nevertheless skeptical of any system whose complexity appeared to
overweigh its application to the observable and observed facts
of the life around us. This pragmatism, or empiricism, has
been often described as a particularly "English" as opposed to
Continental trait of mind; or it may also be explained as the
special genius for observation of the novelist, as opposed to
the social scientist or philosopher. At any rate, it is one of the
hallmarks of Wells's distinctive vision of social possibilities,
and of the chance for utopia. From the beginning, he believed
in the necessity and the reality of social change, or revolution.
But to the end, he wanted his revolution to be both rational
and sensible, both total and civilized.

It can be argued that Wells expressed his fears of revolutionaries most fully in his fiction of the 1890s, and his hopes
for revolution most fully in his fiction of the Edwardian years
and afterward. Just as the Eloi of The Time Machine are partly
a vision of the aesthetes and decadents of the literary and artistic world, the cannibalistic Morlocks who prey upon the
Eloi are a much more explicit projection of the proletariat, the
"mass man" whose emergence Wells feared. His dislike and
suspicion of the dedicated "scientific" anarchist are the basis
of one of his early short stories, "The Stolen Bacillus" (1894).
And his suspicion of abstraction, of theory without humanity,
may fairly be said to run through all his early fiction. Griffin,
the anti-hero of The Invisible Man, and Dr. Moreau of The
Island of Doctor Moreau are both ferociously intelligent
men—the former a physicist, the latter a biologist—who erect
upon their scientific discoveries plans for a new world empire, a new order of things, only to find their structures collapse on them in a suicidal rubble. In The War of the Worlds
and The First Men in the Moon Wells shows us alternate societies—the octopuslike Martians and the insectlike Selenites—that have been built upon an absolutely efficient, rational collectivism, and which are equally anti-human (there is
an important anticipation of both these books in his 1896
story, "In the Abyss").

It is "The Stolen Bacillus," though, that best catches his attitude toward social revolution. This very short story tells how

a pale-faced anarchist steals a phial containing what he thinks is a deadly concentration of cholera bacteria. He intends to empty it into the London water system. But the phial breaks in the cab in which he is making his escape; undaunted, the anarchist greedily swallows the few drops of liquid in the bottom of the phial and charges off amidst the busy London crowds, himself now a living instrument of death and contagion, shouting "Vive l'Anarchie!" Only then do we learn that the phial did not really contain cholera bacteria, but rather a dose of a new compound whose only effect is to turn its recipient bright blue.

What began as a tale of terror ends as a joke: but a joke with a serious point. Men and women really did dread anarchy, and particularly the threat presented by the figure of the anarchist, that outwardly normal, rational man who might, unsuspected, be harboring thoughts and plans of the most unspeakable violence and hatred. If revolution, even in its maddest aspects, could now be "rational"—i.e., philosophically planned and supported—then it was, to all intents and purposes, invisible. Wells's invention of the Invisible Man had been an early, very resonant expression of this fear: the invisible minister of apocalypse, the hyperintelligent terrorist, part of whose terror is that you can't see him. Joseph Conrad, in his novel of 1907, *The Secret Agent,* and G. K. Chesterton in his novel of 1908, *The Man Who Was Thursday,* would both treat the theme of anarchy in ways perhaps suggested by *The Invisible Man:* in terms, that is, of its fundamentally frightening aspects of normality, its terrible quality of being unrecognizable until it is too late.

"The Stolen Bacillus" is a reassuring version of the same situation. The anarchist, for all his dedication and care, has made a stupid blunder; a blunder, moreover, that henceforth will render him immediately, unequivocally recognizable. He will be bright blue, an all too visible man.

We can see the difference between *The Invisible Man* and "The Stolen Bacillus" as part of the difference between the despairing and the optimistic halves of Wells's sensibility. But "The Stolen Bacillus" is also reassuring because it insists that anarchists and their like are not to be feared: their own excessive hatreds will lead them into comically excessive postures

of impotent violence. But, the story insists, they will be led
into these absurdities because of the workings of a slower,
surer, and ultimately more total revolution, the revolution of
scientific thought, which is changing the world daily by making the animosities and class hatreds of the past irrelevant.
The scientist who prepares the "blue" solution does not know
he is thwarting anarchy. But he is, and the single-minded
blindness of his research is revealed to be also the wisdom of
history (Hegelian theme), its comic judgment upon the impulse to mass murder.

Wells, then, heir to a century of metaphysical and social
revolutionaries, was impelled to a version of revolution much
quieter, much more explicitly middle class, than many which
were abroad in his time. This can be thought of as a very English taste in revolution, though Wells was tumultuous
enough in his personal life and far-ranging enough in his
social vision to alienate or scandalize the more conservative of
his revolutionary English friends. Nevertheless, for a while at
least, he found a congenial society among those gentle radicals, the Fabians.

The Fabian Society had begun in the 1880s as a discussion
group dedicated to examining the widest range of programs
for social, spiritual, and economic improvement of the current
state of things. Tolerance rather than orthodoxy, and per-
suasiveness rather than shrillness were the hallmarks of the
Society from its origin, and even during its years of greatest
membership—from about 1900 to the outbreak of the First
World War—it maintained a special and distinctive attitude of
patience toward the most extreme varieties of radical thought
within its ranks. But the Fabians were not simply armchair so-
cialists or elegant, bored triflers with the cause of social
change—even though Wells, in his bitter break with the Society, was to accuse its members of both those sins. In fact, the
Fabians exercised a deep and lasting influence on English
social programs for most of the twentieth century.

They exercised this influence largely because of the talents, dedication, and doggedly practical idealism of Beatrice
and Sidney Webb. The Webbs were of the upper middle class,
and appear in their personal lives to have been almost absurdly bland, temperate, and passionless: during their court-

ship, the then Beatrice Potter wrote to Sidney Webb that he should send her a snapshot of his head, since that was the only part of him that interested her. For pleasure as well as for the good of society, they preferred reading economics to reading fiction. They were not the sort of people, in other words, with whom a man like Wells could be comfortable, and even from the beginning of their association there was tension between his rambunctiousness and their tepid high seriousness.

But tepid or not, the Webbs maintained—and, more important inspired—a concern for the fate of the poor and the improvement of social conditions in England as total, as disinterested, and as saintly in its way as any in the annals of social thought. For these two "passionless" people, the improvement of the common lot may have been the great romance, the great passion of their lives. Their most influential book was the Minority Report of the Poor Law Commission in 1909. It is an unreadable mass of facts, figures, and economic indicators, and a landmark in the literature of social justice which exercised a massive and benign influence on the legislation of England for the next forty years.

The Minority Report is also a quintessentially Fabian document, since its basic assumption is that while a major revolution in social justice is historically inevitable, such a revolution can be effected through already existing channels of legislation, without excessive violence or the wreckage of things as they now stand. The name of the group itself was chosen as a reference to Fabius Maximus, also called Fabius Cunctator or "Fabius the Delayer," dictator and general in chief of Rome during the Second Punic War (218–201 B.C.). His controversial but brilliant tactics were to delay a full-scale confrontation with the invading Carthaginian army until they had come so far into Italy that their path of retreat was closed off. The turn-of-the-century Fabians sought to be "delayers" of this sort in the social sphere, forestalling or avoiding revolution and bloodshed in the streets, working dully, quietly, and obsessively for a revolution within the laws.

Wells, as we have said, joined the society in 1903. His soon-to-follow rupture with them was largely a matter of personal tension and intellectual incompatibility: for all his love of science and "finished ideas," Wells could never really tolerate the boredom of unvarnished facts, numbers, and statistics. And though he understood, and profusely praised, the *Minority Report* when it appeared (after he had broken with the Webbs), he was not the sort of man who would ever think of writing such a book. Nevertheless, just as the aesthetes both attracted and repelled and therefore helped determine his ideas about fiction and the shape of an ideal culture, so the Fabians importantly determined his ideas about fiction and the shape of an ideal society. He was a revolutionary who feared the apocalyptic moment of revolution itself, and the Fabian hope of gradualism was in many ways perfectly suited to the habits of his own imagination.

A number of his early critics were disturbed by the frequency and level of violence in Wells's scientific romances, and the incidence of violence has continued to be an easy cliché for critics discussing his work. And it is true that, especially from *The War of the Worlds* through the utopian visions of *The War in the Air, The World Set Free, Men Like Gods,* and *The Shape of Things To Come,* he imagined a period of chaos and apocalyptic warfare as the inevitable prelude to the establishment of a just state. Indeed, there was something in Wells that took a real delight in scenes of Old Testament-scale destruction and pillage. He wrote to a friend during the composition of *The War of the Worlds,* "I'm doing the dearest little serial for Pearson's new magazine, in which I completely wreck and sack Woking—killing my neighbours in painful and eccentric ways—then proceed via Kingston and Richmond to London, which I sack, selecting South Kensington for feats of peculiar atrocity." It is a lighthearted summary of the book's plot but also an accurate one, and the "feats of peculiar atrocity" Wells enjoyed imagining—or symbolically doing, as the letter makes plain—would characterize his fiction for the rest of his life.

We can explain this taste for disaster in several ways. From his mother's punitive variety of Christianity, Wells retained a sense of God's terrible justice as the eternal prelude to His mercy: all things must end in fire and torment before they can begin again as the city of the saints. From the intellectual life of his early maturity, he retained the *fin de siècle* mood of things wearing out, grinding inexorably toward some sort of irreparable breakdown. And, perhaps most importantly, from his own class background he retained a permanent, potentially violent, hatred of the social structures that but for his own genius and luck would have condemned him to a life of sullen desperation. For a man whose horizon had once been bounded by the fate of draper's assistant, to tear down, wreck, obliterate the suffocating world of dull houses, inept schools, and tomblike shops would, whatever his later success, probably always seem an enticing thing, indeed. Wells would have feared the hate-filled terrorist, in other words, more than most of his Fabian associates, precisely because he was in a better position to understand how one *could* grow so devoted to detonation.

It is important to understand the special quality of violence in Wells's prophecies. In book after book he describes a future that lurches toward a Golden Age across a no man's land of war, pestilence, and reversion to bestiality. But he insists that the ordeal by violence, though highly likely, is not necessary. Again and again in his utopias, there occur observations to the effect that if men had only understood themselves better, had only formed clear and useful concepts of their place in the universe, the Golden Age might have been reached without such an appalling waste of life. "If we had only *seen*": that is the sentiment whose melancholy harmony runs through all his future histories, and it is the central connection between his science fiction and his other writing, where he tried to *make* people see how the kingdom of man could be established without the spilling of blood. For all the violence of his imagination Wells differed from most social visionaries, from the author of the Book of Revelations down to and including Marx, in that he did not believe, or would not let himself believe, that the Golden Age had to be preceded by a Last War. But he feared it would be.

To comprehend the full complexity of his attitude, we must examine a third aspect of Wells's intellectual background, perhaps the most important one. As an heir to the problems and perils of the aesthetic tradition, and to the expectations and fears of nineteenth-century socialism, he would doubtless have written brilliant and successful books. But it is impossible to imagine the Wells we know without

Science (the capital "S" put there by Wells's attitude toward it), and particularly without the awesome edifice of Darwinian evolutionary theory.

A UNIVERSE OF CHANGE

Without Darwin there may literally not have been an "H. G. Wells." As we have seen, Wells's talent for biology and his fellowship to study at the Normal School of Science were what, more than anything else, delivered him from the draper's shop. But besides its importance for the circumstances of his career, evolutionary theory profoundly informed almost every aspect of his thought. Here is a revealing instance of its importance for Wells, from *Ann Veronica*. Ann Veronica Stanley, the independent-minded but hedged-in heroine, is strolling with her very unliberated aunt to a boring garden party. In the middle of their stroll, Ann Veronica (a biology student) has a revelation:

> After all, she found herself reflecting, behind her aunt's complacent visage there was a past as lurid as any one's—not, of course, her aunt's own personal past . . . but an ancestral past with all sorts of scandalous things in it: fire and slaughterings, exogamy, marriage by capture, corroborees, cannibalism! Ancestresses with perhaps dim anticipatory likenesses to her aunt . . . must have danced through a brief and stirring life in the woady buff. . . . Perhaps it was just as well there was no inherited memory.

With Wells even at his most resolutely "realistic," in terms of the conventions of the English novel, there is always this possibility and risk, that the social world he is describing will suddenly open up vistas within itself into another, immeasurably more ancient "reality," that of the vast expanse of geological time and the comparative youth, the flarelike brevity, of the human species. The point of Ann Veronica's amusing insight is not just how innocent her aunt is of the savagery that is her dim genetic past; it is also how shockingly like yesterday that "dim past" is on any scale that measures the real age of the Earth.

What in a novel like *Ann Veronica* is a permanent if muted possibility of narrative is for Wells's major science fiction the constant theme of his imaginings. From *The Time Machine* on, it was generally recognized that no writer had so completely or so perceptively taken Darwin to heart. Wells may not have been the first man to acknowledge the importance of Darwinian theory for the future of civilization and the business of fiction, but he was certainly the first to acknowledge and assimilate that theory, in all its corrosive effect upon ideas of what fiction was for and about.

Let us draw back for a moment and try to imagine what, precisely, the implications of biological science were for a man of Wells's time. Darwin's crucial position in the history of modern thought has by now been so often explained and commented upon that is is likely to seem pointless once again to say how important was *The Origin of Species*. But to examine Darwin in terms of the career of Wells is, in its way, to see him anew, instead of simply "once again": to see him as he affected not only the scientific, but the imaginative life of the age he helped to introduce.

In 1859 Darwin published a treatise called, in part, *The Origin of Species by Means of Natural Selection. . . .* The title is, in itself, part of the astonishing novelty of Darwin's thought. In the middle nineteenth century, despite premonitory rumblings from biological classifiers and the evolutionary theory of the great French scientist Chevalier de Lamarck, it was not generally assumed that species should originate at all. The species of the living world, the insects, birds, reptiles, mammals, apes, and men, were not just varieties of life, continually changing and adapting as the survival-demands of their environment altered. They formed an eternally fixed and divinely decreed order of life, a vital chain of being extending from lowest to highest, from simplest to most complex, incarnating in its elegant subordination and gradation God's eternal plan for the universe.

The evidence for divine supervision and guidance had long since disappeared from the other major area of scientific investigation, physics. A famous anecdote relates how Napoleon met mathematician Marquis Pierre Simon Laplace (author of the five-volume *Mécanique céleste*) with the words, "Monsieur Laplace, they tell me you have written this large book on the system of the universe, and have never even mentioned its Creator." Laplace's haughty reply: "I had no need of that hypothesis." Since the work of Newton in the late seventeenth century, the animate world had ceased to be a convenient place to ground arguments for the necessity of an ordering, purposive God. The emphasis of theological proofs, then, had shifted to the animate world, to the evident and elegant distribution of life forms along a spectrum that, it was claimed, could only be the result of an original and originating plan. Darwin changed all that.

In many ways, Darwin's observations were more an anticipation of the world view to be born than they were an expression, in biological terms, of the world view established by Newton and the Age of Reason. Darwin described an organic world of constant blind flux, struggle, and variation without purpose. What we regard as established species of this process are simply the lucky variants that happen to adapt more successfully to their environment and therefore propagate themselves more efficently than their competitors. We see breaks, of course, and levels of complexity in the range of organic life, and these breaks argue for a hierarchy organized outside the processes of nature. "But," says Darwin in The Origin of Species, "these breaks are imaginary, and might have been inserted anywhere, after intervals long enough to allow the accumulation of a considerable amount of divergent variation."

This implies that nature, left to its own devices, is sufficient to produce the range and variety of the living species we observe. In fact, it implies more than that. It implies, in a single surgical thrust of argument, that all human classifications of nature are nonce-classifications, artificialities imposed upon an intractible and innately incomprehensible flow of reality that always exceeds and baffles our attempts to name it.

Darwin was a very shy, conventional man. He was also one of the great geniuses in the history of Western thought. But his writings are both painstaking and essential, boring and seminal. He was hesitant to draw the inevitable conclusions from his own observations about vegetable and animal variation in varying environments. And after The Origin of Species had been published he all but refused to defend its inevitable conclusions. The history of Western thought probably does not include a more diffident rebel, a more unlikely earthshaker, than this self-effacing and respectably stuffy man. Yet shake the earth he did: perhaps more than his near contemporary Karl Marx (who apparently meditated dedicating his masterwork, *Das Kapital,* to Darwin) or his younger colleague in revolution, Sigmund Freud (whose later ideas about the archaic provenance of the subconscious were at least partly based upon Darwinian theories). Marx explored the dangers and contradictions of history, society, and economics, and Freud explored the dangers and contradictions of the self, the subconscious, and the passions; but Darwin explored what is finally the ground of both those other arenas, the landscape of geological time and its immanent—or nonexistent—purpose.

But so far we have given only a convenient—indeed, a fairly inoffensive—paraphrase of Darwinian theory. To understand fully what he means by "evolution" (a term he was, by the way, very sparing of) it is necessary to understand better *why* the once conventional terminology and mythology of "species" was inadequate to the world he saw around him. And to understand that, we have to understand what Darwin means by his most important concept, "the struggle for existence."

"The Struggle for Existence" is the title of Chapter Three of *The Origin of Species:* and it is also the phrase and concept which, misinterpreted, made "Darwinism" an all-purpose and equivocal banner under which any number of causes in the late nineteenth century could align their troops. But when Darwin used it, what it meant was more revolutionary than any of the revolutionary movements in whose cause it was invoked.

> We behold the face of nature bright with gladness, we often see superabundance of food; we do not see or we forget, that the birds which are idly singing round us mostly live on insects or seeds, and are thus constantly destroying life; or we forget how largely these songsters, or their eggs, or their nestlings, are destroyed by birds and beasts of prey; we do not always bear in mind, that, though food may be now superabundant, it is not so at all seasons of each recurring year.

Thus Darwin discussed the difficulty of the concept, "the struggle for existence." Nature teems with life, life infinitely variegated in its forms and capabilities: so much had been a common conviction at least since the triumph of Romanticism and its attendant natural mysticism. But it teems with life, insists Darwin in the most convincingly cold tones, just because it also teems with death, with the war for survival of every species against every other species, with the eternal and unrelenting struggle of every life form to secure for itself, at whatever cost, an adequate share of the limited food supply which is this garden, Earth.

Species originate, then, in their blind surge to win this elemental, eons-long game of life for food. And the surge *is* blind. A central tenet of Darwin's first formulation of his theory is that "natural selection" as the primary and indispensable mechanism of evolution is purposeless. Change is the only constant in the biological universe. Random mutations—a stronger beak here, a longer arm there, protective coloration somewhere else—will appear in the offspring of already established species. And if these mutations help the offspring find food better and therefore live longer and propagate more offspring, and if they transmit their random mutations to their own offspring, and if those offspring, the mutations transmitted and reinforced in their own bodies, produce offspring of their own . . . then a new "species" eventually comes into existence, a new biological form evolves equipped to fill and defend its niche in the food chain; until of course a better adaptation occurs.

Modern genetics has begun to demonstrate ways in which the genetic code may be broken, ways in which we might actually interpret the surge of life toward order as more purposive, more planned somehow, than Darwin's original description has it. And Darwin himself, in later editions of *The Origin of Species*, revised his opinions in the direction of a more benign, humanly comprehensible idea of evolutionary change: one owing to Lamarck, with which it was possible to argue that artificially acquired survival characteristics could be transmitted, and that therefore evolutionary adaptation was somehow directed or guided by certain universal principles of creative complexity.

Whatever later elaborations of Darwinian theory may have arisen, though—even those articulated by Darwin himself—*The Origin of Species* retains its pivotal position in the history of thought. Before Darwin wrote, it was difficult to understand the role of chance in the living universe; after him it was difficult, even for him, to argue for the importance or presence of plan.

A world in which the blind, violent struggle for life and food is the only constant; a world where the accidental, uncontrollable transmission of an apparently insignificant physical detail to your offspring might make the difference between life and death for the next generation; and above all a world whose history is played out, not on the scale of individual human lives or even on that of the rise and fall of empires, but rather on the unimaginable vistas of geological time: this is the world described by Darwin, and it frightened people.

It also invigorated some of them, later including Wells. Here was an explanation of why things were the way they were that explained not only why life seemed sometimes so crushingly discouraging and overwhelming, but also why sometimes it seemed to be tending toward a better, richer, *different* state of being. For man, after all, even from the beginning of the controversy, was the main point of the thing. In 1871 Darwin published *The Descent of Man*, the long-delayed and inevitable extension of the arguments in *The Origin of Species* to the theme and problem of human nature. If natural selection and the struggle for existence could explain the full range of other beings without appeal to a shaping, divine intelligence, then why should not man himself, that most self-gratulatory of "special" creations, be accounted for the same way? The question had been argued throughout Europe since 1859, and in 1871 Darwin finally answered it:

> Man in the rudest state in which he now exists is the most dominant animal that has ever appeared on this earth. He has spread more widely than any other highly organised form: and all others have yielded before him. He manifestly owes this immense superiority to his intellectual faculties, to his social habits, which lead him to aid and defend his fellows, and to his corporeal structure. The supreme importance of these characters has been proved by the final arbitrament of the battle for life.

It is the last sentence that matters most. The "battle for life," the struggle for existence, the same unconscious and

cosmic force that drives all other seed drives also us. At a
stroke, man and his civilization become the products of blind
chance and galactic accident. Culture, purpose, consciousness
become arbitrary, momentary things: for all the power of reason, reason appears now only a version of survival adaptation,
like the scorpion's sting or the rabbit's hind legs. And those
massive constructs of human intelligence, art, religion, morality, and ethics, become at once terribly endangered and terribly precious. They, more than anything else, are what make us
human. But they, also more than anything else, are what make
our treasured humanity appear arbitrary and—in the cosmic
context of things—vulnerable.

If everything can be explained as an accidental development of life evolved just to preserve its own blind struggle for
existence—everything *including* humanity—then what do morality or civilization finally mean, besides simply a temporary
compromise of the life force with universal entropy, thrown
up as a shelter against the storm and just as readily and as in-
differently torn down? *The Descent of Man* is eloquent in its
explanation of how morality, religion, ethics, and art all develop as necessary defenses for weak, hairless, fangless bipeds
against an array of natural enemies who possess every destructive and protective adaptation except the triumphant one
of culture. And does this finally mean that all our pretensions
to speciality and nobility are nothing more than pretensions,
that man's veneration of man and of the potential godhead
within man is no more than a gigantic and vain self-delusion?
An ancient Greek philosopher wittily observed that, if cattle
could think, they would imagine their gods as supercows.
One implication of Darwinian science was to turn this witty
cynicism into bitter truth.

Darwin was aware of the moral implications of his discoveries, and he was not comfortable with them. The last pages of
The Descent of Man are devoted to a discussion of the disturbing implications of the book's theory. Culture and self-consciousness may arise as species-specific adaptations for survival in the food chain. But, argues Darwin, that does not
mean that "human" is to be equated with "bestial," or that the
classification of biological *origins* is to be taken as the explanation of final *causes*. We can say, Darwin insists, that in man

nature achieves a nobility beyond its innate conditions, and that in the invention of morality man acquires a dignity in excess of that of the universe that gives him birth. In one of his most moving passages, Darwin writes:

> Man may be excused for feeling some pride at having risen, though not through his own exertions, to the very summit of the organic scale; and the fact of his having thus risen, instead of having been aborginally placed there, may give him hope for a still higher destiny in the distant future. But we are not here concerned with hopes or fears, only with the truth as far as our reason permits us to discover it; and I have given the evidence to the best of my ability.

This passage is as subtle as it is rich, both in what it promises and in what it withholds. Man may be proud: but proud of an eminence he enjoys despite, not because of, his own moral effort. We may have great hopes for the future of a creature who has come so far; but those hopes cannot obliterate the facts of our humble, even our violent origins in the muck and struggle of all organic life toward living space. During the decades after the publication of *The Origin of Species* and particularly *The Descent of Man* Darwin and "Darwinism" were to be invoked in defense of a number of social theories, most of which took a very jaundiced view of human aspirations and morality. But it is important to remember that Darwin was, however diffidently, a partner to the debate he engendered—and he entered the debate on the side of charity and decency rather than of rapine and the cult of the main chance.

Darwin's great defender T. H. Huxley—Wells's tutor in his first year at the Normal School of Science—examined the problem of the soul of man under evolutionary principles more explicitly. In 1893 Huxley delivered one of his most famous and most influential lectures, "Evolution and Ethics." It is probably the fullest statement of Darwinian principles as they affect moral and political concerns, and it is a very important anticipation of Wells's own thought on these matters—indeed, it is probably one of the chief influences. Huxley was a better writer, a less profoundly original scientist, and a much more pessimistic man than Darwin. For Huxley, the lesson of evolution is a bitter and possibly a tragic one. Morality, decency, love—all the things we value most intensely as characteristics of our civilization and our distance from the beasts—can be seen, on the cosmic scale, as mere evolutionary excrescences. They are "values," to be sure: but value whose only function is to make possible the banding together and survival of our weak, prehominid ancestors, and having no objective correlation in the structure of outer, physical or biological, reality. The only law nature knows is the law governing the relation of the eaters and the eaten: what humans celebrate as "natural law" is no more natural, no more suggested or echoed by the rest of the universe, than the construction of high-rise apartment buildings or the invention of clothing.

Now two conclusions can be drawn from this set of observations. The first, simpler, and more brutal one is that, since morality and a decent respect for the opinions of mankind are "just" myths, we can dispense with them and live our lives on the "true" ethics of the food-chain relationship, happily eating whatever we can kill, killing whatever looks even partially edible, and observing no hunting limit except the swift and self-ratifying one of not being eaten ourselves. This opinion, that the cosmos underwrites rapine, was mainly the philosophy of "social Darwinism." Its adherents, from the early superindustrialists of the twentieth century (including Andrew Carnegie and John D. Rockefeller) to modern "theorists" like Ayn Rand, tend to be at once curiously cynical and evangelical. We can remember that sociologist Max Weber traced the rise of *laissez faire* capitalism to the Protestant (especially Calvinist) work ethic, in which the sedulous amassing of wealth was a sure sign of the worker's spiritual merit, his membership in the divinely ordained elect. What Darwin did, at least for the people we are now talking about, was to substitute a firmly "scientific" version of justification for the somewhat fuzzier theological concept of salvation. The successful businessman could now claim justification for the mechanics of his success not just on the basis that God helps those who help themselves, but because it had been proved that nature *wants* us, at whatever cost, to help ourselves: salvation is, simply, salivation.

Most will agree that there is something not only innately unpleasant but potentially suicidal in this gospel of success as its own justification. And in the second half of the twentieth century we have been learning more and more, at our own cost, how unrestrained pillage of the environment may finally contribute not to the survival but to the extinction of the human species: how even such marvelously adapted eaters as we are may finally eat so much that we end up by eating, with a triumphantly self-satisfied grin, ourselves. Man in all his ethical obsession and scrupulosity may be different from the rest of nature: but that does not mean he is apart from it. As the only self-conscious, reasoning link in the food chain, he cannot afford, for all his intelligence, to assume that the other links do not matter except as prey.

This is the lesson of ecological studies, and one even our most dedicated social Darwinians have lately learned they cannot afford to ignore. But even before the planet began dying on us—or before we began to notice and measure its death agonies—there was another conclusion to be drawn from the evidence of Darwinian theory, and one directly counter to that drawn by the cheerleaders of unrestrained *laissez faire*. Man with all his ethics and all his pretensions to dignity may be an evolutionary accident, temporarily successful but doomed to extinction; his ideas of honor and nobility, of self-sacrifice and charity may be on the cosmic scale of things no more substantial nor permanent than smoke: but that does not mean such ideas do not matter, or that the human scale, as long as it lasts, may not set itself up against the cosmic one. Huxley, explicitly taking the social Darwinians to task in "Evolution and Ethics," says:

> The practice of that which is ethically best—what we call goodness or virtue—involves a course of conduct which, in all respects, is opposed to that which leads to success in the cosmic struggle for existence. . . . Let us understand, once for all, that the ethical progress of society depends, not on imitating the cosmic process, still less in running away from it, but in combating it. It may seem an audacious proposal thus to pit the microcosm against the macrocosm and to set man to subdue nature to his higher ends; but I venture to think that the great intellectual difference between the ancient times with which we have been occupied and our day, lies in the solid foundation we have acquired for the hope that such an enterprise may meet with a certain success.

In a universe of change, chaos, struggle, and the un-mediated war of all against all, in other words, human ideas of justice and fair play are not only irrelevant, they are brilliant and precious, the only explanations of its own processes nature has thrown up: and whether or not such explanations are finally, "objectively" true (and who but humans could measure such "truth"?) they remain the only explanations we have, the only beachheads we have built against the eternally encroaching, circumambient chaos.

In the work of a writer like Wells's friend Joseph Conrad, this special sensibility is both inchoate and acute. Books such as *Lord Jim, The Secret Agent, Nostromo,* and especially the tale "Heart of Darkness" all insist upon a vision of human society and human fate that is at once novel, tragic, and ominously congruent with contemporary biological and social theory. Man is an evolutionary accident and a brief evolutionary triumph, argues Conrad, whose society and culture for all their elaboration are only masks of the primal, lurking violence beneath such civilizing shams. At any moment the abyss may open, the chimerical norms and social fictions of "culture" may fade away, and we may find ourselves once again face to face with the ravenous beast within—a beast our social conventions only partially and temporarily hold in check.

Conrad's novels upon this theme are among the established and undeniable classic works of English literature in his age. But we can also see them, for all their brilliance, as less complete and comprehensive examinations of the "Darwinian problem" than Wells's best work. Man's proper role, said Huxley, is not to imitate but to resist the cosmic process, to oppose, however unavailingly, the moral force of his tiny microcosm to the cruel exigencies of the cosmos at large. To say this is to argue that, in a universe governed by the Second Law of Thermodynamics, consciousness is the only power that resists the tendency of all things to spin their way down to the level of least energy. It is also to argue that the human enterprise—culture, art, intelligence—is both totally "artificial" and, in being totally artificial, totally "natural." This is the crucial paradox on which Wells's science fiction—and, indeed, his lifework—is based, and if we do not understand it aright we will misunderstand most of Wells.

Nature, such as is our inheritance from Newtonian physics—still the only physics most people learn at school—appears to be a gigantic zero-sum game, that is, a process in which nothing is created or gained but what was originally there, though perhaps in another form, at the creation of all things. *Panta rhei*, said Heracleitus long before Aristotle: all things flow, one into another. It is such a universe, in all its uncertainty and terror, that Wells describes in *Men Like Gods*:

> All the peace and fixity that man has ever known or will ever know is but the smoothness of the face of a torrent that flies along with incredible speed from cataract to cataract. Time was when men could talk of everlasting hills. Today a schoolboy knows that they disssolve under the frost and wind and rain and pour seaward, day by day and hour by hour. Time was when men could speak of Terra Firma and feel the earth fixed, adamandine beneath their feet. Now they know that it whirls through space eddying about a spinning, blindly driven sun amidst a sheeplike drift of stars.

Out of this cosmic uncertainty emerges one fixed thing, accidental, to be sure, in its origin, but nevertheless everlasting, or at least as everlasting as anything except the universe itself can be: thought. Wells insisted upon this from *The Time Machine* to *Mind at the End of Its Tether*: whether or not it finds an echo or a justification in the surrounding universe, intellect and will and common sense—thought, in other words—are a good in themselves and may be man's salvation in the midst of a cosmos that is trying to kill him. His thinking about art, politics, and even himself all come down to this fundamental, distinctively post-Darwinian insight, that human intellect, though divorced from "objective" reality, is nevertheless a reality of its own, with its own innate urge to survive and conquer.

It can be argued that this belief, though seemingly Darwinian, was really part of Wells's inheritance from Romanticism and the Romantic poets he so admired. But it is more correct to say that Darwinian science, as perceived and reflected by a mind like Wells's, is an objectification and expansion of the vision of high Romanticism. Thomas S. Kuhn, in an important study, *The Structure of Scientific Revolutions*, has argued that we need to perceive the history of science, not as a straightforward and unrelenting march from fact to fact and truth to truth, but rather as a dialectical process of evolving, and sometimes contradictory, overall *visions* of the way things work. This process, as Kuhn describes it, seems less like our commonly held ideal of "pure," rational scientific progress and more like the history of philosophical, even literary, systems and mythologies that we have been taught to regard as somehow "unscientific." The history of science is largely the history of the formation of what Kuhn calls its major "paradigms." And a *paradigm*, far from being a mathematically provable or physically demonstrable set of theorems, is more a way of seeing things—a model or a myth, in other words. He writes:

> Paradigms gain their status because they are more successful than their competitors in solving a few problems that the group of practitioners has come to recognize as acute. To be more successful is not, however, to be either completely successful with a single problem or notably successful with any large number. The success of a paradigm . . . is at the start largely a promise of success discoverable in selected and still incomplete examples. Normal science consists in the actualization of that promise, an actualization achieved by extending the knowledge of those facts that the paradigm displays as particularly revealing, by increasing the extent of the match between those facts and the paradigm's predictions, and by further articulation of the paradigm itself.

Kuhn's main examples are drawn from the history of physics and chemistry in the eighteenth through the twentieth centuries; so it is all the more surprising that Darwinian and post-Darwinian biology should satisfy his description of a revolutionary "paradigm" as fully as it does. The implications of Darwin's view, as drawn by Huxley, Wells, and any number of other writers, led to a sense of man and man's wisdom as simultaneously accidental, a supreme caprice of blind nature, and infinitely precious, the one accident in the whole cosmos through which Being could begin to regard and try to explain—however haltingly—its own reality. Anticipated though it was by the lyrical visions of Wordsworth, Shelley, and Goethe, this was indeed a new paradigm, a new way of seeing the total reality of the human endeavor.

More than half a century after Darwin's great work, Werner
Heisenberg formulated his famous "Uncertainty Principle" of
physics, which can suggest that human reason can never—
because of the very nature of reason—understand "things as
they are." Consciousness alters what it perceives in the very
act of perceiving it: and, therefore, science is condemned to
survey and explain *probabilities* of matter, probabilities
whose only certainty is the fictive certainty of human science.
Less well known than Heisenberg is great German-American
mathematician Kurt Gödel, whose most important theory is
even more deeply disruptive than the Uncertainty Principle.
In the thirties of this century, Gödel advanced the theory of
unsolvability, the idea that any mathematical system, however
complete, will always and inevitably produce statements that
are both true and *impossible of being proved* by the axioms of
the system itself.

Gödel's idea may sound harmless enough. But if we remember that, since Newton, mathematics has been the cornerstone of science's claim to describe "reality," then the daring
of the assertion begins to become apparent. Laplace's arrogant
reply to Napoleon, cited previously, could never have been
made, were it not for a long tradition of belief that the world
of numbers and forms, functions and equations, was in some
deep sense the world of an ultimate reality, to whose iron certainties all the messy irregularities of our world would finally
reduce (if only we had the right exponents). It was the one,
the last, the supreme connection between the human mind
and the structure of outer events. And Gödel took it all away,
insisting that mathematics had the structure not of a "real"
world but of an elegant fiction. Gödel's theory may be one of
the most important, as it is certainly one of the most upsetting, in the long history of mathematics; and it is worth noting
that recent developments in formation theory and the theory
of computer programs bear out and even extend the validity of
his astonishing assertion.

Neither Heisenberg nor Gödel worked in fields connected
to evolutionary theory. And yet, if we want to expand on
Kuhn's theory of the scientific paradigm, we can say that both
men, and their most important formulations, fall well within
the implications of the Darwinian world view. For in all three

writers, and in many more diverse areas of modern science, we can see the emergence of a new "scientifically sanctioned" view of man, a view that regards him as isolated from the universe around him not only by virtue of his intelligence, but by virtue of the *limits* of that intelligence.

From almost his first writings, this was the universe Wells dealt with: a universe whose great challenge and great danger was the Uncertainty Principle even before the principle was formulated. He may not have understood relativity, quantum theory, or contemporary mathematics nearly as well as he remembered his early training in evolutionary biology, and yet Wells was able, in his best fiction, to generalize from that training to a vision of man and his place in a hostile cosmos that is still one of the most responsive mythologies we have to the paradigms of modern thought. It was why in art he could be both an aesthete (art is inevitably artificial, isolated from the "nature" it describes) and a realist (art serves a useful function only insofar as it raises the consciousness of its audience to a perception of the true—i.e., artificial—nature of human affairs). It was why in politics he could be both a radical (society *must* change the order of things and the face of the earth, wresting the planet to its own needs) and a conservative (no society—because of the structure of biological reality itself—can long survive that does not take account of its membership in the class of all living things). From this perspective the paradoxes in Wells's personality and career appear as profound regularities. And though he was not always consistent in his ideas, or even in his feelings, he was always consistent in his vision of the way ideas and feelings ought to feel and ought to work.

As recently as 1971, eminent anthropologist J. S. Weiner has eloquently restated the essential Darwinian position in his book *The Natural History of Man*. It is impossible not to see this opinion as "Wellsian," for all that Weiner bases it strictly upon the discoveries of recent archaeological and anthropological evidence and not upon Wells's own work (work much more intuitive and much less rigorously scientific than Weiner's evidence). And in the first pages of his book, Weiner traces successive stages of the human species' empire over the circumambient world, concluding with the present:

In this fourth era . . . the control of the natural world of matter, energy and living forms, seems near to completion. Already the ecological challenge of the future is clear—it is surely the achievement of that social self-control that will ensure the survival of a secure and harmonious world society.

But we return to the crucial date with which we began this discussion of the Wells background, the year 1895. The concerns we have been tracing throughout this chapter occupied Wells for the fifty years of his creative career and inevitably underwent the changes of emphasis, the shifts of perception such an expanse of time must involve. People, like the universe described by Wells, change. But Wells changed less than most. And the remarkable solidarity of his central vision is never more completely, richly, or brilliantly formulated than in the scientific romances that first made him famous. It is to those books that we now turn.

3

EVOLUTIONARY FABLES:
The Time Machine and
The Island of Doctor Moreau

In the last chapter we examined some of the dominant currents of thought that shaped the mental landscape of Wells's youth. But, in the ten years of transition from the nineteenth to the twentieth century, Wells shaped that landscape into a new visionary order. In his essays, his realistic novels, and above all in his scientific romances of these years he both summarized and recast into a distinctively modern form the intellectual and emotional concerns he had inherited.

The very idea of the "modern," of course, is a modern idea. Not until the calendar began to approach the magical number of two thousand years since the birth of Christ did people—philosophers and poets and charlatans alike—begin to think obsessively in terms of what might happen rather than what had always been. The nineteenth century is the great age of the discovery of *History*: that is, of the present as not just a repetition of an immutable social and political structure, but rather as the link between a dynamically changing past and a looming, challenging, and dangerous future. The idea of the "modern," then, is mainly a particular way of thinking about the possibility and the limits of change. As with hypochondria and some kinds of religious conversion,. wishing (or fearing) makes it so. You are "modern" the moment you begin to *regard* yourself as modern. And in this respect it is just to regard Wells as one of the founders of the modern sensibility. His fiction, to be sure, was never experimental in its techniques, and his ideas, even at their most revolutionary, never aimed at a total break with the great traditions of social and political thought. But few men of his age thought as much or wrote as much about what it felt like to live in an era of change, an era coursing headlong toward an uncertain and perhaps terrible fate.

I have mentioned that P. N. Furbank defines the central effort of Edwardian writers as that of redeeming the suburban. This is not a contemptible, nor is it an easy, task to set oneself. It is also not a new one in the history of English letters: and thereby hangs much of our understanding of Wells and his early fiction. Since the emergence, in the middle of the eighteenth century, of Dr. Samuel Johnson as the most distinguished man of letters of his time, there had existed in England the tradition of the middle-class prophet. This is the man of extraordinary intelligence and ordinary sympathies whose energies are devoted not toward the formation of a school or the establishment of a doctrine, but toward just the *interpretation* of modern schools and doctrines for the embattled and distraught, reasonably intelligent and literate common reader. The discipline of explainer may not, finally, be as exalted as that of prophet or originating heresiarch. But it is one that, from Johnson's essays through Arnold's poetry and criticism and Wells's best fiction, has accounted for much of what is most lasting and most humanizing in the history of English prose.

This is the best context in which to view both the original intent and the original success of Wells's first major novels, *The Time Machine* and *The Island of Doctor Moreau*. In both, strains of current confusion are evident—about the nature of society, about the purpose of art, and most of all about that still-threatening concept, "evolution." But both tales, besides merely articulating contemporary fears, transcend those fears in providing fictions that *reconcile* the comfortable sense of the ordinary with the terrifying sense of "what might be." This is not to say that either *The Time Machine* or *The Island of Doctor Moreau* is an optimistic or "uplifting" fiction: both stories end in shattering and, for their time, shockingly original visions of disaster and loss. Nevertheless, even in the imagination of disaster, Wells manages to give a name and a

shape to forces and tendencies that threaten his—and our—
age. And by naming them he helps render them visible and
controllable.

THE TIME MACHINE

Whatever else it is—and it is many things—*The Time Machine* is certainly an exercise in that curious literary subtype
called utopian fiction. As such it belongs to a very old tradition, indeed. Sir Thomas More's tale *Utopia* (1516) gave a
name to the genre: *ou topos* in Greek means "nowhere," and
More's story is about the totally rational, sane, subordinated,
and peaceful society men have developed in an ideal state
which lies—Nowhere.

Even as early as More's book, the fictional description of
an ideal, "utopian" society has always involved an irreducible
element of satire of society as it really exists. But though More
may have given a permanent name to the form, he was not its
first exponent. The visions of the Hebrew prophets, especially
Isaiah and Jeremiah, the description of the New Jerusalem by
the author of the Book of Revelations, the Republic of Plato,
and even the idealized Christian kingdoms hinted at by some
medieval allegorists—all these and many more examples may
be taken as "utopias" before the invention of the term. It is
safe to say that as long as people have lived in society (which
means as long as there have been people), they have had the
tendency to imagine what such society might be like at its
best—or at its worst. And those extremes, once put in the form
of narratives, represent the whole range of utopian fiction.

There is an important difference between earlier utopias
and their nineteenth-century heirs, however, in the concept of
time. The word means "no*where*," and even in Biblical pre-
sentations of an ideal society to come, that society is always
imagined as occupying more a special place (the land of milk
and honey, the New Jerusalem) than a special time. It is a distinctively nineteenth-century—and therefore modern—habit
of mind to imagine that the perfect "place" for an ideally good
or allegorically evil human society may be literally no place at
all except in time, in history itself.

As we said in the last chapter, the beginnings of this phenomenon can be traced to the Romantic movement and its emphasis upon the creative, sometimes mystical, force of historical process. Two of the greatest English Romantics, William Blake and Percy Shelley—both of whom Wells read and admired as a young man—created utopian visions that we can call "futuristic" in the sense we are discussing. Blake's *Jerusalem* and Shelley's *Prometheus Unbound* both imagine history as an immense series of cycles which, at their completion, will liberate man into a new perception of his own godhead. For both writers, of course—as for Marx in his myth of the revolution of the proletariat—the idea of the "fulness of time" also carries strong associations of much more ancient myths of liberation through history, i.e., Messianic hopes or the Christian expectation of the Second Coming. But between Blake and Shelley and Marx, the work of Darwin intervenes. And Darwinian theory, as we have already seen, forever altered the European perception of history and its crucial, inexorable pressure on human events.

Darwin's importance for utopian visions in the late nineteenth century is as great as for other, more "serious" areas of thought. One of the first, and richest, literary responses to the theory of evolution by means of natural selection is Robert Browning's poem of 1864, "Caliban upon Setebos." This complex satire is, at least in part, an ironic commentary on the pretensions of theological speculation in the face of man's newfound, bestial heritage. The poem may be regarded as the first evidence of that new sensitivity to evolutionary change, to the slow, subtle, but all-important grinding away of the geological, ecological clock that later came to inform even the "realistic" fiction of authors such as Thomas Hardy, Joseph Conrad, and D. H. Lawrence. And "Caliban upon Setebos" is also important as part of the background of Wells's grimmest and most deliberately shocking evolutionary parable, *The Island of Doctor Moreau*.

More to the point of *The Time Machine*, however, is the array of more explicitly utopian, sociological fictions that follows in Darwin's wake and takes account of the implications of natural selection for the human community. Edward Bulwer-Lytton's *The Coming Race* (1871) describes an ideal community of gigantic, further-evolved humans existing in the present time in a subterranean world into which the narrator stumbles. Their nobility and their altogether proper-Victorian acceptance of natural dynamism are a comforting assertion that "evolution," whatever its direction, will not lead us astray. Samuel Butler's Erewhon (1872), on the other hand, entertains some darker notions about the implications of natural selection for the future of the human race. "Erewhon" is a dystopia of sorts—literally, it is "Nowhere" spelled (almost) backwards—where machines have evolved an intelligence of their own, and where man is the servant of his superior, more efficient tools. The idea that man might eventually create a "race" of artificial beings who supplant his lordship over the planet has, of course, always been one of the most fecund themes for science fiction, from The War of the Worlds to 2001: A Space Odyssey and beyond. And Butler gets credit for being the first writer to understand that such a theme underlies many of the assertions of evolutionary theory.

Two other utopias, though, are even more central to the background of The Time Machine, for in both of them the idea of the future as the real "place" of utopia is much more explicit. They are Edward Bellamy's Looking Backward (2000–1887) and William Morris's News from Nowhere: Or, an Epoch of Unrest. Both books appeared in 1888—the same year in which Wells wrote the first, very amateurish draft of what was to become The Time Machine.

Bellamy was an American socialist, with a great faith in the benevolence of technological development. In Looking Backward the hero, Julian West, through a strained series of circumstances, falls asleep in Boston in 1887 to awaken in the Boston of the year 2000. It is a Boston miraculously transformed, like the rest of the world, into an orderly, hygienic, mechanically run, and absolutely self-satisfied socialist paradise. Everyone has exactly as much as he or she needs for a modest yet comfortable existence, and everyone contributes to the common fund of labor exactly as much as society and the individual feel is just. Massive networks of producing and calculating machines keep the world supply of goods balanced, and citizens are "paid" for their contributions not in coin or cash, but by tiny cards that register their productivity and their appropriately calculated purchasing power. And all

this wonderful change has come about simply through the inevitable but kindly ministrations of history, without bloodshed or revolution. As Dr. Leete, West's host (and the father of
the girl West eventually marries), explains:

> "It was not necessary for society to solve the riddle at all. It
> may be said to have solved itself. The solution came as the
> result of a process of industrial evolution which could not
> have terminated otherwise. All that society had to do was to
> recognize and cooperate with that evolution, when its ten-
> dency had become unmistakable."

The distance from the threatening technology of Butler's
Erewhon is vast. And *Looking Backward,* though clumsily
written and often mawkishly sentimental, exercised a profound influence over speculation on society and technology
for many years. Of all modern utopias, it is perhaps the most
unabashedly optimistic. Present trends are toward the increasing mechanization of society, Bellamy acutely observes; and,
he insists, those trends can only work to our good, since the
bigger and better machines we keep building will turn the
world into one giant, intricately organized, and brightly lit
city. It is an unfair distortion of Bellamy's passion and earnestness to say that, for him, the vision of the future resolves
itself into a global, climate-controlled shopping center. But it
is a distortion: not, that is, entirely a misrepresentation.

William Morris, if he had known about shopping centers,
would doubtless have used the image as a weapon against
Bellamy and all Bellamy stood for. In *News from Nowhere,*
written explicitly as a refutation of *Looking Backward,* Morris's narrator tells how he falls asleep and dreams that he has
awakened in a future civilization where benevolent socialism
has transformed the world according to anti-industrial, anti-
technological principles. If Bellamy's future can, at its worst,
look suspiciously like a shopping center, Morris's, at its worst,
can look like a romanticized, nineteenth-century painting of a
medieval fair. One of the dreamer's informants explains to
him how the world of cities and machines was changed:

> "The town invaded the country; but the invaders, like the
> warlike invaders of early days, yielded to the influence of their

surroundings, and became country people; and in their turn, as they became more numerous than the townsmen, influenced them also; so that the difference between town and country grew less and less; and it was indeed this world of the country vivified by the thought and briskness of town-bred folk which has produced that happy and leisurely but eager life of which you have had a first taste."

The world at its best, that is, has become a garden; but a garden inhabited by city folk who, for all their pastoralism, retain their city-bred sophistication of taste.

Between Bellamy and Morris, the terms of the modern utopian debate are firmly established. The question is no longer, "How shall we form an ideal society?" It is now, "Toward what kind of society are history and cultural evolution leading us, and how can we best control the process for our own good?" There is an important paradox in that set of questions, one that will govern later utopian thought. For according to strict Darwinian dogma, we are literally *out of control* of history. Evolution will change us into what we will become whether or not we like it—and even before we know we have been changed. But the most persistent of human illusions is that of free will; and almost from the opening of the Darwinian controversy, thinkers were suggesting ways in which our species, blessed and cursed with self-consciousness, might come not only to understand but to guide, to control, the evolutionary process to our own ends (this was the central belief of Wells's great disciple of the 1930s, Olaf Stapledon). The paradox of determinism and free will has always been a crucial one in Western social and religious thought, of course. But Darwin (and, in their different way, Marx and Freud) raised it to a level of particular urgency for their age and ours. Enter Wells, and *The Time Machine.*

It is a risky thing for an author to create a masterpiece in his first published book: success of that sort can be a terrible burden for the writer who then has to go on to his next book, and his next, etcetera. But that is what Wells did with *The Time Machine.* And the next fifty years of his extraordinary career can be thought of as, among other things, a heroic living-up to the promise of that great first book. As late as

1940, in one of his last fictions, *All Aboard for Ararat,* he was still acknowledging the influence and the pressure of that book in his career.

At least part of the novel's genius is the way it catches, crystallizes, clarifies so many current (and still very live) controversies. Jean-Pierre Vernier, a French critic of Wells, has observed of *The Time Machine* that, however dire its implied prophecies and however dark its central vision, it is still primarily an entertainment, a fantasy intended, and taken by its audience, less as a cautionary parable than as a diversion. And Vernier is partly right. The subtitle of *The Time Machine* is *An Invention,* a witty reference by Wells to the "invention" of the time machine within the book, and also to the book itself as a primarily aesthetic, quasi-musical "invention" or fantasia (showing here the strong influence of Wilde and *The Yellow Book* aesthetes on Wells). But in Wells, even from the beginning, the artist was never very far from the social planner and prophet. In an important early essay, "The Rediscovery of the Unique" (1891), he writes of the implications of modern science (mainly, of course, biological science) for man's understanding of himself. And the concluding paragraph of the essay perfectly catches both the popularism and the pessimism of his voice at its best:

> Science is a match that man has just got alight. He thought he was in a room—in moments of devotion, a temple—and that his light would be reflected from and display walls inscribed with wonderful secrets and pillars carved with philosophical systems wrought into harmony. It is a curious sensation, now that the preliminary splutter is over and the flame burns up clear, to see his hands lit and just a glimpse of himself and the patch he stands on visible, and around him, in place of all that human comfort and beauty he anticipated—darkness still.

It is a magnificent passage (and one that helps explain why the young Wells was so eagerly sought out by newspaper editors as a feature writer). And in its tones, we get a startlingly accurate premonition of some of the images of *The Time Machine:* questing man, as a vulnerable character surrounded by darkness trying to light a puny match to illuminate his condition; humanity as imprisoned in a giant building or temple of uncertain origin and not of his own device; and above all, perhaps, darkness itself—that terminal darkness that lies at the end of all our questing and all our struggle, and which Wells, however much he dramatized or popularized it, could never take less than seriously. One way, indeed, of describing the track of his career is to say that he increasingly discovered, and made increasingly explicit, the grim implications of his early, artistically designed scientific romances and sketches.

In *The Time Machine,* he casts a cold eye upon the quarrel between Bellamy's and Morris's visions of utopia. Both versions of the future are there in the year 802,701 to which the Time Traveller journeys. The world has indeed become a massive and smoothly running complex of machines as well as a garden, an Edenic landscape where men and women share an uncomplicated and blissful, toil-free communal existence. But the smooth-running machines have reduced the men who tend them to a state of mindless cannibalistic bestiality, and the inhabitants of the garden world have become dwarfed, childish caricatures of mankind, the unprotesting and ineffectual prey of their once-brothers, the tenders of machines. The brutal Morlocks and the lovely but sickly Eloi of the year 802,701 are very grim visions, indeed, of Bellamy's hyperindustrial and Morris's postindustrial utopians. Where is evolution leading us? According to Wells in *The Time Machine,* at least, it matters little whether it is leading us toward the socialistic garden world of Morris or the socialistic technology of Bellamy: for both are terrible places, and spell the end of mankind as we now know it.

When a species overadapts to its environment, it starts to die: that is a central Darwinian tenet, and is very near the heart of *The Time Machine.* For the environment will inevitably change over the course of geological, cosmological time. And the species that has become too at home in one phase of climate and ecology will probably lose the resiliency to change and meet the demands of another phase. This is to say that, on the evolutionary scale, a certain dis-ease, a certain genetic "restlessness" ought to be built into the structure of a surviving organism. And Wells, that perennially restless man, was quick to adopt the Darwinian generalization as a kind of pledge that the universe was, after all, on the side of his own energetic permanent self-dissatisfaction. It is perhaps why he was able to write such a stunning refutation of the utopias of his Darwinian predecessors. For them, the end point of society would be the point at which the struggle for existence ceased, resolved itself into a new Eden. But for Wells, a world without struggle and tension would be, simply, uninhabitable. This is what the Time Traveller reflects upon after he has encountered the graceful, ineffectual Eloi and before he meets their brutal counterparts, the Morlocks. Man, he thinks, has finally subdued nature, has finally wrested the world to his own imagination of a Golden Age where all effort is unnecessary:

> I thought of the physical slightness of the people, their lack of intelligence and those abundant ruins, and it strengthened my belief in a perfect conquest of Nature. For after the battle comes Quiet. . . . No doubt the exquisite beauty of the buildings I saw was the outcome of the last surgings of the now purposeless energy of mankind before it settled down into perfect harmony with the conditions under which it lived—the flourish of that last triumph which began the last great peace. This has ever been the fate of energy in security; it takes to art and to eroticism, and then come langour and decay.

That "perfect harmony" with the environment is, for Wells, the inevitable and irreversible prelude to decay and death. And, of course, the Eloi with their "hectic beauty"—the delicate beauty of the fevered or the tubercular—and their life of uncomplicated art and eroticism are, among other things, a bitter parody of the aesthetes and decadents of the nineties. But, as the Time Traveller tells us at the end of these reflections, his theories are wrong: he has not yet seen the Morlocks, and not yet learned the great fear under which the Eloi live. When he first meets the Morlocks, and visits their subterranean dwelling among the great machines, he will venture another theory: that the present distinction between rich and poor has become increasingly pronounced in the process of social evolution until the capitalist and laboring class divide into two distinct species, with all the energy of the race concentrated in the antlike, uncomprehending busyness of the wretched and deformed children of the workers. Not until the

Aubrey Beardsley's "A Snare of Vintage," 1894. This is an illustration by Beardsley for Lucian's *True History*—a book Wells often acknowledged as one of his early influences. Beardsley's "decadent" imagination of these strange, seductive, and poisonous sirens is both a perfect example of the graceful eroticism of his school and an obvious source for Wells's invention of the Eloi.

end of his stay in 802,701 does he come to the full realization
of that world's terror, the realization that the two distinct species into which man has evolved are now predator and prey,
acting out a massive and bloody ritual of self-consumption:

> I understood now what all the beauty of the Over-world peo-
> ple covered. Very pleasant was their day, as pleasant as the
> day of the cattle in the field. Like the cattle, they knew of no
> enemies and provided against no needs. And their end was
> the same.
>   I grieved to think how brief the dream of the human in-
> tellect had been.

Three theories of society are in the end put forth by the
Time Traveller, each of them cancelling out its predecessor,
each of them a more complex view of the possibilities of social evolution over an immense period of time, and each of
them more grim. For all the flurry of Darwinian elements or
evolutionary speculation in late-nineteenth-century utopias,
not until *The Time Machine* did the real power, and the real
terror, of evolutionary theory find adequate expression in fiction. I have said that one of the most important shockwaves
cast by *The Origin of Species* was not simply the idea of man's
heritage from lower animals, but rather the disorienting discovery of the immense vistas of time upon which any definition of "man"—or of man's success—has to be imagined. "I
grieved to think how brief the dream of the human intellect
had been," says the Time Traveller in the year 802,701. And,
on the scale of the age of the Earth, the elapsed time between
1895 and 802,701 *is* brief; it is terribly brief, and that is the
whole point of that melancholy line. Here, again, is the Time
Traveller looking up at the night sky as he and Weena, the
Eloi girl who loves him, flee from the Morlocks:

> Looking at these stars suddenly dwarfed my own troubles
> and all the gravities of terrestrial life. I thought of their un-
> fathomable distance, and the slow inevitable drift of their
> movements out of the unknown past into the unknown future.
> I thought of the great precessional cycle that the pole of the
> earth describes. Only forty times had that silent revolution oc-
> curred during all the years that I had traversed. And during
> these few revolutions all the activity, all the traditions, the

complex organizations, the nations, languages, literatures, aspirations, even the mere memory of Man as I knew him, had been swept out of existence.

This, like so many passages in *The Time Machine*, is a passage of great lyrical power, a kind of prose poem. And its theme is time, but "time" imagined in a way that, except for the very act of imagination that calls it into being, reduces all things human to triviality. This is a very romantic sentiment, desperately lonely in its vision of man's place in the universe and desperately assertive in its faith in the power of imagination and language to make that universe habitable. Almost a century before *The Time Machine* Shelley had ended his great meditation, *Mont Blanc*, with the defiant question

> And what were thou, and earth, and stars, and sea,
> If, to the human mind's imaginings,
> Silence and solitude were vacancy?

The answer to that question, of course, can be either "everything" or "nothing," and on the gamble implied rests the central romantic gamble on behalf of man's position in the universe. But note that, while Shelley asks that question in terms of man's position in *space*, i.e., in a potentially infinite universe of things, Wells asks it in terms of man's position in *time*, a potentially infinite universe of duration. In the difference between those two meditations lies much of the emotional history of the nineteenth century as well as much of our own discomfort, not knowing which answer to choose.

The invention of the Eloi and the Morlocks is finally not as central to the brilliance of *The Time Machine* as is the invention of the machine itself, and the consequent imagination of time in its fullest, longest, and most challengingly inhuman dimensions. Here is the description of the model Time Machine that the Traveller first shows to his dinner guests:

> The thing the Time Traveller held in his hand was a glittering metallic framework, scarcely larger than a small clock, and very delicately made. There was ivory in it, and some transparent crystalline substance. And now I must be explicit, for this that follows—unless his explanation is to be accepted—is an absolutely unaccountable thing.

What follows is a description of how the Traveller sends his model into the future. But notice what has happened in this brilliant, and brilliantly vague paragraph. The machine has been described, but nothing of its precise form has been given. It has, in fact, been made real without being at all realized. And in using this kind of description Wells set a precedent for most of his later science fiction. His concern was not really with technology, but with the effects, the human implications, of possible technological advances. Time travel may be (in fact, is) impossible; but Wells really does not care. What he cares about is inventing just enough convincing hardware to allow him—and us—to speculate about the possible fate of the human race as the year 802,701.

The very date, 802,701, as numerous critics and commentators have pointed out, is a kind of hieroglyph of entropy, a numerical metaphor for a machine about to run down, a process about to play itself out. (In the 1894 serialization of the novel, the date the Time Traveller reached was the rather less portentous 12,203.) But it is not simply a matter of numbers or social prophecy. What Wells manages to do in The Time Machine is to articulate, for the first time and distinctively for his age, a vision of the abyss of geological time. The great passage with which the Time Traveller's story concludes, his vision of the end of the world, is one of the most powerfully imagined passages in modern English fiction. But it is powerful precisely because the whole novel has anticipated and adumbrated its dark tones.

We have been discussing The Time Machine so far in terms of the traditions of utopian, social-prophetic storytelling out of which it arises. But it is impossible to think about the tale for long without considering it for what it finally is, a major and brilliant work of literary art. Harold Bloom, perhaps our most perceptive critic of Romantic and modern poetry, has observed that the structure of the archetypal romantic poem involves a visionary dialectics on the part of the speaker. Confronted by a particular problem or paradox, that is, the speaker of a Romantic poem entertains first one solution to the problem, then another (usually unrelated) one, and finally a third one that either resolves or transcends the first two. This is, indeed, the way Wordsworth's Tintern Abbey and Shelley's *Mont Blanc* work; it is also the way *The Time Machine* works, once we begin to understand it as not simply a post-Darwinian utopian fiction but a lyrical meditation on the nature and the terror of time itself.

We have already seen that the Time Traveller, in his visit to the year 802,701, makes up three successive explanations of what he sees. The Time Traveller (and, of course, Wells) is quite explicit about the difference of this narrative procedure from the ordinary course of utopian fiction. Other utopias always involve excessively detailed description of the scenery and architecture of the ideal state, the Time Traveller says. "But while such details are easy enough to obtain when the whole world is contained in one's imagination, they are altogether inaccessible to a real traveller amid such realities as I found here." Wells in a single stroke lets himself out of the boring burden of describing fully the future world in which his hero finds himself, and at the same time (since indeterminacy and confusion are always the best alibis) makes that world more believable, more *notionally* real than it would otherwise have been.

Other utopias also involve, as the Time Traveller is careful to point out, conveniently informative guides or historians to explain how things came to be as they are in the great good (or the great bad) place. But the Traveller has none of these aids. The Morlocks do not talk at all, and of the Eloi, he observes, "their language was excessively simple—almost exclusively composed on concrete substantives and verbs." An ideally Edenic language, but one emptied of the powers of abstraction or a sense of history. The Traveller is confronted with the future in much the same way the Romantic poet finds himself confronted with the inhospitable rockface of nature: a mute, gigantic, threatening, and absolutely uncommunicative presence, about which one can only speculate, only entertain notions. It is one of the most brilliant devices of *The Time Machine* that no one, in the Traveller's narrative of the future, *speaks*. Weena gives the Traveller some flowers she has gathered, which he produces in the only interruption of his narrative. But that gesture, so touching and so sentimental—and so crucial to the end of the story—is also a sign that the future *is* inarticulate, that it has no names except the names we choose to give it. Silence and solitude, Shelley insists, are really not vacancy: but, in the romantic tradition, you can only insist upon that as long as you are willing to take silence and solitude in their full frightening reality. And that is what the Time Traveller does.

The central narrative device of The Time Machine, then, is a first-person narrator entertaining a number of alternate explanations for the phenomena he witnesses, coming to the true conclusion about the reality of things only at the end of his tale. This structure not only recapitulates the movement of a romantic meditation, but also provides the novel with a reasonable facsimile of what was being increasingly celebrated as "scientific method." Faced with the implied question, "What does the future of mankind hold in store?" the narrator, like a good scientific investigator, tries out explanation after explanation of the observed facts until he finally hits on the one explanation that suffices, that explains all the facts as observed and nothing but them.

It is a structure that was to serve Wells in good stead for the next decade. As we shall see, most of his major scientific romances turn on the same process of alternate and progressively accurate explanations of the impossible or the unspeakable. To be sure, there are precedents for this kind of narrative. Herman Melville in Benito Cereno and Nathaniel Hawthorne in The Scarlet Letter and The House of the Seven Gables both give us stories in which an object or set of objects is first presented, then perceived in various ways, and then finally revealed in the full clarity of its meaning. And behind Melville and Hawthorne lies the whole tradition of the Gothic novel in English, that curious amalgam of supernaturalism and narrative indirection that dominated the popular tastes of England and America during the late eighteenth and early nineteenth century. Wells knew this tradition of tales intimately, and in the first version of The Time Machine barely departed from it. "The Chronic Argonauts" is the very Poe-esque (or Hawthorne-esque) story of a mysterious man named "Dr. Nebogipfel" who arrives to take over occupancy of an old manse in an English village, seems to practice arcane and dangerous arts, and is finally revealed to be a traveler from the future, an exile out of time. This information, however, is made known only *after* the major (and unnarrated, since the tale is incomplete) action has taken place—and it is made known by the country doctor who is Nebogipfel's unwilling companion on his journey through time. So that even from its crude beginnings, *The Time Machine* incorporated its central narrative-framing device—having the story told after the voyage into time has taken place, and having the story of the adventurous, eccentric Time Traveller told *through* the mediating voice of a more conventional narrator. This is also the procedure, of course, of one of the most successful and most lasting nineteenth-century tales of horror, Robert Louis Stevenson's *The Strange Case of Dr. Jekyll and Mr. Hyde*, published in 1886, two years before Wells began *The Chronic Argonauts*. And Wells, like Stevenson, was—from *The Time Machine* onward—fascinated with manifestations of dual personality, even, in his early story "The Late Mr. Elvesham," writing a Jekyll-and-Hyde tale of, if anything, more terrifying dimensions than Stevenson's.

Nevertheless, *The Time Machine* as we have it now is as distinct an advance over those early Gothic and post-Gothic frame-tale narratives as it is over previous nineteenth-century utopias. We begin in the most cordial and comfortable of surroundings, a late-nineteenth-century dinner party, where a group of talented men are exchanging serious but politely vague, conveniently mellowed after-dinner views:

> The Time Traveller (for so it will be convenient to speak of him) was expounding a recondite matter to us. His grey eyes shone and twinkled, and his usually pale face was flushed and animated. The fire burned brightly, and the soft radiance of the incandescent lights in the lillies of silver caught the bubbles that flashed and passed in our glasses.

This is the beginning of the tale in its final version, and it is important to note that it is all we ever learn of the Time Traveller's physical appearance: he has grey eyes, and a usually pale, but now animated and flushed, face. He is, in other words, an abstraction: as is his vaguely described machine, and as is appropriate for this most abstract of speculations on the future of the human race. Even his last vision of the end of all life on the planet is abstract and disembodied, although it is also one of the great chilling passages in the history of the English language. This passage was added to the book on the insistence of W. E. Henley, Well's editor. But it is nevertheless one of the finest, most unrelentingly apocalyptic things Wells wrote. Journeying past the year 802,701, past the death of the human species on the planet, the Traveller alights at a time when the Earth is dying. What follows must be quoted in full.

> The darkness grew apace; a cold wind began to blow in freshening gusts from the east, and the showering white flakes in the air increased in number. From the edge of the sea came a ripple and whisper. Beyond these lifeless sounds the world was silent. Silent? It would be hard to convey the stillness of it. All the sounds of man, the bleating of sheep, the cries of birds, the hum of insects, the stir that makes the background of our lives—all that was over. As the darkness thickened, the eddying flakes grew more abundant, dancing before my eyes; and the cold of the air more intense. At last, one by one, swiftly, one after the other, the white peaks of the distant hills vanished into blackness. The breeze rose to a moaning wind. I saw the black central shadow of the eclipse sweeping towards me. In another moment the pale stars alone were visible. All else was rayless obscurity. The sky was absolutely black.

There is little that need be said about a passage like this. Not often in the history of the language has a vision of The End, a vision of the absolute conclusion, collapse, and catastrophe of all things been so powerfully imagined. Wells here is the chosen poet of the abyss, the perfect lyricist of entropy. "All that was over," he writes of the whole range of human and animal life on the planet—and in those four words is compressed a universe of melancholy. In this passage we come very close to looking into what Wells at his most despairing could imagine—and what he refused, at all cost, to let himself imagine.

For if the Traveller and his final vision are cold and inhospitable, the dinner party is not. We know that there is a fire, champagne, and we even know into what shape the incandescent lights over the table are fashioned. We know such things for two important reasons, two related reasons: First, because they are precisely the comforting, recognizable details which the Traveller's grim vision of the future is about to upset; and second, because they are precisely the details of scene and decor that the narrator of the story would remember. This narrator—or editor—of the Time Traveller's story is an important character, and one who, during the rest of Wells's career, will engage in a fascinating and unending struggle with the despairing voice of the Time Traveller. At the next dinner party, a week after the opening scene, the Traveller appears, scarred and shaken by his voyage into and return from the distant future, and tells his awful tale of the Eloi, the Morlocks, and the final journey to the end of all things. But, at the very end of the book, after the Traveller has again departed on a voyage into time (never to return), the final word on the tale's meaning is held in a curious ambiguity between the vision of the Traveller (who sees into the cosmic meaninglessness of things) and the narrator, his friend (who remembers champagne and firelight from dinner parties). "He," says the narrator of the Traveller:

> He, I know—for the question had been discussed among us long before the Time Machine was made—thought but cheerlessly of the Advancement of Mankind, and saw in the growing pile of civilization only a foolish heaping that must inevitably fall back upon and destroy its makers in the end. If that is so, it remains for us to live as though it were not so. But to me the future is still black and blank—as a vast ignorance, lit at a few casual places by the memory of his story. And I have by me, for my comfort, two strange white flowers—shrivelled now, and brown and flat and brittle—to witness that even when mind and strength had gone, gratitude and a mutual tenderness still lived on in the heart of man.

Some readers have taken this final comment by the narrator as an exercise in fatuity, a falsely comforting conclusion to a book whose *real* conclusion is the Time Traveller's preceding vision of the end of the world in darkness and meaninglessness. But to read *The Time Machine* this way is to misread it. The narrator is given the last word for the same reason those two white flowers, which the Traveller produced in the middle of his narrative, are there at all. Wells *wants* the future to remain, however threatening or despairing aspects of it may appear, fundamentally "black and blank"—black and white, that is, depending on the state of mind or soul with which we behold it. The two voices of The Time Machine, in other words, encapsulate between them that elementary tension between cosmic determinism and freedom of the will that we have seen at the heart of all speculation about the future of mankind. Well's achievement in The Time Machine is to fuse that intellectual dubiety into the very structure of his narrative so that, as with a Symbolist poem, what the story means (is the future unrelievedly dark? is there any hope for our species before the tribunal of history?) is absolutely indistinguishable from how the story works (which voice is the "real" one, that of the Traveller who has been to the future and back, or that of the narrator who stays with us to record and interpret his tale?).

Returning to Vernier's observations about The Time Machine as entertainment, we can say that the book works as marvelously as it does as entertainment precisely because of the seriousness and complexity of the intellectual contradictions it incorporates; and, of course, it makes those contradictions so powerfully real for us just because it is such a finely fashioned aesthetic machine for producing ambiguity (much like the Time Machine). For once in his career—and, some would say, for the only time—Wells found the perfect vehicle for his intellectual, artistic, and personal obsessions, the perfect story and method for bringing them all into an intricate, if ambiguous, harmony. And the contradictory voices of hope and despair, the narrative procedure of doubtful and successive explanations of outrageous phenomena, and above all the abiding sense of a great darkness just outside the range of human ken were to remain the major attributes of his genius during the years of his great scientific romances, and perhaps during his whole career.

THE ISLAND OF DOCTOR MOREAU

In his next major scientific romance, Wells was to intensify that sense of darkness just beyond the human limit of perception, and to intensify it to a degree that, for a short while, damaged his career. The Time Machine was an almost unqual-

ified success, and established Wells as one of the very best
and brightest young writers of his time. But when *The Island
of Doctor Moreau* appeared the next year, 1896, the reviewers
were nearly unanimous in their distaste for its violence, its
cynicism, and its disgusting images of man as little more than
a half-trained, cannibalistic beast. Even today, of Wells' five
major scientific romances from 1895 through 1901, it is probably the least widely read or taught.

It is interesting to ask why: what is it about *The Island of
Doctor Moreau* that makes it, of all Wells's science fiction, the
hardest to approach, the most difficult or distasteful to con-
template? Part of the answer, at least, is that as a kind of companion piece to *The Time Machine*, *Doctor Moreau* is another
post-Darwinian utopia, another evolutionary fable about
human society, but one that emphasizes not the possible
dangers of the human *future*, but the animal, chaotic, bloody
origins and hidden nature of the human *present*, of the society
in which you and I live so comfortably at this very minute.

Like *The Time Machine*, this book is the story of a brilliant
scientist's successes and disasters told by a secondary, less
brilliant but more humane character who is obviously intended to be "one of us." But instead of the urbane, sympathetic Time Traveller, the central scientist-figure here is Dr.
Moreau, a mad and ultimately sadistic visionary determined
to create, by vivisection, a more perfect species of mankind
sculpted from the living flesh of lower animals. And instead
of the quiet, reassuring voice of the narrator of *The Time Machine*, the storyteller's voice here is that of Charles Prendick,
an ordinarily intelligent man shipwrecked on the island of
Moreau's horrible experiments and scarred forever afterward
by what he witnesses there. The two voices of determinism
and free will from *The Time Machine* are still there: but in
this novel the tone of both is significantly darkened, until the
idea of "determinism" (Moreau's experiments) becomes a
grim algebra of universal pain and suffering. Even the saving
voice of "free will" (Prendick's narrative—and his survival of
Moreau's island) has become, by the end, only a bitter mockery of man's pretensions to "humanity" in the face of his
animal heritage.

But to say this much about *Doctor Moreau* is to say that it is, among other things, a satire. And satire, if it does nothing else, offends people: it is supposed to. Utopian fiction, as we have seen, aways includes within itself the possibility of satire, since in describing the truly good society one may always reflect upon how truly bad, how stupid or benighted, is the society in which one lives and writes. This, indeed, is the major point of one of Wells' own favorite books, Voltaire's *Candide*. And it is also the point of *Gulliver's Travels*, the single book that more than any other lies behind the narrative procedures of *Doctor Moreau*. But simply to identify it as satire does not quite account for the particular offensiveness or—to use a word common in some of the first reviews of *Doctor Moreau*— the particular blasphemy of Wells's novel. For the book is a satire on an especially broad—and therefore especially dangerous—scale, a scale particularly suited for reducing human illusions to irrelevance. Wells himself later described the novel as "an exercise in youthful blasphemy."

Here is Moreau, in the middle of the action of the book, explaining his horrendous experiment to Prendick:

> "A pig may be educated. The mental structure is even less determinate than the bodily. In our growing science of hypnotism we find that promise of a possibility of replacing old inherent instincts by new suggestions, grafting upon or replacing the inherited fixed ideas. Very much, indeed, of what we call moral education is such an artificial modification and perversion of instinct; pugnacity is trained into courageous self-sacrifice, and suppressed sexuality into religious emotion. And the great difference between man and monkey is in the larynx. . . ."

There is not one of these statements which was not entertained by biologists or anthropologists of the nineteenth century, and which has not continued to be entertained by particular schools of linguistics, animal ethology, or behavioral psychology. But taken together, and presented as they are here, in the dramatic context of Prendick's isolation upon the terrible island of Dr. Moreau, they are outrageous, and outrageously disturbing. They call into question the most basic tenet of the entire tradition of Western humanism: the belief in the speciality, the sublime individuality, the autonomy of the human species on this planet. If "a pig may be educated," it is not really a very long step to the realization that we, for all our culture and all our pretensions to difference from the circumambient animal creation, may be little more than particularly well-educated pigs. And if "what we call moral education" is simply a stimulus-response mechanism so deeply embedded in our genetic material (for the sake of species survival) that we aren't even aware of the embedment, then the whole moral heritage is simply a pathetic sham, and our most cherished ideas of the value of life, of the necessity of charity and compassion, are little more than the learned responses of unusually weak apes whose "humanity" is simply their shared code word for a mechanism that protects them from being eaten by stronger animals. Remember that the Time Traveller "thought but cheerlessly of the Advancement of Mankind": Moreau's vision is the Time Traveller's skepticism raised to the level of moral nihilism. In this very grim, deliberately ugly book, what is being satirized is the nature of man himself. This is another way of saying that in *Doctor Moreau*, thanks both to Wells's intellectual moment and his perceptions, satire discovers a prophetic level that goes beyond the previous possibilities of the form, and in fact anticipates much of the troubled experience of our century. Listen to Moreau again, only a few moments after his disquisition on the education of pigs. He is answering Prendick's objection to the pain he inflicts upon his animal victims:

> "Oh! but it is such a little thing. A mind truly opened to what science has to teach must see that it is a little thing. It may be that, save in this little planet, this speck of cosmic dust, invisible long before the nearest star could be attained— it may be, I say, that nowhere else does this thing called pain occur. . . . Plants do not feel pain; the lower animals—it's possible that such animals as the starfish and crayfish do not feel pain. Then with men, the more intelligent they become the more intelligently they will see after their own welfare, and the less they will need the goad to keep them out of danger."

In his calm, dispassionate, and mad way, Moreau manages to reduce the idea of suffering—and, more importantly, of human sympathy—to a cosmic irrelevance. Note how he repeats the idea that such concern, such empathy, is "a little thing." And this mere epiphenomenon in the history of consciousness will disappear, like all useless organs, when the perfectly rational man is attained. In Moreau's passion for total control and rationality, in his ruthlessness in pursuit of that goal, and above all in his eerily chaste sadism, we can see the origins of a peculiarly modern institution. The concentration camp is becoming possible.

For that, at its heart, is what Moreau's island really is: a landscape of total domination, total pain, and total, brutal irrationality masquerading as the natural order of things, the true state of affairs. Moreau's obsession is to create from the raw stuff of animal flesh and animal nature, a race of perfect and perfectly sane (perfectly *conditioned* would be today's term) human beings; to improve, in other words, upon the work of evolution. For once we assume that what we call morality is only an "artificial modification and perversion of instinct," or what we have more lately come to call a conditioned reflex, then it is not difficult to draw the conclusion that, with the right techniques, we might be able to condition the moral reflex (our own preferred moral reflex) better than it has been done by the slow, almost random processes of natural selection.

Moreau's island is a totalitarian regime—perhaps the first really totalitarian regime imagined by Western man. And Wells is never more brilliant than in understanding the connection between romantic aspiration and tawdry, bestial, murderous practice that underlies so many twentieth-century totalitarianisms. "Each time I dip a living creature into the bath of burning pain," Moreau says, "I say, This time I will burn out all the animal, this time I will make a rational creature of my own." The fatal paradox of his desire is that in his quest for rational perfection he creates a nightmarish world of monsters: in his attempts to burn out the animal, he only disfigures the animals into pathetic caricatures of humanity, but burns out, without even knowing it, the humanity that leavens his own overwhelming intelligence.

Wells, as we have seen, was no stranger to the complexities of biological science, and was neither frightened nor revolted—as were many of his literary colleagues—by the necessary rigors of the laboratory and dissecting room. So that

Doctor Moreau, for all its "mad scientist" overtones, cannot be read simply as an anti-scientific, anti-experimentalist potboiler. Yet it is a very dark book. And part of its darkness is also part of a theme Wells begins to sound here and never really finishes sounding until the end of his career. As passionately as he believes in science, he believes in the reality of the ordinary world, the world we see around us, the good things of the Earth and their inalienable right to survive, regardless of human beliefs about their usefulness or efficiency. Moreau is cast into despair when the mere instinctual animal reasserts itself within the grisly handiwork of his surgical sculpture. And the final chapters of the book, describing the reversion of the whole island of beast folk after Moreau's death, is one of Wells's richest and broadest satires of the pretensions of self-confidently "civilized" men and women. Nevertheless, the return of the beast in the beast folk is in its way the one, measured, victory imagined in this novel; for it asserts something Wells tried to make himself believe throughout his life—that evolution itself is not a blind mistake, that Earth as it is given to us by cosmic, geological history is not simply a massive blunder, and that we might be saved just because the creation which has produced us is ultimately benevolent. We know that Moreau is *wrong,* in other words. But that does not prove—though all our desire is to believe so—that the nature against which he struggles is right.

This is an important and very delicate theme for Wells to have examined in 1896. We have seen that one of the first and most lasting, most disturbing effects of Darwinian theory was to call into question the whole heritage of theological certainty, the belief in the special creation of mankind and the historical centrality of the human race, which had supported humanistic thought for nearly three thousand years. Mankind no longer occupied center stage: Darwin, or Darwin's heirs, effectively banished us to stage left or stage right, but at least to a position definitely less than central to the real scope of the drama of life upon Earth. Hints of the displacement had come, indeed, before *The Origin of Species:* much early-nineteenth-century thought (which is to say, much romantic thought) had played with the notion that human life might be less than crucial to the fate of the universe, or, worse, a kind of *disease* of the universal life force, a fever of matter accidently gifted with self-consciousness and totally unprepared to transform that special curse into a special blessing.

Darwin, however, helped turn such dim romantic forebodings into grim postromantic certainties. The barrier between man and animal, for many, was not only erased by *The Origin of Species*, but was converted into a passageway: and to do that, of course, was to call into question the whole nature of our difference and distance from the life around us. Were we the masters of that life, or merely its products? Or were we something else, perhaps in between, simultaneously the mutated children and the blind gardeners of the eons-long, random, and brutal Eden Darwin seemed to have discovered? Behind this question, of course, lies the debate between determinism and free will in the course of human events that we saw at work in the dialectics of *The Time Machine*, the question of whether we can really hope to control our future, or whether our future is simply the playing out of a hand long since dealt by the cosmos, the inevitable conclusion to a drama that was no drama since it never allowed for freedom of choice.

But in *The Island of Doctor Moreau*, and in the other pre- and post-Darwinian fictions to which it is intimately related, this central question takes on a more serious, a more threatening, perhaps a more fully human tone of urgency. For what is being asked in *Doctor Moreau*—and the really frightening question raised by the whole appearance and aftermath of the *The Origin of Species*—is not just does determinism or free will describe most accurately the human condition? It is this: Is there God? And if so, why does he not show himself?

"I will make a rational creature of my own," Moreau says, but it might equally well come from the first chapter of Genesis. Like many of the things Moreau says and does in the novel, it has a deliberately Biblical, and therefore a deliberately blasphemous, ring to it. For if, indeed, physiognomy, physiology, and clinical psychology (of which Moreau is a practitioner almost before the science is born) define the range of the human, and the range of what *makes* humans human, then it is well within the possibility of a really intelligent man to do what few men previously had dared to do, and what the whole romantic tradition of thought had insisted it was man's right to do: a man could become god. After all, in the absence of a guiding intelligence to the development and sequence of life forms upon the planet, the position is open.

The theological implications of Darwinian theory had been explored, as we have already said, at least as early as 1864, when Browning published his poem, "Caliban upon Setebos." In it, Caliban—the half-human monster of Shakespeare's The Tempest—reflects upon the nature of "Setebos," the god his witch-mother worshipped. And since Caliban himself is cruel, bestial, and sadistic, he imagines a god who shares the same characteristics, a god whose delight is in the tormenting of his creatures and the very arbitrariness of his cruelty:

> "Conceiveth all things will continue thus,
> And we shall have to live in fear of Him
> So long as He lives, keeps His strength: no change,
> If He have done His best, make no new world
> To please Him more, so leave off watching this,—
> If He surprise not even the Quiet's self
> Some strange day,—or, suppose, grow into it
> As grubs grow butterflies: else, here are we,
> And there is He, and nowhere help at all."

The poem is, at first glance, difficult reading because Caliban's semiarticulate musings are meant to sound like one long growl: but it is a growl struggling toward a kind of reason. The image of Shakespeare's beast man is, for Browning and for his age, the perfect metaphor for man as he comes to understand himself after the Darwinian revolution. We are all beast men: and where does that leave our theologies and our hopes for transcendence? To be sure, there might, just might, be something like Grace—the "Quiet" Caliban speaks of—and that might finally absorb and transvalue the cruelty and bestiality of the god who seems to rule this world. But that is only a hope: and otherwise, as Caliban says, "here are we,/And there is He, and nowhere help at all."

If Caliban is the perfect image of man under the post-Darwinian dispensation, Setebos, the god Caliban invents on the basis of his observations of the way the world works (a perfectly consistent and rational "natural theology") is a perfect metaphor for that "Nature," blind, random, unconsciously cruel, which is the central mechanism of natural selection, the mainspring of the creation of life. Browning's poem is neither a satire of Darwinian ideas, nor quite a satire of traditional human pretensions seen in the light of Darwinian ideas. But it is a severely honest, visionary estimation of the chances for not human survival but human pride in the not-so-brave new world charted by The Origin of Species.

It is impossible not to hear, in Caliban's simultaneously cringing and angry disquisition upon Setebos, an anticipation of one of the most stunning passages in The Island of Doctor Moreau. Before he learns the truth of Moreau's experiment, Prendick thinks that Moreau might, for some unspeakable reason, be surgically transforming men into beasts: he gets the process exactly backwards, but his mistake only emphasizes the larger, grimmer point that the border line between human and nonhuman is being erased. Fearing that he might be the next victim of Moreau's vivisection, he flees into the heart of the island, where he stumbles upon a cave inhabited by the beast men. Mistaken for one of them, he is told he must "learn the Law" if he is to be truly a Man, and thereupon the leader of the beasts takes up a chilling litany in which the others join:

> "Not to go on all-Fours; that is the Law. Are we not Men?
> Not to eat Flesh nor Fish; that is the Law. Are we not Men?
> Not to claw Bark of Trees; that is the Law. Are we not Men?
> Not to chase other Men; that is the Law. Are we not Men?"

It is, of course, a bitter parody of the Ten Commandments handed down by the vengeful God of the Old Testament; Moreau's own set of conditioned responses to raise his new creation to the level of full rationality. And the litany concludes with a chant that underscores even more strikingly the blasphemous nature of Moreau's experiment:

> "His is the House of Pain.
> His is the Hand that makes.
> His is the Hand that wounds.
> His is the Hand that heals."

Moreau takes it upon himself singlehandedly to recapitulate and improve upon the process whereby men evolve from beasts. And in doing so he makes himself a parody god, a botched version of that inhuman force, the blind struggle for existence, which has supplanted the image of benevolent creative deity.

But the parody cuts two ways. For if Moreau has dissipated his humanity in his attempt to become a microcosmic god, his creation of the beast folk and the religious awe he burns into their flesh also remind us (as, indeed, does the natural theology of Browning's Caliban) how ludicrous, in the light of the evolutionary facts, appear our attempts to locate or describe a god—how silly, weighed against the immensity and incomprehensibility of universal process, are the mythologies we invent to render that process human. After Moreau has been killed by renegade beast folk, Prendick and Moreau's drunken assistant Montgomery are left alone upon the island. Prendick saves both their lives by the simple expedient of continuing the myth of Moreau. The beast folk, stunned and confused by the sight of Moreau's mangled body, are on the verge of reverting fully, abandoning the Law that restrains them from murder and the eating of flesh:

> "Children of the Law," I said, "he is not dead."
> M'ling [one of the beast folk] turned his sharp eyes on me.
> "He has changed his shape—he has changed his body," I went on. "For a time you will not see him. He is . . . there"—I pointed upward—"where he can watch you. You cannot see him. But he can see you. Fear the Law."
> I looked at them squarely. They flinched.

After the mock-decalogue of the litany of the Law, this is the mock-gospel of the dying and reviving god: Moreau has been transformed from a post-Darwinian Jehovah into a post-Darwinian Christ, and both manifestations are equally sham, equally disturbing reflections of our disease of thought as well as Moreau's. How much, we are forced to ask, is our belief in the afterlife simply an expression of our fear—fear that the dead, our fathers, may still be looking on and judging our lives? Passages like this one, in the full scandalousness of their implications, help explain the outcry that greeted the novel's appearance. This, indeed, is one of the special, subtle, and distinctive qualities of the early science fiction of Wells;

that it manages to indicate not only the inhumanity and brutality we risk when we deliver ourselves over to the reign of pure rationality, but also the foolishness and bestiality we risk if we refuse to allow rationality, science, the cosmic view of things their due.

Moreau is a "mad scientist" (to use the phrase that has become almost shorthand for his numerous descendants in science fiction). But he is a mad scientist of a very peculiar sort, which must be carefully distinguished from the others of his kind who had populated English fiction before Wells began to write. The creation of a new man, that arrogantly godlike act, is of course not only the aspiration of Moreau and the special frenzy of his Darwinian mind. It is also, as we have said, part of the essential romantic dream, the essential romantic quest to remake the world in the image of human aspiration, to wrest reality, through revolution or vision, to the scale of human hope. And in this connection it is necessary to think of Wells's Dr. Moreau in connection with and contrast to another "mad scientist" figure, perhaps the most famous one devised by the European mind in the last two centuries: Mary Shelley's Dr. Frankenstein.

Superficially, the two tales are quite similar. They are both, in the Gothic novel tradition, frame-tale narratives, in which a minor, more "normal" character (Walton in *Frankenstein*, Prendick in *Doctor Moreau*) meets the title character whose experimental career has led him beyond the bounds of ordinary human experience, and into regions of thought and discovery either godlike or demonic in their energy. Both tales, moreover, are about the creation of artificial consciousness through scientific means, and in both, the scientist who performs this miraculous feat is explicitly associated with the God of Genesis, but as a *failed* creator, a would-be deity blinded by the excessive light of his own rationalism. To that extent, both novels are critiques of the romantic vision at its most expansive, cautionary fables about the limits of human aspiration for control or understanding and the dangers of overstepping those limits.

But there the similarity between the two books ends. Mary Shelley's tale emphasizes the success of Dr. Frankenstein's experiment, and the terrible price he has to pay for that success.

He does, indeed, create a rational being, a grotesquely ugly creature who is nevertheless fully rational, sensitive, even poignant in his loathing of his condition and his terrible loneliness. For Mary Shelley is concerned, mainly, with writing a cautionary parable about the entrapments of the untrammeled romantic imagination. The mind, freed of all restraints, inhibitions, and socially embedded barriers, might become godlike: but, argues Frankenstein, the price of becoming godlike is to become solipsistic, isolated from ordinary human concerns and ordinary human warmth, so absolutely and so severely that it is to be looked on as a kind of hell. The isolation suffered by Dr. Frankenstein's sole creation is the projection, the double, of the isolation suffered by his creator himself.

Wells's Dr. Moreau, on the other hand, is a less successful creator. His beast men never attain the intelligence or the articulateness of Frankenstein's monster, and their very creation—unlike the almost instantaneous alchemical process of Mary Shelley's novel—is achieved only through a slow, excruciatingly painful and bloody surgery. If Mary Shelley wants us to understand the particular traps laid for the autonomous, imperial romantic imagination, Wells wants us to be aware of how fallacious, how self-serving and ultimately mad, that imagination is in itself. Moreau is a version of Frankenstein, but a Frankenstein chastened, humbled by the intransigence of nature to his grandiose schemes.

Of course, the Darwinian revolution in thought, along with the massive expansion of European imperialism and colonialism in the eighteenth and nineteenth centuries, accounted for a great number of stories in which the man/animal distinction was raised and resolved to the advantage of a Western, white, and Christian idea of what makes a "man." It is important to remember, while reading Doctor Moreau, that only a hundred years previously, serious debates had been carried on about the humanity of the "native" populations of Asia and Africa just coming under European domination. And at the very time the book was being written, there was still widespread feeling that the "savages" being colonized by the Europeans were largely nonhuman until they could be trained to humanity by their white captors and governors. This theme, too, is prominent in the background of the action of Wells's novel: particularly so, since Darwinian (or misunderstood Darwinian) arguments for the evolution of the human race could easily be invoked as proof of the semicivilized, semihumanized nature of non-Western populations, and therefore as justification of the right of more civilized peoples to control and exploit such "beast folk."

The imperial theme was nowhere more strongly sounded than in the work of Rudyard Kipling, whose first *Jungle Book* appeared in 1894. Kipling's stories of Mowgli, the manchild reared among wolves and yet somehow superior to, more successful and more heroic than his animal foster-parents, are thinly veiled allegories for the inevitable triumph of Western (i.e., truly "human") civilization over savagery. This theme—an important one in the formation of the modern European and American world view—was of course to find its fullest expression twenty years after the appearance of the first *Jungle Book* and eighteen after *Doctor Moreau* when the American Edgar Rice Burroughs published the first novel describing the exploits of the ultimate white imperialist, *Tarzan of the Apes*.

In *The Jungle Book* the major strains of the Tarzan theme are already sounded. Mowgli is exiled from the wolf pack in which he has been raised by his own intelligence, his own innate superiority to the animals around him—an optimistic, but distinctively post-Darwinian way of expressing man's uniqueness. And very early in *The Jungle Book*, he asks his friend, Bagheera the black panther, why it is that the other animals (Mowgli does not yet know what it means to be a man) will not accept him. The passage that follows is one of Kipling's finest, and one of the century's most important:

> "But why—but why should any wish to kill me?" said Mowgli.
>
> "Look at me," said Bagheera. And Mowgli looked at him steadily between the eyes. The big panther turned his head away in half a minute.
>
> "*That* is why," he said, shifting his paw on the leaves. "Not even I can look thee between the eyes, and I was born among men, and I love thee, Little Brother. The others they hate thee because their eyes cannot meet thine; because thou art wise; because thou hast pulled out thorns from their feet—because thou art a man."

To be a man is a fine, commanding thing for Kipling. As in the Tarzan stories of Burroughs, it is no wonder that the animals can speak, that they, too, might be gifted with powers of discrimination, morality, even with something approaching a Law. For humanity, manhood, in Kipling's universe is something beyond those merely physiological attainments of speech or organized behavior, language and society. It is a quality almost like a sacramental sign, a magic seal that raises the truly human above the simply animal (and hence, of course, the truly European above the simply human): "the others they hate thee . . . because thou art wise," says Bagheera. But this kind of "wisdom," more than anything else, is the expression of a last-ditch faith in human speciality almost without rational cause. The more the romantic or imperial imagination is undermined by fact, the more strenuously and mythologically it asserts its reality.

But though it may be no wonder that the beasts of The Jungle Book speak, it is part of the central horror of The Island of Doctor Moreau. According to Moreau, "the great difference between man and monkey is in the larynx." Animals who may be trained to speak call into question the whole identity of the human species, for Wells, good modern that he is, assumes that it is only such accomplishments as speech and social organization that distinguish the human species, not anything as insubstantial or questionable as "soul" or, in Bagheera's (Kipling's) terms, "wisdom." It is all the more striking then that, early in Doctor Moreau, Wells describes a scene which is, either consciously or not, a direct version and inversion of the scene we have quoted from The Jungle Book. Early in his stay on the island, Prendick is wandering through the woods when he finds himself being watched by one of the strange, half-human, half-bestial creatures who are the island's inhabitants:

> Setting my teeth hard I walked straight towards him. I was anxious not to show the fear that seemed chilling my backbone. I pushed through a tangle of tall white-flowered bushes, and saw him twenty yards beyond, looking over his shoulder at me and hesitating. I advanced a step or two looking steadfastly into his eyes.
> "Who are you?" said I.
> He tried to meet my gaze.

"No!" he said suddenly, and, turning, went bounding away
from me through the undergrowth.

"He tried to meet my gaze," Prendick observes of the beast
man in the forest. But his failure to meet the narrator's gaze is
not an earnest of human superiority over the animal, as is
Bagheera's experience with Mowgli. It is, rather, the mark of a
further confusion between human and animal, between imperialist and subject—for the beast man's shamefacedness at
Prendick's gaze is not natural but *conditioned*: and conditioned precisely by the training Moreau has instilled into him,
cut into his flesh, in order to make him more fully "man."

The Island of Doctor Moreau, in other words, is, at this
level of reading, a critique not only of the biological and theological but also of the social implications of Darwinism misunderstood. The erroneous view of the theory of evolution
might lead us to believe that the line between man and beast
is so thin, so artificial, that no moral sanctions really exist at
all save as social conventions; it might lead us to believe that
man, as the only conscious agent in a universe of blind flux,
has the right to assimilate godlike powers and godlike arbitrariness; and it might lead us to justify, in terms of our own
triumph in the struggle for survival, our brutality and tyranny
over "races" or non-European members of our species less
visibly civilized than ourselves. All three of these misreadings
of Darwin are diseases of thought, and cancers of the soul, according to Wells in this novel. As both satire and evolutionary
parable, *The Island of Doctor Moreau* manifests its fullest
complexity as just such a vivisection of mental errors. If *The
Time Machine* had taken the idea of evolution seriously
enough to predict the worst that might lie in the human future, *Doctor Moreau* takes the same idea seriously enough to
anatomize the worst misconceptions of the human present.

As in *The Time Machine*, the structure of the book is perfectly suited to the acting out of its themes. Prendick narrates
the events after they have all taken place: a first-person narrator with important similarities to that other first-person narrator, Swift's Lemuel Gulliver, who was so dear to the young
Wells. Shipwrecked during his voyage on the *Lady Vain*,
Prendick finds himself adrift in an open boat with two other
men, without provisions, for a seemingly interminable period

of time. As often happens in such open-boat narratives (and as often did happen in fact), the men decide to resort to cannibalism to stay alive: they draw lots to see who will sacrifice himself so that the other two might live. But by an absurd accident the other two men are cast overboard, leaving Prendick alone and delirious until he is picked up by a ship bearing supplies, animals, and Montgomery to Moreau's island.

Abandoned on the island with Montgomery, Moreau, and the beast folk, Prendick enters more and more deeply into the nightmare world and nightmare perceptions that constitute the major atmosphere of the book. But the brief introductory chapters have made an important point: they not only carry us out of the "real" world into the abstract, fevered world of Moreau's island but they establish that in that so-called "real" world such things as cannibalism, the reversion of man to self-destructive bestiality, and the warfare of the species against itself and its very survival are all quite distinct possibilities—if the comforting assurances and rituals of the "normal" are a little suspended. Prendick, the ordinary man who experiences and narrates this scarifying story, in other words, is crucial to the tale not only because of his normality, but also because we feel, and he is willing to let us know, how close he and we can come to the brutal abnormality which Moreau and the beast folk represent.

As in *The Time Machine*, the "plot" of the novel is largely a matter of the alternative, successive explanations Prendick entertains about the strange and uncanny things he encounters on Moreau's island. We have observed that the satire of the novel is directed against three levels of misinterpretation of the Darwinian message, the social/imperialist, the humanistic, and the theological. And it is no accident that Prendick's successive explanations of the oddities he witnesses are in terms of these three progressively more complex and threatening accusations against the very idea of "human nature."

At first, confronted with the disgusting, inexplicably unnatural appearance and demeanor of the inhabitants of the island, Prendick merely assumes that they are a particularly degenerate species of human being, quite rightly pressed into slavery and submission by the superior intelligence of Moreau as standard-bearer of Western culture and all its accoutrements. Later, having learned that they are not "natural" beings at all, he assumes that they are in fact deformed men, humans translated by Moreau's demonic surgery into animal parodies of the human: living demonstrations, that is, of the fictitiousness and the impermanence of the barrier between "human" and "other than human." When Prendick finally learns the truth of the island, and the truth of the grisly experiment Moreau is carrying out, learns in fact that Moreau has set himself up as a tragicomic god of instant evolution, it is already too late for that knowledge to make any difference. The beast men are already beginning to revert to the cannibalism which Moreau fears so much, and the prohibition of which is such a central tenet of the Law he instills in his creation. The border line between man and beast may be crossed: in this, at least, Wells agrees with the optimistic fairy tales of Kipling and Burroughs. But to cross that border line, to deny finally that there is a difference, is not so much to accept the burden of evolutionary truth as to indulge in a suicidal "wisdom" whose final effect is not to dignify the animal in us as much as it is to degrade the human.

I have described the novel as an early, prophetic vision of the world of the concentration camp. That prophetic vision is nowhere more stunning than in the final, full irony of the novel as a whole, its insistence that the man who denies the special quality of human consciousness, for however legitimate and honorable scientific reasons, ends by denying the very possibility of consciousness at all. *The Island of Doctor Moreau* cannot be taken as a sermon against behaviorism, only because behaviorism as a science or pseudo-science did not come into existence until nearly a half-century after its writing. Nevertheless, its bitter strictures remain as powerful today as they were in 1896.

But the bitterest of its visions are reserved, not for Moreau the mad scientist, but for Prendick the "normal" observer of the nightmare experiment. After Moreau dies, and Montgomery is later killed, Prendick is left alone upon the island with the beast folk. And, until he is rescued, he is forced to witness them revert to their animal natures: but to their animal natures with something of the human still left in.

> The Monkey Man bored me. . . . He assumed, on the strength of his five digits, that he was my equal, and was for

ever jabbering at me, jabbering the most arrant nonsense. One
thing about him entertained me a little: he had a fantastic trick
of coining new words. He had an idea, I believe, that to gabble
about names that meant nothing was the proper use of speech.
He called it "big thinks," to distinguish it from "little
thinks"—the sane everyday interests of life.

It would be difficult, even among the work of Alfred North
Whitehead and Bertrand Russell, almost contemporary to the
writing of *Doctor Moreau*, to find a more efficient or more eloquent satire of the self-serving, metaphysical pretensions of
the philosophical community. Just as the novel began by leading us from a relatively "realistic" incidence of cannibalism
into the dreamworld of Moreau's island, so it ends by leading
us back to a perception that, however fantastic the vivisec-
tionist's experiment might have seemed, we really are animals, really *are* well-trained pigs (or monkeys or whatever).
After Prendick builds a raft and escapes from the island to return to civilization, he, like Swift's Gulliver at the end of his
voyages to the Lilliputians, Brobdingnagians, Houyhnhnms
and others, finds his perceptions of "ordinary" life irreparably
distorted by the satirical truth he has seen underneath that
comforting ordinariness.

> Then I would turn aside into some chapel; and even there,
> such was my disturbance, it seemed that the preacher gibbered
> Big Thinks even as the Ape Man had done; or into some li-
> brary, and there the intent faces over the books seemed but pa-
> tient creatures waiting for prey.

Moreau's experiment, to this extent at least, has been a
success: it has taught Prendick to be less certain of his self-
confident "humanity," less arrogant about the naturalness of
his own civilization. It has shown him, and the reader, the potential abyss that lies on the other side of everything we believe in as civilized. It is the Time Traveller's vision of universal futility carried into a perception of the everyday, the here
and now. But the here and now, the "sane everyday interests
of life" that the Monkey Man and his cohorts ignore, was
always for Wells the final salvation, the origin and the end of
human thought. And in his next books of importance that saving ordinariness was to take its revenge against the abstraction
of the Moreaus of this world.

4

REALIST OF THE FANTASTIC:
The Invisible Man and
The War of the Worlds

"Frankly—it is uncommonly fine. . . . Impressed is the word, O Realist of the Fantastic! whether you like it or not." This is what Joseph Conrad wrote to Wells, on December 4, 1898, about *The Invisible Man,* published in 1897.

Wells had begun his career as a novelist two years before. But it is important to realize—what Conrad and few of Wells's later commentators realized—that this novel represented a new direction, a new orientation of his talent. *The Time Machine* and *The Island of Doctor Moreau,* for all their power, were essentially parables: stunning and disturbing in their mapping out of the implications of the new vision of science, but nevertheless abstract, almost disembodied in their presentation of character and locale. We have already noted that the Time Traveller is ghostlike in his lack of specific qualities. He is a pure observer, a seeing eye into the future—or a possible future—without any visible characteristics. In much the same way, though Prendick and Moreau in *The Island of Doctor Moreau* have "real" names and even the rudiments of a personal past, they play out their grisly melodrama in a landscape, on an island, which is precisely nowhere (as is proper for a utopia, even an evil one), a generalized, surreal backdrop for a struggle whose very terms seem to preclude the possibility of everyday reality. Even *The Wonderful Visit,* that minor but delightful novel of 1895, shares this abstract, allegorical quality: though set in the southern suburbs of London, its action and its characters are obviously of an aesthetic and decorative rather than a realistic origin.

Nevertheless, in his next major scientific romances, Wells did unite the cosmic anxieties of his earliest tales to a sense of the real, the everyday, the *ordinary*. Only a few years later, with the publication of the first of his major "realistic" novels (*Kipps* in 1905), he was to be hailed as the natural heir of Charles Dickens for his convincing grasp of the details of middle-class life and his gift of presenting those details in the full dimensions of their humor. It was an analogy Wells disliked very much—not because of any distaste for Dickens, but because of the implied snobbism of assuming that a chronicler of the middle classes could be only a comedian, that the mercantile classes, at their best, could be only humorous. There is a passage in *Kipps*, near the end of the book, when Wells confronts this misunderstanding head-on. Artie Kipps, the working-class hero, and his wife, Ann, are feuding in what seems to be a conventionally comical way about their social position and the propriety of receiving calls from their neighbors. But Wells characteristically interrupts the comedy to make a serious, even a jarring, point:

> The stupid little tragedies of these clipped and limited lives!
> What is the good of keeping up the idyllic sham and pretending that ill-educated, misdirected people "get along well," and that all this is harmlessly funny and nothing more? You think I'm going to write fat, silly, grinning novels about half-educated, under-trained people and keep it up all the time, that the whole thing's nothing but funny!

This is the sort of preachiness, the tone of direct moral urgency, that Henry James thought so detrimental to Wells's real gifts as an artist. And, of course, there is something undeniably preachy about a passage like this one. But there is also something very moving about it; it is a moment in which we hear the voice of Wells in its fullest, most identifiable tones. Ordinary, limited, only superficially cultured the lives of these characters might be, Wells is saying. But the "clipped and limited" quality of their lives, the silliness of their bourgeois tragedies, are not "harmlessly funny and nothing more": they are the chief disease of civilization at the present

time, since they doom thousands of potentially creative men
and women to live out a mere parody of what their lives, in a
truly enlightened society, might have been. This is, of course,
the liberal's myth of universal education, the belief that if only
people could be trained properly, they would behave nobly.
And by 1905 it was far from a radically original idea. Yet
Wells in his best fiction and his most passionate essays
breathed new life into the dream, mainly through the ferocity
with which he himself believed it—and had lived it. In a
famous essay of the twenties, Virginia Woolf, a great novelist
and a great snob, took Wells (and middle-class fiction generally) to task for misunderstanding and distorting not only the
nature of fiction but the nature of the middle class. But it is at
least arguable that Wells understood both terms better than
his distinguished opponent—and understood them both as
well as he did because he understood them together.

Wells may fairly be said to have helped change the course
of English middle-class fiction simply by insisting that the ordinary details of so-called "real life" are also details that show
the pressure of cosmic, eons-old forces: that real life matters,
and matters in more than a local, comic way, since it is, however unconsciously, the playing out of the very forces that
move the planets in their orbits and the protozoa in the direction of thought. George Eliot and particularly Thomas Hardy
had already articulated this special sense of the massive
grinding of universal forces against even the most undis-
tinguished of lives, in their fiction. But with Wells the terms
become more severe, the interference of universal forces with
the everyday business of life more pronounced. A "realist"
Wells may have been, in some of his best novels published
before the First World War. But, at least for an English writer,
his realism was of a very peculiar quality indeed: a blend of
low comedy, high seriousness, and scientific accuracy unlike
much that had come before. His realistic novels and his
science fiction, in other words, were not really as far apart as
many of his critics have suggested.

Even before *Kipps* in 1905, Wells had explored this level of
realism. His *Select Conversations with an Uncle,* published in
1895 before *The Time Machine,* is a series of sketches, very
Dickensian in character, which describe the responses of a

healthily skeptical, middle-class mind to the pretensions of contemporary society. And in 1896, following *The Island of Doctor Moreau*, there was *The Wheels of Chance*.

The Wheels of Chance is a minor work, written generally in a light, coy tone reminiscent of *The Wonderful Visit*. But it is also, in some important ways, the direct ancestor of *Kipps*, and even of *The Invisible Man* in 1897 and *The War of the Worlds* in 1898. Here, for the first time, Wells presents the countryside that was the landscape of his own youth, the counties south of London; and here, also for the first time, he confronts the theme of the middle-class, undereducated, and yet immortally longing *homme moyen sensuel*, that bourgeois, venal, confused, somehow infinitely interesting figure whom we can almost call the "Wellsian man."

The Wellsian man of *The Wheels of Chance* is not as complicated or as self-conscious as he will become in his later incarnations. Hoopdriver, the hero of the novel, is a draper's assistant in a small London firm, who decides to bicycle south to Chichester, on the sea, on his vacation. Along the way he encounters two other cyclists: the beautiful Jessie Milton, daughter of a famous and scandalous woman novelist, and the evil Bechamel, with whom Jessie has made the mistake of eloping. She is trying to escape from Bechamel's clutches, and Hoopdriver, in spite of himself, is forced to become her deliverer and protector, in a headlong cycling flight from the seducer, until she is finally rescued by her distraught mother and her mother's clownish friends.

It is fairly flimsy stuff, even for a novel as brief as *The Wheels of Chance*. And yet some important features for Wells's later work emerge from it. First of all, is the idea of social class, so painfully a part of Wells's own youth and so perennial a theme of his mature work. Hoopdriver is a draper—is, in other words, what Wells would have become except for his genius, good luck, and absolute incompetence at bookkeeping. More to the point, Hoopdriver knows—as, surely, did the young Wells—the degree to which his undertraining dooms him to a life of stunted intellect (which will appear "comic" to the superior classes) and closes him off from any real grasp of what can make life sublime or beautiful. Or, rather, Hoopdriver does not know, but learns these unpleasant facts in the course of the book. He falls in love with Jessie Milton, but so severe is the cultural gap between them that he can never bring himself to express that love. In a delicate scene at the end, he promises to read, to better himself, and Jessie suggests that in six years a man may make much of himself: it is as close to a promise of love as they come.

In later novels, of course, Wells's middle-class heroes will be much more energetic, more ferocious in their grasping at life. That grasping is the second major theme sounded in The Wheels of Chance: the desperate solitary struggle of the individual to control the social forces that surround him and to wrest them into a more human shape, for the sake of his own fate and that of others like him. In a way, it is the obverse of the utopian strain in Wells. For if he was driven to think of the future of society as a massive evolutionary process that men working together might seek to understand and control, he was also driven, for obvious autobiographical reasons, to value the sheer force of will through which a single individual can sometimes wrestle successfully with the "way things are." It was one reason Wells often annoyed his fellow utopians of a more doctrinaire, Marxist sort. For if the Wellsian hero could sometimes look like the true selfless revolutionary hero, he could also at times look like that hero's anti-type, the Samurai (as he called the leaders of his 1905 A Modern Utopia), or the gangster.

Hoopdriver is far from being a full-fledged intellectual gangster, although he may be regarded as the larval form of later, stronger figures in Wells. But in another respect he touches very close to the heart of a crucial Wellsian theme. He is a man in flight. The whole action of The Wheels of Chance occurs during his brief cycling vacation—that miserable pittance of time (in the Wellsian view) allotted the prisoners of urban shops for their pathetic attempts at escape to finer air, larger vistas. And after Hoopdriver rescues Jessie from her seducer, their journey becomes a real flight—from Bechamel, but also more subtly from the social structures, the elaborate web of privilege and dominance that separates them from one another. The flight is circular, finally a failure. But it is the exhilaration of escape, however brief and foredoomed, that underlies much of the real energy and charm of the novel.

Such moments of escape, of frantic flight from an intolerable situation, are a recurring motif in Wells's fiction, as they were a recurring temptation in his own life. It has been said that whenever Wells took a new mistress, he built himself a new house. But it went deeper than that. Restless and often despairing about the human condition and his own, Wells was particularly vulnerable to an elementary urge all of us share to one degree or another: the longing to break and run, to get out. Artie Kipps resolves an engagement he has contracted by eloping with Ann, his true love. Mr. Polly in *The History of Mr. Polly* (1910) is a heroic arsonist: he burns down the shop he has run for fifteen years, is assumed to have died in the fire, and thereby frees himself from both a drab life and a drab wife.

We can also think of Prendick, fleeing from the reverting beast men on Dr. Moreau's island. At his grimmest, Wells tends to imagine the state of human society as cannibalism of one sort or another, and the city as a hellish place which is (or ought to be) burning. A remarkable number of Wellsian heroes are seen, or remembered, at their most vivid in headlong flight from a universe of man-eaters and burning structures.

Class differences, the necessity of personal struggle against those killing differences, and the temptation of flight, escape to a new freedom from the awful state of things: these are certainly the characteristics of the realistic, socially conscious novel, the kind Virginia Woolf disliked so much. But they are less obviously elements of science fiction; much less so than the utopian, Darwinian, and cosmological themes we discussed in the last chapter. The integration of these two levels of thought and imagination is precisely the accomplishment of Wells, as "realist of the fantastic," in *The Invisible Man* in 1897 and *The War of the Worlds* in 1898.

THE INVISIBLE MAN

The title itself is resonant, ominous; although, after nearly a century in print, its resonance may have become a little muted through repetition. What *is* an invisible man? A walking emptiness, a disembodied voice uttering mad and dangerous things, a threat both anarchic (he can do anything he wants) and intimately terrifying (he may be right next to you). But also, because he is a walking emptiness, a violation of the natural order of things, he is a peculiarly virulent threat to the comfortable everyday assurances of "normal" life—in which men are decent to one another precisely because they can keep an eye on one another. And the pun in that last sentence is, the novel insists, not really a pun at all. "Keeping an eye on" your neighbor is, at a grim level of realism, the founding act of the whole elaborate web we think of as social morality. A half-century after *The Invisible Man,* the existentialists were to insist that seeing and being seen are among the most crucial and most morally determinative of human experiences. And, of course, one of the most ancient and suggestive ideas of God as the fountainhead of all morality is that of a giant, all-seeing eye (an image still preserved on the back of the dollar bill).

But what if a man could become unseen? What if, like a primitive deity, he could transform himself into an invisible but murderously powerful presence? Would this, at a single stroke, free him from the bounds of ordinary morality and into a new, savage, absolutely individualist universe? As we have already observed, there were a number of arguments abroad at the end of the nineteenth century that the next stage of social evolution might lead to a "new man" who would be godlike in his potency and demonic in his freedom from conventional ideas of morality. Nietzsche had profoundly explored and articulated this possibility in his image of the Übermensch to come, and both Robert Louis Stevenson in *Dr. Jekyll and Mr. Hyde* and Oscar Wilde in *The Picture of Dorian Gray* had rendered cautionary, moral fables about the dangers of coasting too close to the border line between knowledge and forbidden knowledge, approaching too nearly the science or alchemy that might free (or exile) a man from all moral restraints.

And yet despite these precedents there is a special sense of urgency, a special sense of the apocalyptic, in a scene like the following, when the Invisible Man first reveals himself and runs amok in the small town of Iping, where he has been conducting his experiments:

> There were excited cries of "Hold him!" "Invisible!" and so
> forth, and a young fellow, a stranger in the place whose name

did not come to light, rushed in at once, caught something, missed his hold, and fell over the constable's prostrate body. Half-way across the road a woman screamed as something pushed by her; a dog, kicked apparently, yelped and ran howling into Huxter's yard, and with that the transit of the Invisible Man was accomplished. For a space people stood amazed and gesticulating, and then came Panic, and scattered them abroad through the village as a gust scatters dead leaves.

This is one of the earliest of those descriptions of mass confusion, mob panic, which for many readers came to characterize Wells. And it is important to realize that the power of the passage stems not only from its concentration upon specific detail (the woman screaming, the kicked dog, the homeliness of "Huxter's yard"), but also from its insistence on the pressure of the uncanny upon that everyday specificity. An Invisible Man, after all, is running mad among this very conventional crowd; and Wells imagines the effects of such an unseen terror as powerfully as he does just because he is able to hold in mind, at the same time, both the reality of the everyday and the awesomeness of the uncanny. The last sentence, with its three phrases of unequal length, is a model of Wells's technique at the height of his powers. "For a space people stood amazed and gesticulating"; the detail is convincing because it is the way people in mobs really behave after some public disaster. "And then came Panic"; the literary sounding, semipersonalized appearance of "Panic" makes sense here just because "Panic" in this sense is a primordial, allegorical power that reduces the mob to a terrorized, Panic-ridden abstraction. "And scattered them abroad through the village as a gust scatters dead leaves"; by its end the sentence has transformed the mob panic into a poetic image of apocalypse (ultimately, the image is from the "Ode to the West Wind" by Wells's beloved Shelley) that we believe, just because we believe in the carefully imagined detail that has gone before. Indeed, the image of the wind blowing the dead leaves before it works as well as it does because, among other reasons, the wind itself, like the Invisible Man (and like the force of revolution or apocalypse in Shelley) cannot be seen except through its effects.

This is writing of a very high and self-conscious order indeed—so self-conscious as to mask its artifice as a naturalistic description of events. But to say that is also to imply that *The Invisible Man*, besides being a major turning point in Wells's career, is also a subtle and corrosive critique of the conventions of the "realistic" novel.

The novel, after all, is a comparatively young form among the varieties of fiction. Arising in the mid to late eighteenth century, it was the classic, and classically appropriate, expression of the aspirations and fears of the mercantile middle class: the perfect vehicle for a vision of society very like that of Adam Smith's *The Wealth of Nations* (1776), in which the structures of capitalist society are assumed to function, on the whole, benevolently and efficiently, and to assign every man finally to his proper place in the system. Critics as different as Wolfgang Iser and Edward Said have remarked upon the peculiarly sociological quality of the nineteenth-century novel, the way its characteristic plots, from *The Red and the Black* to *David Copperfield*, assert that every hero, with however many errors and misdirections along the way, will eventually discover the key to success within the prevailing system, and make himself successful (i.e., visible) within that system.

For the world of the conventional novel is one of almost exclusive visibility. To be a hero, or to become a hero, is to be or become *visible*: to be noticed by others, to be seen, to be *there* (on a given rung of the social ladder) and not be ashamed of it. The successful man, that is, is one who has learned the rules of his society and has managed to manipulate those rules to his own advantage, which is to say to his own increased *presence* in the society.

David Copperfield, Julien Sorel of *The Red and the Black*, Dorothea Brooke of *Middlemarch*, and any number of other characters are all somehow more "present" at the end of the novels describing their careers than they had been at the beginnings. The novel as capitalist fable is about the ways people increase their presence in a world imagined as closed to the infinite or the uncanny, insulated by its own efficiency from anything like an intrusion from the ab- or supra-normal.

But what if a man discovered a way to be, not more, but less present? What about a hero who violates these conventional expectations of the conventional novel? His mere existence, of course, would challenge the assumptions about "success," "reality," even "heroism" of ordinary fiction. And the more unconventional, the more *absent* he is from the ordinary world and ordinary conventions of the middle-class novel, the more severe would be the implicit challenge he offers the society that produced and sponsored that novel.

We have asked two questions, one theological and one sociological: What if a man could be unseen yet active among mankind? and, What if a man could be absent from yet still present in his society? *The Invisible Man* is an examination of both these questions. And not the least part of its genius is that it manages to answer them both at once, as if they were being asked at the same level of realism.

Griffin, the man who discovers the secret of invisibility, is both the perfect expression and the perfect refutation of the implied ideals of the ordinarily middle-class novel. Like a good bourgeois hero, he has discovered a secret, a hidden rule, that allows him unlimited mobility and power within his society. But that secret also excludes him from the fellowship of other men: at the same time it gives him power over society, it makes him the most extreme of exiles from society, a worse-than-monster since his monstrosity cannot even be seen.

From *Frankenstein* through *Dr. Jekyll and Mr. Hyde* to *The Island of Doctor Moreau*, the monster poses a single bothersome question: how awful can a man become and still be a part of the human community? Or, to put the question another way, how much can you take away from a man and still be able to call him a man?

But the monster of *The Invisible Man* is different: different from the conventional ideas of the monstrous, and different also from the accepted idea of the hero. Griffin is neither the Time Traveller nor is he Doctor Moreau: he is neither the sublimely removed, uninvolved observer of the course of human events, nor is he their demonic reorganizer. He is, rather, a meddler in the course of those events, a *terrorist*. And in that identity, for Wells, lies both his victory and his inevitable defeat, his sublimity and his absurdity.

The terrorist, after all, is as much the victim as he is the agent of the terror he produces. And here Wells is, perhaps, as prescient about political realities as he ever was to be in his long career. Griffin has discovered the secret of invisibility, and that secret allows him to move, unseen and unperceived, among other men. It allows him, in fact, to be the perfect revolutionary, the perfect terrorist, the perfect agent of a new society about to be born out of the ashes of the old: but that new order is one of selfishness and madness, an egotistic anarchy that is worse than the cannibalism of Doctor Moreau's reverting beast folk, since it is a fully conscious malevolence. "It is killing we must do, Kemp," says Griffin calmly to the doctor he tries to enlist as an ally.

> "Not wanton killing, but a judicious slaying. The point is, they know there is an Invisible Man—as well as we know there is an Invisible Man. And that Invisible Man, Kemp, must now establish a Reign of Terror. Yes—no doubt it's startling. But I mean it. A Reign of Terror . . . And all who disobey his orders he must kill, and kill all who would defend them."

A century of rationalized violence has perhaps inured us to statements like this one; but there is still something chilling about Griffin's obsessive repetition of the word, "kill," and especially about the phrase, "a judicious slaying," which perfectly catches the dissonance of orderly, rational planning and lunatic, uncontrolled violence which is Griffin's mind. Indeed, it is significant that it is this particular novel of Wells's that Conrad singled out for praise. In his own grim novel of anarchism, *The Secret Agent* (1905), the frightening character of the "Professor," a scientist and bombmaker purely devoted to destruction for its own sake, probably owes a good deal to the Invisible Man; especially in the celebrated last scene of the novel, where the Professor is described as passing, unseen, like a plague among men. Conrad dedicated the book to Wells.

The Invisible Man proposes a "Reign of Terror," but in fact his intended empire of fear and violence never gets beyond a comparatively petty, suburban apocalypse. He only kills one man, actually—and that one pointlessly, in a fit of rage after he has been betrayed by Kemp. During the original Reign of Terror after the French Revolution, Robespierre uttered the famous and awful statement, "Virtue without Terror is powerless." And in that statement speaks all the self-assured, in-

souciant certainty of eighteenth-century rationalism, a belief
that the moral universe of right and wrong could be explored
and analyzed as certainly, and with the same speculative in-
struments, as the physical universe of force and mass. But
even at the height of that optimistic period, doubts and dis-
sents were being expressed about the ultimate predictability
or rationality of human events. We have already mentioned
Frankenstein, and it is important to realize that the archetypal
figure of the monster is born out of the same foment of European thought that produced the dreams of the revolutionaries
and social planners. For if the monster poses the question,
How much can you take away from a man and still call him a
man? he also poses that question in its sociological key: How
much of what we call "human" can exist outside the elaborate
system of checks and balances which is human society?

"In all my great moments I have been alone," cries Griffin
to Kemp as he narrates his discovery of invisibility. And
Kemp later reinforces that observation as he is organizing a
party of villagers to track Griffin down: "The man's become
inhuman, I tell you. . . . He has cut himself off from his kind.
His blood be upon his own head." A great deal of debate in
the history of political theory turns on the question whether
man is naturally or only culturally human: that is, whether
those values of honor, dignity, and heroism we think of as
most distinctly human are the cause of society or the result of
it. In its way, of course, this is a chicken-and-egg problem, finally unanswerable: presumably the same impulses that lead
men to band into societies are later reinforced and refined by
the societies they form. But nevertheless the history of the
argument is a revealing one for the way men feel about the origins of their own nature.

Since the mid-nineteenth century, most thought has
tended to support the primacy of social organization over any
ideas of the pre-social, "natural" humanity of humans. And
Wells's Invisible Man is a powerful image of that argument.
Stevenson's Dr. Jekyll bartered his soul for hidden knowledge
and was damned, just as Wilde's Dorian Gray bartered his soul
for pleasure and was damned. But Griffin is the most political
and, perhaps, still the most contemporary of these grand-
children of Faust. His sacrifice is for power. And the paradox

of his sacrifice is that the very means through which he achieves power also cut him off from his kind and severely limit and trivialize the exercise of that power. Griffin is damned, that is, not as a result of but in the very terms of his devil's bargain. His crime *is* his punishment.

An Invisible Man, he soon learns, cannot act too soon after eating, or the yet undigested food in his stomach will still be visible; he must avoid rain, in which his outline will appear, and snow, in which his tracks can be seen; indeed, he cannot effectively function at all without at least one accomplice or lieutenant who *is* visible. Observations like these are, of course, part of Wells's power as a storyteller, evidence of his ability to imagine the extraordinary in terms of the most convincingly ordinary details. But they are more than that. They are dramatic realizations of the degree to which man, triumphantly and arrogantly cut off from society, is nevertheless still abjectly the product and perhaps the prey of that society he so despises.

For it *is* society, the simple and ordinary society of the small English town, which finally tracks down and destroys Griffin in all the mad egotism of his isolation:

> In another second there was a simultaneous rush upon the struggle, and a stranger coming into the road suddenly might have thought an exceptionally savage game of Rugby football was in progress. And there was no shouting after Kemp's cry—only a sound of blows and feet and a heavy breathing.

The brilliant analogy between the crowd falling upon and killing the Invisible Man and "an exceptionally savage game of Rugby football" is, at one level of reading, another of those commonplace details that moor Wells's perception of the fantastic so firmly in the real. But it also, at least partially, redeems the violence of this scene from mere subhuman randomness—the kind of randomness hinted at in Griffin's own plans for a reign of terror. A rugby team, after all, is a social organization, like all teams; and however violent its activities, they are bounded by a clear set of rules, objectives, or purposes. The disorganized mob that first fled the approach of the Invisible Man, in other words, has by the end of the book become something other than a mob. In reaction against the threat posed by Griffin (which is implicitly a threat to the very survival of human society) it has become, however violently or murderously, a group.

It is a distinctive feature of Wells's perception of the middle class that he does not romanticize them. The mob may have become a group, an appropriate representation of society marshaled against the threat of the isolated terrorist, but that does not make them or what they do pretty. "Cover his face," shouts a man as the mutilated Griffin slowly, for the first time in the book, becomes visible. "For Gawd's sake, cover his face!" It is an eloquent and grim epitaph, not only for the bloodshed Griffin had envisaged, but for the bloodshed he had called forth upon himself. As we have said before, Wells believed to the end in the reality and the *value* of ordinary things, of all those concerns and commitments so important to the daily functioning of human society. But he also believed, and articulated in a thousand different ways, that these home truths were *not enough* to form a truly efficient society—and that, moreover, many of them were warped and deformed by the inherited weight of custom, misplaced religious awe, and pusillanimous moralism. *The Island of Doctor Moreau* had argued that man may be no more than a well-trained animal. *The Invisible Man* argues that that well-trained animal is still the best chance we have for survival as a species—certainly a better chance than the pure disembodied intelligence and greed of the Invisible Man himself—but it does not allow us to rest secure or comfortable in that knowledge.

Indeed, Wells's ambivalence about the group versus the individual, the one versus the many, led him in 1910 to write "The Country of the Blind," the most powerful and bitter of his short stories, and a stunning reversal of the situation in *The Invisible Man*. The same basic tale is repeated, except that our sympathies and our identification are with the individual figure, the isolated hero rather than with the group, the society, that destroys him. In *The Invisible Man* Griffin describes his first experience of invisibility this way:

> "My mood, I say, was one of exaltation. I felt as a seeing man might do, with padded feet and noiseless clothes, in a city of the blind. I experienced a wild impulse to jest, to startle

people, to clap men on the back, fling people's hats astray, and
generally revel in my extraordinary advantage."

But, in fact, as Griffin soon finds, it is not entirely an extraordinary advantage to be invisible among a crowd of seeing people. And, as Wells's later story makes plain, it is also not entirely a joyful thing to be a "seeing man . . . in a city of the
blind."

"In the country of the blind, the one-eyed man is king,"
runs the old saying—itself an ironic commentary on the relative proportions of wisdom and stupidity in human affairs.
But Wells reverses the conventional wisdom of the saying in
"The Country of the Blind" to give us a tragic vision of the
fate of the gifted man at the hands of his inferiors—almost a
vision, in other words, of Griffin as he would probably like to
have been perceived. The story begins by describing a remote,
almost unapproachable South American valley populated by a
group of settlers who, because of a unique virus, are all blind
from birth. Into this country of the blind stumbles Wells's
hero, Nunez, gifted with sight and enthusiastic to use his gift
to make himself the dictator of the sightless by whom he is
surrounded. It is, of course, exactly the situation of the Invisible Man, except that since we, the readers, are also sighted,
our sympathies and identification are with Nunez rather than
with the valley's inhabitants. But Nunez soon learns that his
power of sight is not an advantage but a handicap: the villagers, over generations of sightlessness, have honed their
other powers of perception to such an acute degree that it is
the sighted man who is at a loss confronting them. Nunez's
claims that he possesses a sense they do not have are, moreover, met with disbelief, mockery, and completely logical religious and metaphysical refutation by the philosophers of the
world he has entered. Finally, given the choice of imprisonment or blinding in order to join the community, Nunez attempts to escape from the terrible valley and dies of exposure
on the surrounding mountains.

It is a very somber tale, narrated with masterful poise and
an ironic distance from the absurdity and terror of the events
that only emphasizes their absurdity and terror. But, reading it
in relation to The Invisible Man, it is impossible not to see it

as the completion, almost the underside, of the earlier tale. At least as a political parable, "The Country of the Blind" insists that the gifted, the special individual does have his special rights and special social sanctions (and here, to be sure, Wells was probably again thinking of his own personal career): and that the fate of a man, even an Invisible Man like Griffin, may not be an altogether glorious triumph for society.

We can call this ambivalence about the rights of the individual and the group a profound confusion at the heart of Wells's social thought, or we can call it a particularly mature and balanced tolerance of the necessary paradoxes of democratic society. In either case, it is an ambivalence that characterized his fiction and his discursive writing throughout his career. And its full complexity is well caught in the balance of characters in *The Invisible Man*. The "two voices" we have previously seen at work in the scientific romances, the adventurous, cynical one and the conservative, at least mildly optimistic one, are present in the personalities of Griffin and Kemp: the mad scientist and the country doctor, the fanatical solitary and the loyal member of a community. But the balance between these two voices, so evident and schematic in the first two scientific romances, is enriched and complicated here by a third figure. We can hardly call him a "voice," for he is all but inarticulate during and after the events of the tale, but he is nevertheless a novel and a crucial character. This is Mr. Thomas Marvel, the amiable, quite disreputable, and completely self-interested vagabond whom Griffin early on tries to bully and cajole into aiding him in his conquest of the world.

Marvel is a rogue, a coward, and the character around whom most of the comic elements of *The Invisible Man* revolve. He is, in fact, one of Wells's most unusual figures, a lower-class clown (in both the ancient and modern senses of the word), nearly untouched by elements of sensibility or tragedy. And yet it is Marvel, in all the unthinking self-confidence of his ordinariness, who is the last person we see in the book. After Griffin has been killed and Kemp and Kemp's society vindicated in their trust in the normal conventions of humanity, Marvel is—absurdly but somehow appropriately— rewarded with some money Griffin has stolen, since no one can determine from whom he originally stole it. More crucially, though, Marvel has secured the three volumes of notes Griffin has made about the secret of invisibility—volumes of immense importance to the scientific world, but totally incomprehensible to Marvel, who nevertheless refuses to disclose their existence to anyone: anyone, that is, except us, the omniscient readers of this strange tale. Every Sunday morning, when the pub he has bought with his windfall is closed, Marvel retreats to the bar, and over a glass of gin peruses the notes of the Invisible Man's terrible experiment: notes which he understands not at all, except as a kind of trick beyond his own poor powers of scheming:

> So he lapses into a dream, the undying wonderful dream of his life. And . . . no human being save the landlord knows those books are there, with the subtle secret of invisibility and a dozen other strange secrets written therein. And none other will know of them until he dies.

It is a strange ending for a strange book. Why should Marvel, that most crass and unredeemed member of the working (or non-working) class, be the heir, the final actor, of the struggle between Griffin's anarchist revolutionism and Kemp's humane conservatism? Perhaps because Wells wishes to insist that neither Griffin nor Kemp, ultimately, is right, that neither the pure individual nor the committed group man is quite the figure needed to carry on and advance the course of human civilization. So that the magic books, the essential manuscripts containing the strange and frightening secret of invisibility, are given in the end to a man too stupid to use them, but also too ordinarily decent to try and exploit them. They are given to Marvel, that is, just because Marvel is the embodiment, not of a utopian intelligence, but of an anti-utopian, generous ignorance that knows its own limits, and in recognizing its own limits asserts or incarnates something important about the limits of human capability.

It may be said of Wells as it has been said (by George Ridenour) of Wells's hero Shelley, that he was infinite in hope but sober in expectation. By bequeathing Griffin's notebooks to the drunken, bumbling Marvel (the name itself is a joke), Wells indicated as finely as he ever did both how little and how much he was prepared to hope for, in 1897, from the class that had given him birth.

We return to the image we began with, that of the Invisible Man, the isolated agent of apocalyptic change who is so immensely attractive and so deeply frightening to the Wells of the 1890s. It is possible that the novel is finally a kind of exorcism by Wells of those elements he distrusted most in himself: the abstract, absolutist intelligence (Griffin), the conservative, socially responsible sensibility (Kemp), and the everyday, sensual loafer (Marvel). But to say that, of course, is also to say that *The Invisible Man* is a failed exorcism, since it exorcises *all* of what was most characteristic of Wells. Its very realism of description and locale, though, does seem to indicate a desire to externalize the conflicts and contradictions of the earlier tales, to ground them in a recognizable world. Wells may have become a "realist of the fantastic," in other words, just because "reality" was always the basis, and increasingly became the test and the justification, of his serious fantasies.

The increasing subtlety of the interplay between "realism" and "fantasy" is, at any rate, one of the most salient features of *The Invisible Man*. And it is significant in this respect that *The Invisible Man* is the first of his major works to be written in the third person. Both *The Time Machine* and *The Island of Doctor Moreau* are first-person stories. But in *The Invisible Man* Wells breaks with that tradition, giving us this most unconventional of stories in the most conventional (for the nineteenth century) of narrative frames, the third-person tale. Indeed, we never know more of Griffin, the Invisible Man, than he reveals or tells to the other characters in the book. There is real grace and supreme narrative skill, in fact, in the way Wells conveys to us the reality of Griffin without ever narrating *any* act or thought of Griffin's that he himself does not reveal to someone else in the novel. The "Invisible Man" is also "invisible" in terms of the narrative technique itself: for while we are privileged to see Kemp, Marvel, and even minor characters in moments of reflection or private action such as are usually granted us by the third-person omniscient narrator, Griffin, the central and crucial character of the tale, appears only in his *effect upon others*, only in those moments when he *chooses* to violate his invisibility in one way or another. The reader who goes through *The Invisible Man* a second or third time checking for this special effect will probably be surprised at the scrupulousness with which Wells maintains this narrative quarantine of his main character. Such a quarantine is natural in a first-person tale—where, after all, only one character relates his thoughts or feelings—but is striking in a third-person narrative and serves to highlight and (to use the word again) exorcise the mind and spirit of the character so isolated. Indeed, as if to emphasize this particular quality of the narrative, the novel frequently purports to be simply a compilation of contemporary testimony to the events. As the Invisible Man is fleeing from Kemp's house, for example, Wells writes:

> No one knows where he went nor what he did. But one can imagine him hurrying through the hot June forenoon, up the hill and on to the open downland behind Port Burdock, raging and despairing at his intolerable fate, and sheltering at last, heated and weary, amid the thickets of Hintondean, to piece together again his shattered schemes against his species.

There are a number of scenes like this, though none so extended or, perhaps, so finely executed. For here we *see* everything about Griffin's flight except, of course, Griffin himself. It is not simply a *tour de force* of storytelling skill (though it is that); it is also a realization, on the level of language, of the moral theme of the novel. The man who has allowed his intelligence to remove him from ordinary reality has become the victim of that reality, the man who has chosen to become "other" for his own selfish purposes has become in fact "other" not only to the world he loathes, but to the only world in which he can live. In a brilliant parallelism of theme and form, the crime of the Invisible Man in exiling himself from society is doubled in his exile from the very novel whose antihero he is. He is known only through report; he is, in the most frightening sense of the word, like a true invisible man, not really there.

THE WAR OF THE WORLDS

During the 1890s Wells was, as he later said in his autobiography, "writing away for dear life." A sickly young man with a family (and a former wife) to support, and no way of knowing how long he had to live, he wrote as much as he did at least in part as a form of life insurance. And with a writer as productive, as fast as Wells it is no surprise that themes, situations, even specific scenes should be repeated, with variations and expansions, from book to book. There is an especially interesting case of this echo effect between a minor incident in *The Invisible Man* and a major narrative device in *The War of the Worlds*, which was serialized (in *Pearson's Weekly*) in 1897, the year *The Invisible Man* appeared in book form.

As the Invisible Man is fleeing the villagers of Burdock, heading for the house of Dr. Kemp, Kemp is sitting in his study, writing. The calm of the evening is broken by shouts and pistol shots from the town, and Kemp goes to the window to see what the commotion is, deciding it is merely a brawl at the local pub.

> After five minutes, during which his mind had travelled into a remote speculation of social conditions of the future, and lost itself at last over the time dimension, Doctor Kemp roused himself with a sigh, pulled down the window again, and returned to his writing-desk.

Soon afterward, the Invisible Man breaks into Kemp's house. Simply as a dramatic effect, the scene at the window is a fine detail, emphasizing Kemp's placid unawareness of the danger coming toward him—and, of course, intensifying our own sense of that danger.

But there is also a curious, and revealing, dissonance in the passage. Why, gazing out his window at what he believes to be a common brawl, should Kemp be led into "a remote speculation of social conditions of the future"? At one plot level, the answer is surely that the genteel Kemp is also an intellectual, and quite naturally might wonder what developments in society might eliminate the wasted energies of drunkenness and pointless fighting. But at another level, reading the book in terms of Wells's previous evolutionary parables, we can also say that Kemp is led to speculate on the future of society precisely because the future of society, or a possible future of society, is at that very moment approaching his house from the village, ready to break into and destroy forever his confidence in the way things are. For the Invisible

Man, as we have already seen, is the emissary of that society, a society abstracted from the ordinary concerns and verities of middle-class existence and dedicated to a "Reign of Terror" that is actually the triumph of pure selfishness over those balances of right and responsibility that hold society—any society—together, and that in fact constitute all we are prepared to call fully human.

This theme, though, is sounded only faintly in the scene of Kemp at his window. It is merely a passing thought for Kemp, and merely a passing note for the narrator: Kemp's speculation fails to surmount the "time barrier." But we know of course that Wells himself had already surmounted that barrier in his very first novel. And he would surmount it again, in a very different way, in The War of the Worlds.

In the first chapter of The War, the anonymous narrator describes the complacency of Earthlings even as the cylinders that carry the Martian invaders course across space toward our planet, and observes of himself: "For my own part, I was much occupied in learning to ride the bicycle, and busy upon a series of papers discussing the probable developments of moral ideas as civilisation progressed." The ironic collision of the triviality and the high seriousness of these two concerns makes its own point. But it is also important to notice that the narrator's "series of papers" is a version, not just of Kemp's vague speculations at his window, but of Wells's own major themes as a scientific journalist in the years preceding the publication of his great prophecy, The Time Machine. In the next chapter the landing of the first Martian invasion craft, or "falling-star," is described:

> I was at home at that hour and writing in my study; and although my French windows face towards Ottershaw and the blind was up (for I loved in those days to look up at the night sky), I saw nothing of it. Yet this strangest of all things that ever came to earth from other space must have fallen while I was sitting there, visible to me had I only looked up as it passed.

Later, tired of writing, the narrator strolls out to buy his morning newspaper and learns of the arrival of the spacecraft not five miles from his home. Thus begins, first in placid ignorance, then with mild curiosity, and at last in growing panic and despair, his and the Earth's close encounter with a threat of cosmic violence and indifference to the very survival of the species. Like Kemp, the narrator is given to speculation on the future of society: but he not only dreams about it, he writes about it. And like Kemp, he is sitting comfortably by his study window as the nightmare answer to his speculations approaches: but he is even more unaware than Kemp of the approach of the monstrous, and the monstrous itself—not an Invisible Man but a threat from the massive, all too familiar and sublimely cold night sky—is correspondingly more ominous.

This crucial motif of the narrator at his window reappears at the very end of the novel. After the Martian invasion has been defeated (significantly, through no human effort or plan), the narrator returns to his abandoned house, and goes up to his study, where an interrupted essay is still lying on his desk:

> It was a paper on the probable development of Moral Ideas with the development of the civilizing process; and the last sentence was the opening of a prophecy: "In about two hundred years," I had written, "we may expect—" The sentence ended abruptly. I remembered my inability to fix my mind that morning, scarcely a month gone by, and how I had broken off to get my Daily Chronicle from the newsboy. I remembered how I went down to the garden gate as he came along, and how I had listened to his odd story of "Men from Mars."

At this point the narrator's wife, whom he had feared lost, also wanders into the abandoned house, and the two embrace in a scene of what could be, but is not, swooning sentiment. What saves the reunion from sentimentality is, simply, the context in which it occurs. The comfortable, everyday, reassuring warmth of the family unit has been reestablished after the eruption of the threat from beyond. But how effectively, really, has that threat been banished? Here at the end we finally see what the narrator was writing while the first Martian cylinder crashed into the English countryside: an essay on "the development of Moral Ideas with the development of the civilising process," or technology. "In about two hundred years, we may expect—" But the canny reader will notice that the whole book, the whole story of *The War of the Worlds*, is a completion of that broken sentence. For the Martians represent not just an invasion from space, but an invasion from time, from the future of man himself. The "time barrier" that defeats Kemp's speculations at the window in *The Invisible Man* had already been broken by Wells in *The Time Machine*, when he sent a man from the present into a possible future. And in *The War* Wells breaks the barrier another more violent way, by sending the cruel and passionless emissaries of a possible future squarely into the midst of the comfortable, smug present.

Near the very center of the novel, Wells also emphasizes this aspect of his tale. Trapped in a ruined house right next to which another Martian cylinder (the fifth) has impacted, the narrator has a chance to witness at close range the physiognomy and behavior of the Martians as they construct their seemingly invincible machines of destruction: it is a famous passage:

> They were heads—merely heads. Entrails they had none. They did not eat, much less digest. Instead, they took the fresh, living blood of other creatures, and injected it into their own veins. I have myself seen this being done, as I shall mention in its place. . . . Let it suffice to say, blood obtained from a still living animal, in most cases from a human being, was run directly by means of a little pipette into the recipient canal. . . .

The last detail, though it appeared (somewhat differently phrased) in the original serialization of *The War*, was deemed too ghastly for inclusion in early British students' editions of the novel, and so was deleted. And the people who deleted the passage were, in their way, reading the novel very perceptively indeed. For it *is* ghastly. We have already seen how disturbingly fascinated Wells was with the theme of cannibalism in *The Time Machine* and *The Island of Doctor Moreau*. But the cannibalism of the Morlocks or of the beast folk of Moreau's island is, at least, a straightforward if horrible fact of genetic reversion: as men become more like the beasts from which they evolved, they naturally revert to the disgusting practices of the beasts. Here, however, the Martians have refined cannibalism to an exquisite perversity. They are not less

A Martian, from W. Goble's original illustrations for *The War of the Worlds*. Note the powerful Martian war machine in the background, and the pathetic, almost laughable, vulnerability of the monster who occupies the foreground of the picture. The contrast between the two is very largely the point of Wells's novel.

but more "civilised" than their human victims. And they are not, properly speaking, cannibals at all but rather vampires. The evolutionary future invading and sucking the lifeblood from the human present: that is the image Wells means us to have of his tale of an invasion from Mars, not simply the idea of the clash of two alien species, Earthling and Martian. For the Martians are not, after all, aliens. They are ourselves, mutated beyond sympathy, though not beyond recognition.

The narrator makes this point directly after his mention of the invaders' vampirism. Conscious life on Mars, he speculates, must have evolved along parallel lines to conscious life on Earth. But just as Mars is an older planet than Earth, so the evolution of consciousness on that planet must be far in advance of ours. The Martians, then, represent not the simple danger of the monstrous and the unknown, but rather the danger of what we ourselves might become. There have even been anticipations of this grim possibility represented by the invaders, the narrator remarks. He observes that "a certain speculative writer" had published a "prophecy" (the same word he applies to his own, interrupted sentence at the end of the book) about the probable development of the human body in the technological age:

> His prophecy, I remember, appeared in November or December, 1893, in a long defunct publication, The *Pall Mall Budget*. . . . He pointed out . . . that the perfection of mechanical appliances must ultimately supersede limbs; the perfection of chemical devices, digestion; that such organs as hair, external nose, teeth, ears, and chin were no longer essential parts of the human being, and that the tendency of natural selection would lie in the direction of their steady diminution through the coming ages. The brain alone remained a cardinal necessity.

The "certain speculative writer," of course, is Wells himself, and the sketch the narrator so accurately paraphrases is "The Man of the Year Million," published November 6, 1893, in the *Pall Mall Gazette*. The self-reference here is not (or not only) a witty bit of literary recycling. It is also an indication of how consistent—and how consistently Darwinian—remained Wells's central concerns during the period of his first great scientific romances.

Years later, in the Preface to Knopf's 1934 collection of his early science fiction, Wells confesses that "now and then, though I rarely admit it, the universe projects itself towards me in a hideous grimace," and he goes on to say that *The War of the Worlds* like *The Time Machine* was another assault on human self-satisfaction."

It is significant that Wells grouped *The Time Machine* with *The War of the Worlds*, for the two stories are, in their way, mirror reflections one of the other. And of all his work, they have certainly exercised the strongest influence over the later development of science fiction. Ordinary, quotidian man may be impelled into an alien and ominous future world, or that alien and ominous future world may explode into the present of ordinary quotidian man: those are the alternatives posed by these two tales, and a great deal of science fiction written since their publication can be seen as a reexploration or expansion of one theme or the other. And of the two, it is surely *The War of the Worlds* which has had the most imitators.

But Wells did not write the novel merely as an exercise in prophecy or as a variation on the themes of *The Time Machine*. Crucial as the influence of *The War of the Worlds* has been on later science fiction, the novel takes its origin from a very popular, though now largely forgotten, subgenre of late-nineteenth-century writing. It is a subgenre we can conveniently call the "tale of invasion."

I. F. Clarke, in his book *Voices Prophesying War*, catalogues and examines these tales, all of which, we can now see, were fictional anticipations of the mechanized disaster that was the First World War. As we have already said, to many perceptive minds of the age, the most surprising thing about the First World War was not that it broke out, but that it broke out as late as it did. Since the 1880s, at least, the major European armies (except England's) had been engaged in a massive buildup of personnel; all the countries of Europe were contributing to that technological revolution in armament and weaponry which the *Encyclopaedia Britannica* disingenuously calls "the Golden Age of the machine gun"; and any number of relatively minor conflicts, particularly the Franco-German War of 1870, had indicated as strongly as possible that a worldwide conflagration was not far off, and that it would be fought, when it came, with ferocity and with machines of destructive efficiency—and indiscriminacy— hitherto unknown. As Clarke puts it, "already in 1871, the First World War was being prepared in fact and in fiction."

The first writer to begin preparing for the war in fiction was an Englishman and a soldier. Sir George Tomkyns Chesney had served with the Army in India, and in 1871 was an instructor at the Royal Indian Civil Engineering College. In 1871 he also published, in *Blackwood's Magazine*, his novel *The Battle of Dorking*, which began an international craze of imitations and retellings. Chesney's narrator, a former Volunteer in the English forces years after the war, tells how England had been caught unprepared, underarmed, and understaffed by a German invasion. Because it played upon national insecurity, the book was an immediate success, and soon versions of it appeared in almost every country of Europe and in America—each nation, of course, imagining itself as the complacent and unprepared victim of a surprise attack from one or another of its neighbors. By 1897, when *The War of the Worlds* began to appear in *Pearson's*, the conventions of the invasion story, and particularly the prediction of futuristic, terrible machines of destruction, had been long and well established. What Wells did with this minor, though popular, form was both simple and brilliant. He raised the very idea of invasion from an international to a cosmic scale, and in doing so raised the invasion story from the level of propaganda to that of art.

Dorking, where the decisive defeat of the British forces occurs in Chesney's story, is less than twenty miles south of London, in the heart of Surrey. One of the most striking elements of *The Battle of Dorking*, and of the many imitations it spawned, was its imagining of the great war to come as fought not on the conventional, more or less isolated battlefields of classic warfare, but in the very streets and towns, the safe civilian locales that even the most ferocious wars had, in the past, largely left untouched. Considered by itself, this detail represents a striking—and very widespread—anticipation of one of the giant horrors of the First (and, of course, the Second) World War: the idea of total war, war in which there are no real civilians since everyone is a potential target of the new and terrible versions of weaponry.

The plot of *The War of the Worlds* is a deliberate allusion, then, to Chesney's book and the genre of the invasion tale. The first of the Martian cylinders lands on Horsell Common, just outside Woking, a Surrey town not fifteen miles west of Dorking. Thereafter, the invasion proceeds on an almost exact northeast diagonal into the heart of London. The seven cylinders whose landings are described on seven successive nights can be easily mapped along this line, the last one landing on Primrose Hill, just north of Regent's Park. More important than the simple topographical realism of the story, though, is Wells's precise and sympathetic understanding of the effect of panic on "ordinary" people, the varieties of cowardice and courage of which they are capable, without the usual melodramatic embellishments of "literary" heroism. The "realism" of *The Invisible Man* is often the realism of comedy: the various innkeepers and villagers who cross paths with the Invisible Man react with the kind of unintentional absurdity that is common in Victorian treatments of lower-class characters. ("It was then observed that his head was invisible," says one character, painfully paraphrasing a newspaper article on the Invisible Man's activities.) But there is little of this sort of comedy in *The War of the Worlds*. Rather, there is a strong and self-confident will to allow the "little men" who are the victims of the cosmic invasion the dignity of their own nature—even the dignity of their own panic.

This is simply another way of saying that the difference between *The War of the Worlds* and the minor works that precede and shape its conventions is the difference between genius and skill. But until we understand the skill of his predecessors, we cannot really understand the genius of Wells. As we have said, Wells has been called the Shakespeare of science fiction: and excessive as the comparison of course is, it is nevertheless true that Wells and Shakespeare have at least one important thing in common. They were both *popular* writers, writers who deliberately dealt in the exploited conventions of popular entertainment, and who wrote (as Northrop Frye has observed of Shakespeare) for the best reason anyone has yet thought of for writing: to make money.

Thus, as much as it rises above most of the voluminous fiction of warfare in the late nineteenth century, *The War of the Worlds* would not really be possible without those books. Wells never saw a battlefield, never fought in a war. But on the basis of the invasion-story tradition, and of his own gift for anticipation, he managed to create a vision of total war that tallies, sometimes uncannily, with the recorded experience of those who lived through the horrors of the First World War. Here is the narrator describing how he fled from the first wave of the Martian invasion; the English countryside upon which he looked has been devastated by the Martian heat-ray:

> Halliford, it seemed, was deserted, and several of the houses facing the river were on fire. It was strange to see the place quite tranquil, quite desolate under the hot, blue sky, with the smoke and little threads of flame going straight up into the heat of the afternoon. Never before had I seen houses burning without the accompaniment of an obstructive crowd.

It is the last detail that has the authentic ring of prophecy. Quiet villages are burning, and no crowds gather to watch the fire: because all the people have been either killed or driven to headlong panicked flight. And in this context, the mysterious heat-ray and the ungainly, deadly efficient Martian war machines take on their own kind of grim realism: the century of long-range artillery, aerial bombardment and, ultimately, intercontinental missiles and laser guns is already, in 1897, being chronicled.

Wells, to be sure, was not particularly interested in technological forecasting for its own sake. He may have claimed to have anticipated the development of the tank in his 1903 story, "The Land Ironclads," but unlike most writers in the invasion-story line, and unlike great technologue and prophet Jules Verne, it was not his concern to predict, however intricately, the next extrapolations from the present state of the art. (In a famous interview of 1901, Verne huffily dismissed comparisons between himself and Wells by observing of the latter, "*Mais—il invente!*") His business, rather, was the more visionary one of imagining, or trying to imagine, how humanity might fare under *technology*: technology, that is, understood not as discrete series of inventions or improvements in the quality of life, but rather as an ongoing, evolving force—an adaptive mechanism in human evolution—which might ironically, threaten to overadapt the species to the point of extinction. This had been the central concern of Wells's scientific romances from *The Time Machine* on, but it is perhaps not too much to say that in *The War of the Worlds* that concern achieved its fullest and most complex articulation.

The invading Martians represent a threat to the everyday from the depths of outer space; they represent the fear of the war to come which had already possessed Europe for at least thirty years when the book was written; and they represent the terror of a possible future for mankind in which mankind has ceased to be even recognizably human. All these elements are important to the power of Wells's dark novel. And all of them are caught in the single perception, which runs throughout the story, that the Martians are somehow a form of natural life that, through its own self-mechanization, has grown unnatural, monstrous. They are "heads—merely heads," intellect dissociated from passion, and are dependent on the cold efficiency of their machines for their very movement. They are in their way the final development of the disinterested cruelty of Moreau, the abstract rage of Griffin, and, more than that, they are a combination of the Eloi and Morlocks of *The Time Machine*, a single species combining the frailty, the dead-end weakness and vulnerability of the masters of the machines and the barbarous cannibalism of the machines' slaves.

This particular kind of monster is, indeed, one of Wells's great original inventions. There is almost nothing like the Martians of *The War* in any previous literature, for they are a nightmare that had to wait until Wells's special moment in history, and Wells's especially sensitive imagination of that moment, to emerge.

We have already said a great deal about monsters in Wells and in the writers whose works preceded, and variously influenced, his own. But it is important to remember, from the earliest stories told in the world to the most recent, what the monster really is: he (or she, or it) is *what you fear most,* what your culture and environment have taught you is the worst thing that could happen to you, the situation over which you would have the least degree of control.

A revealing history of civilization could probably be written in terms of the definitive monsters imagined and feared by successive ages, from the apocalyptic armies in the sky of the middle ages through the ghouls, the man-made creatures of the early nineteenth century, to the mind-controlling aliens and soulless computers of contemporary science fiction. And in that history, Wells's Martians occupy a special place. For they raise in its fullest urgency the question which has remained central to technology: how may we, as humans, survive the invention of increasingly complex tools which, as they make our survival as a species easier, also threaten that very survival by separating us—in a kind of second version of the myth of the Fall—from the natural life of the planet which gave us birth? During the 1960s, much was said and written about what Alvin Toffler, in a famous book, called *Future Shock*: the panicky realization on the part of contemporary man that he is living in the future, that changes in his life and his perception are being forced upon him faster than he can assimilate them by developments in technology. But the shock was really nothing new in the sixties. It had begun to be felt at least as early as the mid-nineteenth century, and Wells's work is one of the first, most complete, and still useful explorations of its implications.

The great opening paragraph of *The War of the Worlds* sounds all the themes we have been discussing so far, and weaves them into a prelude that has to be one of the finest and most complex pieces of writing Wells ever produced. It must be quoted in full, for like the invocation of a classical epic poem, it both invokes and, by anticipation, resolves the major elements of the tale it introduces:

> No one would have believed in the last years of the nineteenth century that this world was being watched keenly and closely by intelligences greater than man's and yet as mortal as his own; that as men busied themselves about their various concerns they were scrutinised and studied, perhaps almost as narrowly as a man with a microscope might scrutinise the transient creatures that swarm and multiply in a drop of water. With infinite complacency men went to and fro over this globe about their little affairs, serene in their assurance of their empire over matter. It is possible that the infusoria under the mi-

croscope do the same. No one gave a thought to the older worlds of space as sources of human danger, or thought of them only to dismiss the idea of life upon them as impossible or improbable. It is curious to recall some of the mental habits of those departed days. At most, terrestrial men fancied there might be other men upon Mars, perhaps inferior to themselves and ready to welcome a missionary enterprise. Yet across the gulf of space, minds that are to our minds as ours are to those of the beasts that perish, intellects vast and cool and unsympathetic, regarded this earth with envious eyes, and slowly and surely drew their plans against us. And early in the twentieth century came the great disillusionment.

"And how are all things made for man?" ends the quotation from astronomer Johannes Kepler which is the epigraph to The War. Kepler's question, of course, like the first paragraph of the novel, is really a form of the more disturbing question, "Are all things made for man?" From its very beginning, the novel poses the question of human survival in the most chillingly absolute terms. Before the Martian invasion, observes the narrator, men thought of Mars, if at all, as the possible object of an imperialist and missionary enterprise. But, of course, the Martians reverse the direction of that imperialist desire, baffling and overcoming the humans whose world they invade with the same ease—and the same lack of conscience—with which Europe had for the last hundred years baffled and overcome the native populations of the rest of the world. We have already mentioned, with reference to The Island of Doctor Moreau, Wells's concern with the imperialist expansion of Europe and the moral questions that expansion raised. It was, after all, fundamentally a triumph of technology. But what did the technological supremacy of the white race imply for the future—not only the future of the subjugated "native" populations, but for the Europeans themselves? The original dedication of The War of the Worlds was to Wells's brother Frank, and H. G. later recorded how an observation of Frank's was the inspiration for the whole novel. One day, strolling through the countryside of Surrey, Frank idly asked H. G. What would happen if beings from another planet, armed with superior weapons, should descend upon that landscape. Would not the Earthlings be as defenseless and terrified in the face of this threat as were the non-European nations in the face of Western guns and cavalry?

The anti-imperialist theme of the book is explicitly sounded or implied at a number of crucial moments in the action, but it is finally a version of the much larger, more adventurous question posed by the novel's first paragraph. What is man, and, in the face of his continuing development of machines that threaten to destroy his own humanity, what are his chances for survival?

This is also the question the narrator himself writes upon in that "series of papers" whose placid composition is delayed by the landing of the first Martian cylinder. And if the whole book is a completion of his interrupted sentence, "In about two hundred years, we may expect—," it is also a dramatization of the place of man in nature, a demonstration, Darwinian and unglamorous indeed but also bitterly hopeful, of how the species might survive even the growth of its own technology. But in order to reach that final measured vision of hope, the narrator has first to experience two alternative versions of despair.

From *The Time Machine* on, as we have seen, Wells liked to develop his scientific romances along the line of alternate explanations of the central uncanny phenomenon, each successive explanation including more of the truth of the matter and each one being completed, filled in, by the one that succeeds it. In *The War of the Worlds* those successive explanations are incarnated in four major characters who, at one time or another, involve our attention in the unfolding of the Martian invasion of Earth. They are the Curate, the narrator's brother in London, the Artilleryman, and the narrator himself.

The Curate, with whom the narrator falls in in his flight from the first Martian attack, is one of the most unsympathetic characters in all Wells's fiction. Cowardly, hysterical, and infantile, he is nearly a compendium of everything Wells found most loathsome in organized religion. And yet he is important to the novel, for his response to the Martian invasion is both the most "natural" and the one that allows the narrator to ask what we have seen is the central question of the book. When they first meet, the Curate is babbling in a mixture of self-pity and Biblical allusion about the invasion:

"Why are these things permitted? What sins have we done? The morning service was over, I was walking through the roads to clear my brain for the afternoon, and then—fire, earthquake, death! As if it were Sodom and Gomorrah! All our work undone, all the work—What are these Martians?"

"What are we?" I answered, clearing my throat.

Of course the Curate does not really hear the narrator's counter-question, but it is the question that resonates through the rest of the narrative. Willing as the Curate might be to allow himself to be terrified into insensibility or paralysis by the threat of the unknown (the threat of technology, the threat of the future), the narrator will not allow himself that easy a defeat. Terror, Wells seems to be saying, is the most inefficient of responses to the terrible. And there is surely a kind of exhilaration—at least for Wells—in the scene that ends the Curate's unhappy career, as he and the narrator are trapped in the ruined house outside the Martian cylinder's landing, and the narrator is forced to brain the Curate—who is finally eaten by the Martians—to protect his own life.

The narrator and the Curate are together from Chapter Thirteen of Book One of The War through the opening five chapters of Book Two. In Chapters Fourteen through Seventeen of Book One, Wells does something very striking. He shifts the scene of the action from the Surrey suburbs to London, and shifts the narrative voice from the first person to the third: the narrator relates the adventures of his brother, a medical student in London, during the invasion. This shift of scene and narrative voice allows Wells to achieve a particularly stunning effect. Since the scenes of violence in London, by far the most apocalyptic in the book, are narrated at second hand rather than by an eyewitness, they become paradoxically more believable, having, as it were, a double frame of narrative authority. And the narrator's brother, though he remains a relatively anonymous, undifferentiated character, also represents a possible response to the terror of the Martian invasion, and an important counterpoint to the Curate's headlong cowardice. He is a conventional, and conventionally unassuming, hero, a good man who, in his own flight from London, bravely assists a lovely young woman and her guardian in the exodus. The brother's function in the narrative, then, is not simply to be a crucial witness to the scenes of greatest Martian violence, but also to represent a kind of immediate, unreflective common decency in the face of disaster that, conventional as it may be, is still one of the most admirable and most important of human survival mechanisms.

At the opposite end of the scale of response from the Curate's terror, and as a kind of hyperthyroid extension of the simple resourcefulness of the narrator's brother, are the giant ambition and blustering heroics of the Artilleryman, whom the narrator meets in Book Two as he wanders away from the ruined house where the Curate has died.

The Artilleryman has appeared before. The narrator encounters him, even before he meets the Curate in Book One, as a frightened, defeated, deserting soldier falling back before the initial onslaught of the Martian war machines. But by the time the narrator comes upon him as "the man on Putney Hill" in Book Two, he has overcome his initial fear and is dreaming grandiose dreams about the future.

He is a curious character, a kind of parody of all those powers of will and self-realization that, as we have seen, Wells valued so highly: a clownish version of the Nietzschean superman, and of Wells's own most fondly imagined heroes. But clownish he is, after all. Man is defeated, he tells the narrator. "This isn't a war," he says. "It never was a war, any more than there's a war between men and ants." But out of that certainty of despair he has constructed a vision of the world to come, where the few free men who escape Martian captivity will lead an underground revolutionary life, waiting for the day and the hour when they can arise and destroy their alien masters. And the narrator is, for a while, drawn into the fever of his plan. But it is, finally, a selfish and a self-defeating plan, a revolutionary philosophy not for the sake of the survival of the species, but rather for the sake of the survival of class hatred and class warfare. The Artilleryman, for all his energy, all his heroics, is the kind of revolutionary Wells dreaded most, the revolutionary whose real interest is to perpetuate, rather than to render obsolete, the class distinctions that warp society. It is a program based on hatred of what he cannot have, what he has never been allowed to enjoy:

"There won't be any more blessed concerts for a million years or so; there won't be any Royal Academy of Arts, and no nice little feeds at restaurants. If it's amusement you're after, I reckon the game is up. If you've got any drawing-room manners or a dislike to eating peas with a knife or dropping aitches, you'd better chuck 'em away. They ain't no further use."

It is angry bluster, even, in its way, moving bluster (Wells in his later novels was to make this sort of class anger, frequently, very affecting and sympathetic indeed). But it is, after all, bluster. If the Curate fails to respond humanly to the threat of the Martians through excessive cowardice, the Artilleryman fails through excessive, and excessively self-serving, bravery, through an assertion of the will that leaves no room for the exercise of intelligence. The narrator discovers this as he begins to help the Artilleryman construct his fortification on Putney Hill, only to find that this self-assertive rebel is in fact a lazy, indolent lout more interested in scavenging the wine and cigars he can find in abandoned houses than in pressing forward his plan for a new society.

The chapter describing the Artilleryman's fantastic plans was not originally part of The War of the Worlds. It was added to the book, obviously, to complement the chapters describing the Curate's theological terror. And it also helps us to identify, between these two excessive responses to the Martian threat, the ultimate sanity to which the narrator wins. It is a sanity less visibly, less actively heroic than that displayed by his brother in London, but that is almost the point of it. For it is a sanity of the fully self-conscious intellectual, a sanity that does not so much control the course of events as understand that course and interpret it. After leaving the Artilleryman to his mad dreams of a lower-class empire, the narrator wanders into London (he has all along followed the track of the Martian invasion), bereft of all hope and willing to die before the first Martian fighting machine he encounters. But in the midst of abandoned London, on Primrose Hill, he comes upon the last landing place of the cylinders and the last, dying fighting machine. The Martians have been defeated, not by any human agency, but by the very bacteria of the planet Earth that the

Martians themselves, in the purity of their own technological triumph, had banished ages ago from their own world:

> Against the sky-line an eager dog ran and disappeared. The thought that had flashed into my mind grew real, grew credible. I felt no fear, only a wild, trembling exultation, as I ran up the hill towards the motionless monster. Out of the hood hung lank shreds of brown, at which the hungry birds pecked and tore.

The birds pecking and tearing at the dead, dried Martian meat are in their way, too, a metaphor for the essential conflict and tension in this novel. For the Martians have been defeated by their vulnerability to bacteria—the "transient creatures that swarm and multiply in a drop of water," announced in the very first paragraph—but they have also been defeated by the very fact of life upon Earth, by the very complexity and interrelationship of what later generations were to learn to call the "ecology" of the planet. As the narrator witnesses the death of the last Martian machine, he reflects that the invasion itself was foredoomed from its inception: "For so it had come about, as indeed I and many men might have foreseen had not terror and disaster blinded our minds."

For "terror" and "disaster" we may read, if we wish, the alternative responses to apocalypse incarnated by the Curate and the Artilleryman: unthinking and self-lacerating terror at the approach of the unknown, or unholy and self-serving celebration—the looter's joy—at the approach of an apparently terminal disaster. The narrator, however, has learned to respond in neither way, but rather precisely in terms of the bitter but hopeful proposition with which the paragraph—and the threat of the Martian invasion—ends:

> Already when I watched them they were irrevocably doomed, dying and rotting even as they went to and fro. It was inevitable. By the toll of a billion deaths man has bought his birthright of the earth, and it is his against all comers; it would still be his were the Martians ten times as mighty as they are. For neither do men live nor die in vain.

"For neither do men live nor die in vain": already by 1897 it is a trite sentiment, a cliché, a standard and, since so often used, a meangingless thing to say about the dead. Except that

Wells, in this great passage, actually *reclaims* the cliché from triviality, and gives it new meaning by taking it literally, in its most biologically precise sense. Through countless generations of inherited, transmitted, and increasingly augmented immunity, man *has* purchased his birthright on Earth, *has* established his own membership in the ecology of the whole planet, has become part of a "world" that—if he only has the clarity of mind to recognize it—is proof against the heartless abstraction represented by the Martians.

The War of the Worlds, then, is literally about the war of the worlds: the worlds of present and future, the worlds of everyday security and cosmic danger in collision with one another, but most specifically the ecospheres of Earth in all its richness and Mars imagined as a pure (and therefore sterile) alternative possibility for Earth. At the heart of this dark vision of apocalypse there is something very like a romantic assertion of the permanence of the good things of the earth. It is true, if odd—and quite characteristic of Wells's paradoxical mind—that in this, the most cataclysmic of his early romances, he comes closest to asserting the triumphant possibilities which await man if only he can remain rational in his confrontation with his cosmic vulnerability. The sequence of universal disaster, cosmic despair, cultural self-discovery and rebirth was to become, in Wells's later utopian fictions, a rather predictable forecast (or hope) for the future of mankind. And in *The War of the Worlds* the emphasis is certainly upon the first grimmer phase of that process. Nevertheless it is difficult not to see in this novel something of what came to be the later Wellsian vision, the belief that only by facing squarely the hopelessness of the human condition can man begin to construct something in which, absurdly and heroically, to hope. The realist of the fantastic had not yet become the prophet of a fantastic reality to come; but he was on his way.

5

DREAMS OF THINGS TO COME:
The First Men in the Moon,
The Food of the Gods, and
In the Days of the Comet

Wells's first novel was a version of that oldest of fantastic forms, utopian fiction. But Wells did not really become a utopian novelist until some years after *The Time Machine*. This is strange, since it is as a utopian novelist and prophet that Wells is most remembered—at least by those who grew up under his influence when it was at its height.

To say this, though, is to indicate a curious contradiction in Wells's career. In his early scientific romances he is mainly a prophet of the dangers of the new science, an immensely talented fabulist of what could go wrong if the threatening new knowledge of late-nineteenth-century science were to be extended too far. Science, that is to say, is for the early Wells a kind of forbidden knowledge, to know which is to risk damnation and exile from the human community. We have seen how, in *The Time Machine*, *The Island of Doctor Moreau*, *The Invisible Man*, and *The War of the Worlds*, Wells varies this insight to produce tales which explore not only the grimmer implications of Darwinian and post-Darwinian theory, but also our chances and hopes for survival. But however complex, however paradoxically hopeful are the first major scientific romances, it cannot be denied that they are, in their most basic elements, dark stories indeed.

Wells thought he was dying when he wrote them: reason enough, one would think, for their darkness. But they were written, also, at the very end of a century that had witnessed some of the greatest technological triumphs and the greatest scientific disillusionments in history. And despite their darkness, Wells is—or was until recently—most often thought of as the optimistic, self-assertive, bouncy, and indefatigable herald of the brave new world that could be ours if only we would wake up and deal with ourselves and our problems rationally.

There is not really as much of a contradiction between the early and the later Wells as some critics have indicated. The possibly consumptive, troubled young man who could mourn the brevity of the dream of human intellect aged—or evolved—into the urgent, earnest, and rambunctious prophet and social critic who tried to show how that dream, that precarious occupancy of the planet by our species, might be extended. There may even be a point to observing that a certain kind of despair, a certain kind of apocalyptic sensibility, belongs by right to the young, and mellows inevitably into a more temperate, but also a more hopeful, view of things as youth begins to pass. This does not, of course, deny the power or the importance of the young writer's imagination of disaster, nor does it deny that other and far larger visions of despair may await the writer who survives past middle age.

In 1901 Wells was thirty-five years old. His first son, George Philip Wells, was born, and he had settled in Spade House, Folkestone, the imposing home he built for himself out of the royalties on his early, immensely successful books. He was to be plagued by ill health and by his own private demons of restlessness and depression for the rest of his long life; but it was clear that with the turn of the century had come a happy turn in his fortunes. Furthermore, in 1901 Queen Victoria died and was succeeded by her son, the *bon vivant*, energetic, and obviously very un-Victorian Edward VII. Few successions of power have been more symbolic, or more historically apt. Indeed, one critic, William Bellamy, has traced the radical change in Wells's fiction during these years to the crucial distinction between late-Victorian and Edwardian sensibility. Wells's books of the early years of the twentieth century, argues Bellamy, present us with a vision of culture-free, independent, *liberated* man—man free, for once and all, of social constraints—that is in direct contradiction to the exhaustion and paranoia of late-Victorian fiction.

This view of the transition from late-Victorian gloom to the false dawn of the Edwardian sensibility is, to be sure, an over-simplification. Writers do not, any more than other people, pace their imaginations to conform with so-called "periods" of history. But, in the case of Wells, the historical and the personal turning points do seem to coincide in a remarkable way. In 1901 he published *The First Men in the Moon* and also his first collected essays in social prophecy, *Anticipations of the Reaction of Mechanical and Scientific Progress upon Human Life and Thought*. It is worth noting that the full title of *Anticipations* describes a set of speculations very like those Dr. Kemp entertains briefly in *The Invisible Man*, and those upon which the narrator of *The War of the Worlds* is writing when the first Martian cylinder lands. We have already said a great deal about the "two voices" of Wells's fiction, that of the cosmic doubter and that of the more hopeful, more "ordinary" constructor of solutions to the human riddle. And it would not entirely be a distortion to say that, with the turn of the century, Wells himself turned from the former to the latter voice. The optimism of the Edwardian age, its newfound freedom in social, literary, and sexual matters, and its trust that these matters could be efficiently and creatively handled by nothing more than common sense—such attitudes may strike us as naive, even childish, particularly considering the debacle of the First World War, the shipwreck of all those hopes that lay only fourteen years ahead into the new century. But it was out of such naivety that emerged the major novels of Joseph Conrad, the first stories of James Joyce, and the first poems of T. S. Eliot: the first evidences, in other words, of what we have come to think of as the modern literature. And Wells, if he was not in the vanguard of that movement, was nevertheless the perfect representative of the state of mind that made its revolutionary sensibilities possible.

What turns an apocalyptic novelist into a utopian? What kinds of psychological and spiritual alterations are necessary to transform the writer of *The Time Machine* into the author of *Anticipations* or, in 1905, *A Modern Utopia*? Acquired wealth, an improvement in health, or the turning of a new century are all fairly easy explanations for such a change in attitude—and, like most easy explanations, explain nothing.

Wells was a man possessed by a number of contradictory demons. Heir to and student of the chilling vision of man bequeathed by nineteenth-century science, he was also—and never really forgot that he was—a member of the middle class, heir to and product of the vulgarity, the tawdriness, and the hopelessness that were the birthright of the not quite poor. And furthermore, he was the possesser—though not the natural heir—of the literary and cultural tradition; it was an acquisition he had made stealthily, almost by theft (like that other thief of fire, Promctheus) in his afternoons and evenings in the library of Uppark.

It is no surprise that the demons, in his early years, spoke to Wells mainly about the inevitable and ineluctable doom of mankind before the tribunal of universal necessity and cosmic time. But it is also—or should be—no surprise that these demons, after a few years, began to speak in a different way, ultimately a more reassuring one. Mankind might be condemned to death, in the largest possible view of things; entropy and Newton's Second Law of Thermodynamics may, indeed, be the only sure truths in the world. But if that is so, as the narrator of The Time Machine says, it remains for us to live as if it were not so.

For the narrator of The Time Machine, "living as if it were not so" may mean something fairly unexciting and conventional: responding to the void by the simpleminded (but, none the less, courageous) technique of ignoring it. Wells later, however, was to exalt and extend the sensibility and vision of this anonymous narrator—was to make it, in fact, the sensibility and the vision of his most energetic, if not his greatest, work. For living as if it were not so, living and planning as if man were not under sentence of death, came to mean, for Wells and the generation he influenced, the chance for a kind of earthly paradise, a world where the natural, biologically conditioned violence, acquisitiveness, and rapaciousness of the race would be controlled and channeled into creative directions by an enlightened, scientifically organized body of administrators. Wells's specific plans for this ideal future society changed a great deal in successive books. His ideas about the most equitable distribution of capital, about the division of labor, and about who precisely should rule changed almost as often as he invented different utopian fictions. But these inconsistencies, though they were the delight of his critics—especially his Marxist critics—for nearly a third of a century, are not particularly important. The details may have been vague—what vision of an ideal society is not vague?—but what remained consistent, and consistently central, in Wells's vision of the future was the belief that only a massive exercise of reason, common sense, and will could save the human race from planetary suicide; and, even more importantly, the belief that such an effort of will could, really, be made and could *work*. The grim lesson of Darwinian theory had been well learned, in other words. But Wells was also a product of the age that produced Samuel Smiles's *Self-Help*, and that lesson, too, he did not forget.

"Millennialist" is the term we apply to those who believe, for one reason or another, that the Kingdom of God is about to be established upon Earth and all things made clear. It is an attitude, at least in the European tradition, most associated with the apocalyptic expectations of radical Protestantism. And though Wells may have outgrown or repudiated the *content* of the millennialist, visionary, romantic faith that obsessed his mother, he never escaped its violent scenario.

Apocalypse and utopia, after all, are not really opposite as much as they are complementary states of mind. The wish that the unbearable world in which you live might disappear in one gigantic conflagration, and the desire to construct, or at least dream, a state of affairs that might make the work less unbearable have at least this in common: they are both expressions of a mind fundamentally dissatisfied with things as they are. They are both, in other words, expressions of an elementary, metaphysical *restlessness*. This is true of the most ancient fictions of both apocalypse and utopia, and it is certainly true of Wells, that most restless of men. The transition from his late-Victorian to his Edwardian tales, the much-discussed transformation of his work from the articulation of a universal gloom to the athletic heralding of a better world to come, can be regarded as a natural growth rather than an arbitrary reversal of direction. In assuming the second, more optimistic and more generously humane of his two voices, Wells was not so much shifting his position as developing what had been implicit in his vision of human affairs from his very earliest writing. And if those early writings, amid their darkness, contain radiances he later celebrated, his later writings also contain, amid their self-confident radiance, shadows to remind us that Wells never really thought or willed himself fully out of the dark. It is this honesty to his own perceptions, if nothing else, that makes him even at his most strenuously positive still a valuable and complex writer.

But, in 1901, the optimistic and prophetic Wells was only beginning to emerge. After *The War of the Worlds*, that great paradoxically reassuring narrative of cosmic disaster, Wells apparently went through a period not so much of transition as of exhaustion. But *The War of the Worlds* had been serialized in 1897, to appear in book form in 1898: the fourth in a series of indisputably brilliant tales within three years. He had, against all odds, established himself as a writer and was beginning to establish himself as a social, as well as a literary, lion. It was a time to rest, but Wells was apparently as incapable of rest as he was of remaining silent. Changes, and important ones, were taking place in his life (he had become wealthy; he was moving to a new home). And important changes were occurring in the public life of his time (Victoria was dying; Europe was arming).

What was a young man to do? What Wells did was continue to write, and continue to write stories that developed and ironically reversed even as they repeated the themes of his first successful books. Between *The War of the Worlds* and *The First Men in the Moon* he produced only one important scientific romance, *When the Sleeper Wakes: A Story of Years To Come*, serialized in 1898–99 and published in book form in 1899. In the same period he wrote his first, tentative, but nevertheless scandalously realistic novel of love and marriage, *Love and Mr. Lewisham*, published in 1900. The realist of the fantastic, as Conrad had called him, was finding it more and more difficult to separate reality from fantasy, to distinguish between the precise description of the middle-class life he saw all about him and the perception of that life as it might appear to an interplanetary observer, an intelligence "vast and cool and unsympathetic" (to quote *The War of the Worlds*) that could observe human life, in all its silliness and gigantic expectations, without flinching. The young man of no particular possibilities had become a successful writer. The successful writer had not yet become, but was becoming, the self-designated prophet of the age. And the man who was all these things was also tired and disorganized. Remarkably, out of this jumble of conditions he was able to write a book, an important book.

When the Sleeper Wakes has never been one of Wells's most popular books, though Wells thought enough of the story to revise and reissue it in 1910 as *The Sleeper Awakes.* Considered simply in terms of literary virtue, it is a fairly shoddy performance for a writer of Wells's skill, and certainly a falling-off from the subtleties of narrative technique achieved in *The Time Machine, The Island of Doctor Moreau, The Invisible Man,* and *The War of the Worlds.* But Wells was concerned with more than narrative technique. While he may have begun his career "writing away for dear life," he had learned that writing was also how he could save his soul (he thought he had a soul) and the soul of his culture as well. *When the Sleeper Wakes* is a novel not simply about a possible future for mankind, but about the future course Wells's own writing would follow. It is a very odd book, but it is also an important prelude to his seriously utopian novels.

The sleeper of the book's title is Graham, a late-nineteenth-century intellectual who is driven to the brink of madness by his intricate speculations (on the probable development of Moral Ideas with the development of the civilizing process?) and who, in the first chapter of the novel, falls into a deep, deathlike, unnatural sleep. But he does not die. Miraculously preserved in his trance, he awakens two hundred years later to a world in which he is both a foreigner and a messiah. The world has become, in effect, one gigantic city, walled-in, climate-controlled, a dream of technology triumphant, supported and powered by gigantic wind-mill dynamos which lie outside the city domes. And Graham is the master of all this scientific marvel. For while he has been "asleep" for two hundred or more years, his once-meager finances have been held in trust and have accumulated interest to the point where

An original illustration for *When the Sleeper Wakes*. Graham, the "sleeper" of the novel, looks down upon the elaborate, brilliant—and unfortunately sinister—city that has evolved during his slumber.

his immense wealth is the (untouched and untouchable) cornerstone of the world economy, and he is, literally, the richest man in the world!

The narrative device of having a man fall asleep and wake up in the distant future may be a sloppy one, but the story is an almost perfect realization of a Wellsian daydream; a modern intellectual who escapes the world of our present agony and confusion to awaken in a future that looks like the quintessence of all that science, technology, and rational planning can offer civilization.

But the dream veils a nightmare. The triumph of order and rationality, the cities like palaces of light, the flying machines—all have been achieved at the cost of a social injustice more disturbing than the division of Eloi and Morlocks in *The Time Machine* because less fantastically, apocalyptically overblown. The multitudes of workers who maintain the city in all its splendor are controlled by a council of strongmen—an anticipation, actually, of the gangsters of fascism—headed by the powerful and sinister Ostrog, who becomes Graham's main guide to the new world and later his major adversary. For over the centuries the sleeper has become a figure of myth and millennial expectation among the working class, and the phrase, "When the sleeper wakes" has come to signify their hope that, somewhere in the future, lies their liberation from bondage. Graham awakens then to both a dream of order come true and a situation fraught with violence and struggle, a situation that tests the reality of civilization's pretensions to justice as well as order, and, moreover, a situation in which he is cast in the role of an unwitting messiah.

Messianic considerations are never far from Wells's utopian imaginings, or from his descriptions of himself in his more self-pitying and self-congratulating moods. But in *When the Sleeper Wakes* the associations are at their strongest. Uneasy with his newfound eminence and smitten with love for a beautiful young woman who is among the leaders of the workers' revolt, Graham flees Ostrog's palace to become the still rather unwilling leader of the revolution. But the revolution fails. If the industrial overlords have grown too heartless to understand the human price of their magnificent cities, by the same token the workers who built and maintain those cities have grown too dependent and too mentally and physically weak to take control of their lives. Graham dies in a final airplane duel against Ostrog (who also dies), and his mangled body is discovered by a simple shepherd, an heir to the immemorial cycles of pastoral life, who understands nothing of the great struggle that has been waged in a city he has never seen.

It is a grim utopia indeed. But it is also one which catches and establishes the central themes Wells will sound in his fictions to come. It is almost as if Graham is the Time Traveller reimagined, and stopped halfway on his journey to that black future where reason and muscle, administration and labor, have divided permanently into two separate species. When the Sleeper Wakes, for all its darkness, suggests the ascendancy of that second, less pessimistic, voice of Wells's: what can be done, or what could be imagined, to halt that division into mutually murderous species? Reason and intelligence alone will not be enough to construct the first truly creative and waste-free human society. The book is clear on at least that much, as it is also clear on the necessary survival of the most ancient and most "reactionary" of human emotions, love (Graham's real reason for joining the revolution) and the love of the good things of the earth (symbolized by the shepherd who is the only witness to Graham's death and one of Wells's most important characters).

Even as Wells turned his energy and attention to the construction of possible saving futures for mankind, then, he retained much of the complexity and darkness that had characterized his early scientific romances. And in the three major romances he published during the first decade of this century—The First Men in the Moon, The Food of the Gods, and When the Sleeper Wakes—one can almost see him feeling and thinking his way toward what might be the ultimately satisfactory Wellsian utopia. He was trying out, rejecting, and modifying certain aspects of his vision of man, society, and the universe until he could finally imagine a way in which those three overwhelming forces might at last be held in a creative and humanizing balance. The great tragedy of his career, of course, is that the closer he came to working out the terms of that balance the farther he got from the art of fiction. But to invent a utopia as a storyteller and to mean it as a social and political thinker are perhaps always irreconcilable habits of mind. What makes Wells an important and remarkable utopian is that he managed to maintain this *internal* balance for as long as he did.

THE FIRST MEN IN THE MOON

The First Men in the Moon is Wells's only major tale of space travel: and that in itself is a significant fact, since science fiction as a genre is popularly assumed to consist, if not entirely at least overwhelmingly, of stories of this sort. It is, moreover, surprisingly different, lighter in tone, from the earlier scientific romances. The atmosphere of menace, of an overwhelming threat from the biological heritage or the sociological future, which we have noted in the other major novels, is absent here—or is oddly deflected. Instead, the tale has a dreamlike, comic quality, even when events are at their most sinister.

Its narrator, Bedford, is also different from the sensitive, intellectual, and usually anonymous first-person narrators of the other romances. He is much more like the eager, scruffling middle-class heroes of Wells's so-called "realistic" novels; much more like, that is, Wells's own memory of his youthful self. Bedford is out to make his fortune, but after failing rather noticeably in some undefined business enterprises, he retires to Lympne in Kent: he can live more cheaply there, and furthermore, he now plans to write a play—not out of any aesthetic yearnings, but because playwriting seems an easy way of making money. (There is an echo of this joke about playwriting as a get-rich-quick scheme in *Kipps*.)

Once established at Lympne, he meets his neighbor, an eccentric, absentminded, apparently totally impractical scientist named Cavor. At first annoyed, and later amused by Cavor, he soon learns that his new friend has made a startling discovery: he has invented "Cavorite," a substance that is opaque to gravity as most solids are opaque to light and as asbestos is opaque to heat. Cavor is interested in the substance only for its scientific properties, but Bedford's immediate reaction to the news is quite otherwise—and important for the tone of the whole book:

> Among other things I saw in it my redemption as a business
> man. I saw a parent company and daughter companies, appli-
> cations to right of us, applications to left, rings and trusts,
> privileges and concessions spreading and spreading, until one
> vast stupendous Cavorite Company ran and ruled the world.
> And I was in it.

It is the voice of the entrepreneur, comically overblown but
nevertheless unmistakably earnest and egotistic: "And I was
in it." Moreover, it is the voice of the entrepreneur of early-
twentieth-century big business, an age of *laissez faire* capitalism that can seem to us almost mythical in its untrammeled
profits, its profligacy, and its irresponsibility. It is the dream
of wealth, as Bedford argues to Cavor (and quoting Samuel
Johnson) "beyond the dreams of avarice."

That is what the discovery of anti-gravity means to Bedford, and that, at the beginning, is all it means. Cavor, with
some misgivings, agrees to let him into the "Cavorite Company," and between the two of them they decide that the most
profitable first venture would be the construction of a Cavorite
sphere, a space ship, to take them to the moon: Cavor to explore the satellite and Bedford to begin mining it for the min-
erals in which it must be rich.

Their voyage in the Cavorite sphere is described, with
some of the effects of weightlessness in space remarkably anticipating the effects experienced—and observed on live tele-
vision—during real space voyages seventy years after the
novel appeared. But once the voyagers land on the moon, any
resemblance between Wells's moon and that reached by
NASA disappears. During the lunar day, that half-month
when the Earth-facing side of the moon is exposed to the sun,
the atmosphere frozen during the lunar night is warmed back
to its gaseous state. And in this atmosphere vegetation begins,
miraculously, to grow:

> Every moment more of these seed-coats ruptured, and even
> as they did so the swelling pioneers overflowed their rent dis-
> tended seed-cases and passed into the second stage of growth.
> With a steady assurance, a swift deliberation, these amazing
> seeds thrust a rootlet downward to the earth and a queer
> bundle-like bud into the air. In a little while the whole slope

was dotted with minute plantlets standing at attention in the blaze of the sun.

This famous passage is a remarkable anticipation of the effect of extreme slow-motion film. Bedford describes the same slow-motion effect in his description of the leaping strides he and Cavor take in the moon's light gravity. But no sooner does the vegetation appear than the Selenites, the insectlike inhabitants of the moon's interior, also appear, driving the giant, wormlike "mooncalves" that are their food source out to pasture.

Hiding from the Selenites, Cavor and Bedford are overcome by hunger and begin eating the mushroomlike plants in which they are concealed. They get drunk on the plants—in one of Wells's funniest scenes—and are taken prisoner, taken below the surface. Hence the odd *"in"* of the book's title—which is also, of course, a joking reference to the folklore "man in the moon."

Once below, they discover that the Selenites, for all their monstrous appearance, have constructed a highly advanced, mechanized civilization, and have honeycombed the interior of the moon with their dwellings. Cavor, overcome with curiosity and admiration for their alien technology, tries to establish a basis of communication with them. But Bedford keeps insisting that their only hope for survival lies in flight. He has also noticed that the most common material of Selenite civilization, out of which the very chains binding him are made, is gold. Better to flee back to Earth with as much gold as they can carry, he insists, and return properly armed, to deal with the natives from a position of power.

We have already noted Wells's frequent references to and implicit criticisms of the idea of imperialism. And here, linked explicitly with Bedford's dreams of avarice, that criticism is particularly mordant. Even before their capture, as they get progressively drunk on the mushrooms, Bedford has voiced the imperial theme in a blunt, hiccuping burlesque of Kipling (and Cecil Rhodes):

"We must annex this moon. . . . There must be no shilly-shally. This is part of the White Man's Burden. Cavor—we are—*hic*—Satap—mean Satraps! Nempire Caesar never

dreamt. B'n all the newspapers. Cavorecia. Bedfordecia, Bedfordecia. Hic—Limited. Mean—unlimited! Practically."

But Cavor finally agrees that they must flee, and with
much slaughter of the fragile Selenites they make their way
back to the surface and there part company to search for the
sphere. Bedford finds it but, returning to the agreed-on meeting place, discovers a hasty bloodstained note from Cavor to
the effect that he is about to be recaptured. The lunar night is
closing in, and any attempt to rescue his friend is hopeless.
Bedford makes it back to the sphere, with the gold he has
managed to carry off, just in time, and manages to navigate his
way back to Earth, landing—amazingly enough—just off the
coast of England.

He carries his gold with him to the nearest inn, surrounded by awestruck villagers. But he loses the sphere (an
unfortunate boy has entered it and accidentally returned it—
and himself—to infinite space), and with it the secret of Cavorite, the chance to save Cavor, and of course the chance to
make himself even wealthier.

At this point, in the original serialization of the novel, appears a passage not usually reprinted in later editions:

> Here the story, as we originally received it, ends. But we
> have just received a most extraordinary communication which
> certainly gives a curious and unexpected air of conviction to
> the narrative. If our correspondent is to be believed, Mr. Cavor
> is alive in the moon, and he is sending messages to the earth.

This spurious "Editor's Note" is followed, in the next issue
of The Strand Magazine, by the conclusion to the novel. A few
months after his return, Bedford learns that Cavor has survived, has managed to establish a common language with the
Selenites, and is sending his discoveries, in Morse Code, back
to Earth. And, in a fashion by now familiar to readers of the
scientific romances, Cavor's fragmentary concluding narrative
now clarifies the alien wonders the book has so far shown us.
But there is a difference: for if Bedford has been vaguely untrustworthy all along, because of his obvious self-interest,
Cavor has been, and remains, untrustworthy for the opposite
reason, because of his total, nearly inhuman abstraction from
any ordinary passion.

The Selenites are, indeed, insects, but according to Cavor, they are "not merely colossally superior to ants, but . . . colossally, in intelligence, morality and social wisdom, higher than man." Inevitably, this reminds the reader of the ominous description of the Martians at the beginning of *The War of the Worlds:* "minds that are to our minds as ours are to those of the beasts that perish." And the rest of Cavor's messages bear out the association. After the manner of ants and bees, but with vastly superior intellects, the Selenites have created a culture in which each individual is physically and mentally conditioned from birth to perform one and only one specialized task, be it herdsman, warrior, philosopher, or drone: "Every citizen knows his place. . . . The elaborate discipline of training and education and surgery he undergoes fits him at last so completely to it that he had neither ideas nor organs for any purpose beyond it."

The Selenite culture is, as Cavor later calls it, "a world machine." And despite Cavor's evident admiration for it, the phrase may remind us of the technologically perfect, heartlessly repressive world machine encountered by the hero of *When the Sleeper Wakes.* But in its full totalitarianism, its surgical and educational excision of free will itself from its "citizens" (the word is wonderfully ironic), it anticipates one of the most celebrated twentieth-century visions of a nightmare future: Aldous Huxley's *Brave New World,* where artifically grown human embryos are also conditioned from birth for the mental and physical characteristics requisite to their preassigned life tasks.

The moon, in other words, is a nightmarish dystopia, a society from which everything that makes human life valuable has been irrevocably expunged. And the bitter reflection of this nightmare upon contemporary working conditions was as much the point of Wells's description as it was later to be of Huxley's. At one point Cavor comes upon a laboratory where young Selenites destined to be machine manipulators are being transformed into pathetically stunted, deformed bodies with immense, grotesque, and hypersensitive hands. Even Cavor is shaken by this regimented bruality:

> "I hope, however, that may pass off and I may be able to see more of this aspect of this wonderful social order. That wretched-looking hand sticking out of its jar seemed to appeal

The Grand Lunar, from an original illustration for *The First Men in the Moon*. The drawing catches the true Wellsian nightmare, the triumph of a being who is all brain and no passion.

for lost possibilities; it haunts me still, although, of course, it is really in the end a far more humane proceeding than our earthly method of leaving children to grow into human be-ings, and then making machines of them."

A passage like this, in its cold savage irony, reminds us that one of Wells's earliest found and most treasured writers was Jonathan Swift.

But if Cavor's creator understands the darker implications of Selenite perfection, Cavor himself does not. He is finally taken for an interview with the "Grand Lunar," the monstrous—and also preconditioned, predetermined—brain who controls and administers the entire range of the society's activities. The interview does not go well. In trying to explain Earthly civilization to this purely, even grotesquely, rational being, Cavor makes the mistake of admitting that Earth has no such orderly, proportioned society as the moon, and even that men, in order to solve their disputes, resort to that most wasteful and most insane of activities, war. He also makes the mistake of revealing enough information for the Selenites themselves to be able to produce Cavorite, should they wish to invade our comparatively disorganized and atmosphere-rich planet. At the end, he is a desperate prisoner whose fate is uncertain but surely grim; and his last message, inexplicably cut short, is a meaningless jumble: "uless"—perhaps his hurried attempt to spell "useless."

The satire cuts two ways. If the insect society of the moon is a cruel parody of inhuman economic conditions on Earth, it is also, in its absolute if chilling sanity, a damning contrast to the bloodlust, the emotional chaos of which man is capable. Here once again Wells demonstrates his debt to Swift, particularly the Swift of *Gulliver's Travels*. For the Selenites invoke the same profound moral ambiguity as do the Houyhnhnms, the purely rational horses whose island Gulliver visits in his fourth voyage. As a realized standard of rationality, they show us how far pure reason falls short of a fully human standard; but by the very same token, they show us how miserably we fail to control and channel those passions that do make us human.

But the implications of the voyage to the Selenites extend farther. We have already referred to the "dreamlike" quality of the action of *The First Men in the Moon*. Bedford, throughout his part of the narrative, speaks of the stupendous voyage and its incredible discoveries as being like a dream. Indeed, his last words before the section describing Cavor's messages from the moon demand to be taken seriously:

> So the story closes as finally and completely as a dream. It fits in so little with all the other things of life, so much of it is

utterly remote from all human experience, the leaping, the
queer eating, the hard breathing of those weightless times, that
indeed there are moments when, in spite of my moon gold, I
do more than half believe myself that the whole thing was a
dream.

It is not the end of the story; but it is the end of Bedford's
story. And what dreams *has* he dreamed, and to what point?
For Bedford too, Gulliver-like, travels to an alien landscape
that reveals not only its own secrets, but some of the internal
secrets of the voyager himself.

On the voyage out, Bedford is driven enough by his
dreams of success and wealth that, remarkably enough, he
does not even pay much attention to the immense, ego-
shriveling void through which he travels. And after he returns
to Earth, a wealthy man, he can at last enjoy the dream of
leisure he has always cherished. He is writing his tale, as he
tells us in its opening sentence, "amidst the shadows of vine-
leaves under the blue sky of southern Italy"—in a petit
bourgeois paradise of success. And in this setting, his experience on the moon quite naturally appears to be the dream, and
the vine shaded comfort of southern Italy the reality.

On the moon, however—within the dream, as it were—
things had appeared otherwise, and Bedford at least remembers that they had. After he and Cavor have escaped from
the Selenites and separated to search for the sphere, Bedford—
alone, in an alien world—has a very Wellsian insight. "Why
had we come to the moon?" he asks himself, almost as if he is,
for the first time, really comprehending what he has done and
where he is.

> What is this spirit in man that urges him for ever to depart
> from happiness and security, to toil, to place himself in
> danger, even to risk a reasonable certainty of death? It dawned
> upon me there in the moon as a thing I ought always to have
> known, that man is not made simply to go about being safe
> and comfortable and well fed and amused. Against his inter-
> est, against his happiness he is constantly being driven. . . .
> Sitting there in the midst of that useless moon gold, amidst
> the things of another world, I took count of all my life. Assum-
> ing I was to die a castaway upon the moon, I failed altogether
> to see what purpose I had served. . . .

It is Bedford's discovery of the cosmic perspective, his first real vision of the way the infinitude of space, the infinitude of the universe, both dwarfs and renders all the more precious the struggle which is human life. Whatever the force is that drives men to attempt the impossible, to strive endlessly against the final-extinction to which they are doomed, it is a noble force—perhaps the only force which really gives to man the chance of being noble. And Bedford's self-seeking entrepreneurship, though tawdry and grasping, is actually a warped expression of that competitive energy, that athletic attitude toward life itself, which Wells in his major utopias will identify as the highest, indeed the essential, pitch of human existence.

To be sure, Bedford forgets—or at least fails to remember vividly enough—this view of things after he has returned to Earth and the petty seeking after wealth and comfort that is its besetting social disease. But this momentary vision on the moon has made its point. Bedford and Cavor are both dreamers; they are extensions, almost caricatures, of that dualism we have seen in Wells's fiction from *The Time Machine* on, the resolutely practical man whose very practicality is a kind of fantasy, and the abstract visionary whose whole life is a potentially dangerous dream. Both dreamers come to rude awakenings of different sorts in the "dream" which is their voyage to the moon. Both awakenings, furthermore, tell us something important not about the "real" nature of the moon or space travel (Wells, like most great science-fiction writers, is really only slightly interested in such details), but rather about the image of a truly just, truly civilized society as it might appear on this planet.

We have said that the invasion of Earth from outer space in *The War of the Worlds* is best understood as an invasion of present society by a possible, and horrific, future. But the journey into outer space, at least as Wells treats it, is not simply an inversion of the first theme. Rather than a voyage into a possible *future*, it is almost a voyage into *the idea of utopian fiction*. And this, perhaps, is why the air of menace, of foreboding, so familiar in the earlier novels is so noticeably lacking in this one. For Wells really is exploring new territory. In the disparate figures of Bedford and Cavor, and in the curiously remote, curiously ambiguous figures of the Selenites, he is as it were examining the *elements* of a positive utopia, the separate parts of an efficient road map for the human future, before beginning to assemble them into a fully articulated whole. Thus, if the novel is the most lighthearted, even the most playful, of Wells's early scientific romances, it is also the most tentative, and in some ways the most self-conscious, of his later social and political polemics.

From *The First Men in the Moon* we receive a hint, and a fairly broad one at that, of the direction Wells's ideas about an ideal society were taking. It would be organized—as highly and totally organized as that of the insectlike Selenites, as rationally grounded as a pure intellectual like Cavor could desire. And yet it would also be designed not only to accommodate but to encourage and nurture the bustling, competitive, self-assertive energies that made Bedford what he is—but to nurture them in more creative, more socially responsible channels than the mere accumulation of wealth or leisure time. We have already said that, to the despair and anger of many of his more socialist or Marxist colleagues, Wells remained to the end of his life an enthusiastic bourgeois. (Though he applauded Marxism for its visionary aims, he always held Marx himself in faint contempt as a pompous pedant, and expressed only the most qualified admiration for the beehive ideal of the communist state.) And at this stage of his career, when he begins to move, as it were, from apocalyptic lyricism to prophecy, the issue becomes very important.

Most orthodox varieties of socialism tend to envision the ideal social situation as one in which the individual finds true peace in *surrendering* his ego and the whole baggage of individualism our ancestors brought out of the caves (or, more correctly, down from the trees) to the good of the state. But for Wells, the only state worth living in was one that supported and *expanded* the claims the individual ego is able to make on life. There are psychological reasons for this peculiar characteristic of his social thought, to be sure: he was an egocentric and could be a very selfish man. But there are also more philosophical, and perhaps even nobler, resonances to the matter. If orthodox socialism imagined the good society as one in which each man could admit and be content with his littleness before the great business of the state, Wells wanted, and tried heroically to describe, a state that could allow each man to be, in passion and achievement, a giant. And his next scientific romance made this desire perfectly, even grotesquely, clear.

THE FOOD OF THE GODS

In 1903, Wells joined the Fabian Society. The Webbs thought that Wells, with his literary celebrity and his inexhaustible enthusiasm, would be the perfect popularizer of Fabian aims and ideals; and they also thought that they might be able to temper and redirect—actually, to civilize—his own more disruptive qualities. It was a mistake. Within four years, as we have seen in the first chapter, Wells had begun an unsuccessful, noisy, and disruptive challenge to assume leadership of the Society, and was involved in a scandalous love affair with the young daughter of a leading, and very unamused, Fabian. But the rift was, or should have been, obvious much earlier than that. In 1904 Wells had published *The Food of the Gods*, a fable about the literally gigantic future of humanity expressing as graphically as any of his books his belief that fierce individualism, if redirected and creatively rechanneled, could be the salvation rather than the bane of the race.

The story of *The Food of the Gods* is so simple, and so generalized, as to be hardly a "story" at all. It is rather a series of speculations on the possible consequences of a single fantastic event. Two scientists, Bensington and Redwood, discover a chemical which when fed to infants of any species (including plants) multiplies the growth rate by a factor of nearly ten. They begin their experiments with the Food—which they call "Herakleophorbia"—by feeding it to hens about to lay. But, due to the sloppiness and irresponsibility of the couple they hire to run their experimental farm, some of the Food is improperly disposed of, and soon the peaceful countryside is plagued, not only with giant runaway chickens, but giant wasps, rats, and vegetation. Furthermore, Redwood has begun giving the Food to his sickly infant son, with alarming results: for not only does the Food increase growth, but it is apparently addictive, necessary to the life of its recipient up to a certain stage of maturity.

Bensington and Redwood, abstract and impractical men of pure science, are at a loss as to how to deal with the unforeseen consequences of their experiment until an energetic and supremely practical engineer, Cossar, helps them dispose of the giant rats and wasps that have been terrorizing the countryside. But Cossar insists on giving the Food to his own children, three healthy sons. And Redwood's pediatrician, the unscrupulous Doctor Winkles, capitalizes on the Food by offering to give it to the infant daughter of a noble European house, the young Princess of Weser Dreiburg. Even the wife of the unreliable keeper of the original experimental farm, Mrs. Skinner, has escaped from the giant wasps, etc., to a remote village, carrying some of the Food with her for her infant grandson, young Caddles.

The children grow to be giants; not only physically but mentally, since their vastly increased brain capacity allows for a vastly increased practical intelligence and wisdom. And as they grow, they spread fear among the "little people" who surround them. A politician named Caterham seizes the opportunity to make himself the leader of an anti-giant, anti-Food faction and becomes widely celebrated as "Jack the Giant-killer." Young Caddles, who, unlike his giant brethren, has been kept in a state of ignorance and carefully disciplined servitude all his life, even makes his way to London, where he is shocked and outraged to discover the rich, bustling life of the cities from which he has been so cruelly excluded. His baffled entry into London is one of the book's most poignant scenes, as he asks (his voice, of course, a roar):

> "What are ye for, ye swarming little people? What are ye all doing—what are ye all for?
> "What are ye doing up here, ye swarming little people, while I'm a-cutting chalk for ye, down in the chalk pits there?"

But the mere presence of this disadvantaged, potentially revolutionary giant is an intolerable threat to the little world he enters: Caddles is shot and killed.

His death is the signal for a massive popular revulsion against the presence of the other giants. What had been only potential violence now erupts into a concerted attempt to contain and exile, or destroy, the children of the Food (who are also, by this point in the book, quite clearly the children of the Future, the first realizations of a fully human, fully self-possessed society). But, aided by their small yet visionary parents Cossar and Redwood (Bensington has long since retreated in panic from the whole business), the giants defend themselves against the first wave of their tiny enemies. The book ends on the eve of all-out war between the giants and the little people, with a stirring speech by one of the sons of Cossar:

> "To-morrow, whether we live or die, growth will conquer through us. That is the law of the spirit for evermore. To grow according to the will of God! To grow out of these cracks and crannies, out of these shadows and darknesses, into greatness and the light. . . . Till the earth is no more than a footstool. . . . Till the spirit shall have driven fear into nothingness, and spread. . . ." He swung his arms heavenward—"*There!*"

It is a mighty, truly apocalyptic, conclusion for a very strange book. And since its first publication, readers have been ill at ease, undecided how, exactly, to take *The Food of the Gods*. We end with the ringing assertion that mankind's future is gigantic, Promethean, literally godlike. But the book opens—and proceeds for some hundred pages—in a resolutely comic tone, emphasizing the absentminded, irresponsible nature of scientists and the absurd (if also dangerous) effects of the first experiments with the Food.

There is something irresistibly *funny* about the idea of a giant chicken invading a village. And there is something irresistibly noble, primally heroic, about the idea of a gigantic man standing in the moonlight, raising his fist to the stars themselves. But how can we possibly get from the one idea to the other? And why should Wells write a book that tries to incorporate both ideas?

It is important to remember that throughout his later career Wells was often attacked or satirized by orthodox or conservative opponents precisely in terms of his "vulgar" preoccupation with *bigness*. While pure Marxists found him too sentimentally spiritual, pure Christians found him too underbred, too materialistic to enter into their kingdom. C. S. Lewis articulated the fullest and most influential attack on the Wells "cult" of gigantic materialism in his space trilogy of the thirties, *Out of the Silent Planet, Perelandra,* and *That Hideous Strength.* But the attacks and satires began as early as the first reviews of *The Food of the Gods,* where the theme of gigantism is sounded so strongly, even grotesquely. G. K. Chesterton, a close friend of Wells and a staunch, witty adversary of his ideas, observed in his book *Heretics* (1905) that *"The Food of the Gods is the tale of Jack the Giant-Killer told from the point of view of the giant";* an ancient and orthodox fairy tale of heroism, in other words, perversely turned on its head. And, he goes on to say.

> The old and correct story of Jack the Giant-Killer is simply the whole story of man; if it were understood we should need no Bibles or histories. But the modern world in particular does not seem to understand it at all. The modern world, like Mr. Wells, is on the side of the giants; the safest place, and therefore the meanest and most prosaic. The modern world . . . talks of being strong and brave: but it does not see the eternal paradox involved in the conjunction of these ideas. The strong cannot be brave. Only the weak can be brave.

Chesterton is, as usual, brilliant and richly suggestive. But, for once, he is also off the point. As we have seen, in the figure of the demagogue Caterham, Wells acknowledges that *The Food of the Gods* is a version, or an inversion, of the tale of Jack the Giant-killer. But he does *not* —or, at least, not at the beginning—tell it "from the point of view of the giant." He tells it, first, from the point of view of the little men who stumble on the Food; then from the point of view of men visionary enough to understand the true implications of that revolutionary giantism; and then, only then, and very delicately, from the point of view of the supermen, the new men, the children of the Food who have been nurtured not only on "Herakleophorbia," but also on the enlightened educational and social wisdom of their small but heroic fathers.

Chesterton helps us see that the novel is not really "about" the giants as much as it is "about" the men—Bensington, Redwood, and Cossar—who make possible the coming reign of the giants. These men, at first unwittingly and then deliberately, stage-manage the ascendancy of the new men. They are, in other words, utopian planners. And in telling their *tale,* Wells is continuing the activity he began in *The First Men in the Moon,* preparing his own distinctive voice as social prophet and social planner.

Thus, the book's modulation from comedy to earnestness is part of the modulation of Wells's own stance at this moment of his career. As long as humans remain immersed in their frantic preoccupation with the everyday, they will remain trivial, tiny creatures, unintentionally comic and perpetually endangered by the cosmic mechanism of revolution. But, once they begin to take stock of themselves and their true position in the universe, once they begin to *think* both realistically and energetically about the business of living, they can, Wells tells us, indeed become the fathers of gods, the founders of a humanity that might resist even the universal principles of entropy and extinction.

The key to this transformation, in *The Food of the Gods* and in Wells's later work, is education. Indeed, we can take the whole book not only as Wells's trying out of a properly utopian voice, but also as a treatise on the nature—and necessity— of education for a truly human civilization.

Chesterton is right, as far as he goes, in insisting that the "strong" cannot be "brave," and that the only truly brave men and women are those who, in spite of their weakness, face and overcome stronger, sometimes apparently. insuperable, forces. But Wells suggests there is another level of bravery, another kind of courage even more difficult to summon up than this elementary kind: and that is the courage to accept *one's own strength,* to face up to one's own power and potential without recourse to the conventional and comforting evasions of false humility and cowardly "ordinariness." The engineeer, Cossar, articulates this central assertion midway through the story. Bensington and Redwood, afraid of the new race they may have created, are all for backing out of the experiment. But Cossar insists that they must go on, not only for the sake of the future, but for the sake of their own self-respect:

> "Here you are, fearfully and wonderfully made, and all you think you're made for is just to sit about and take your vittles. D'you think this world was made for old women to mope about in? Well, anyhow, you can't help yourselves now, you've got to go on."

This announcement of a higher purpose for life is, of course, very like the sudden realization Bedford comes to in *The First Men in the Moon,* the realization that, on the cosmic scale, mere considerations of everyday respectability do not really matter. The great advance Wells makes in *The Food of the Gods* over the earlier novel, at least for his emerging sensibility if not for the art of subtle fiction, is that he now can announce this revolutionary message *in terms of* the ordinary life of this world, rather than in terms of an allegory of an alternate society and planet.

This is why the figure of young Caddles is so crucial and so poignant an element of the novel. His adversaries notwithstanding, Wells is not just saying that bigger is better. He never, really, says that. He is saying, rather, that bigger can be better, if we are wise enough to understand, assimilate, and creatively manipulate the terms of bigness. Caddles is a tragedy because he is a superman whose superiority is *limited* to mere size, deprived of education. His local vicar and his local noblewoman (Lady Wondershoot) keep him, until his brief escape and unnecessary death, in a state of pious and brutally cruel submission to things as they are. The merely material revolutionary force is foredoomed to failure in Wells's universe: as much as he may sympathize with its unjust disenfranchisement, or its inalienable right to anger at that disenfranchisement.

Wells, that is, is more realistic, less sentimental than many of his socialist colleagues about these things. For him, the mere rage of the working class at its bondage was never *quite* enough to free it from that bondage. Caddles is a superman in physical power only: a giant without a giant education. And so he must die, even though our sympathies, and Wells's, are with his hopeless struggle against the hypocritical doctrines of false religiosity and class snobbery.

The future, however, belongs to the beneficiaries of intelligence: those, in other words, who have been trained according to the best that has been, or can be, thought and said on the side of hope, freedom, and the universal liberation of mankind from the shackles of old superstition. Near the middle of the story, Redwood and Cossar build a nursery for their giant children. And the nursery they build is a marvel, a splendid anticipation of what we have since learned about the best conditions for childrearing in the so-called "real" world:

> They had the walls and woodwork painted with a cheerful vigour; for the most part a slightly warmed white prevailed, but there were bands of bright clean colour to enforce the simple lines of construction. "Clean colours we must have," said Redwood, and in one place had a neat horizontal band of squares. . . . These squares the giant children should arrange and rearrange to their pleasure.

The child psychology of Jean Piaget, and the inspired practice of the Montessori schools throughout this century, have both borne out the wisdom of Wells's ideas about the early training of children in creative play. And, after the stage of creative play, lies the truly important stage of education (for Wells, at least), the stage of literary training, the development of the literary imagination. As Redwood says, some pages later: "That, after all, is the crown of every education. The crown—as sound habits of mind and conduct are the throne. No imagination at all is brutality; a base imagination is lust and cowardice; but a noble imagination is God walking the earth again."

Wells was, perhaps, never more straightforward about his valuation of the imagination, or about his idea of the place of literature in the construction of the ideal society, than here. "God walking the earth again" is a strong claim, indeed, to make for the human imagination. But it is a claim Wells devoted most of his life as a writer to proving.

The giantism of *The Food of the Gods*, that is, is not simply the vulgar and materialistic dream of an underbred revolutionary. Rather, it is Wells's difficult act of thinking his way through to a utopian vision that might satisfy both his rational expectations for the future of society and his apocalyptic hopes for the future of mankind. The giants, as we have said, are not really the focus of the story: the focus is on the careers, and the sensibilities, of the men who make the reign of the giants feasible. In this way, if in no other, Wells makes the novel a kind of daydream of his own best hopes for himself and the effect of his writings.

But *The Food of the Gods* is a daydream in another way, too. Think of tiny, insecure, undereducated, and undertrained H. G. Wells: a literary success only in his thirties, welcomed into the homes and salons of the cultured only because of his journalistic triumphs, perpetually (it may have seemed to him in 1904) condemned to be the cute kept darling of pallid, vapid intellectuals who welcomed him into their charmed circle only because of his picturesque difference from themselves. What man, under such circumstances, would not dream of the chance to rise, gigantically, above all the shabby/genteel triviality surrounding him? And what man, possessed of Wells's genius and Wells's passion for change, would not convert that dream (or daydream) into a major fiction? We have already noted the bitter realism of *Kipps*, published the year after *The Food of the Gods*. But that bitterness was *always* a part of Wells's imagination, even at its most hopeful. He hopes for mankind were gigantic, his expectations for mankind were optimistic, at least as much as he could will them to be. But his image of mankind, his idea of society at the most intimate level of his imagination, was always a dark one: it was the image of the little petty people who kill the giant who might be god.

IN THE DAYS OF THE COMET

We have seen that Wells in 1901, in *The First Men in the Moon*, began to examine the narrative possibilities of Utopia. In 1904, in *The Food of the Gods*, he explored those possibilities more completely, moving from fantastic, comic speculation about alternate futures for mankind to serious concrete propositions about the best possible future for mankind. But even in *The Food of the Gods* Wells had not yet become fully a utopian writer, had not yet fully abandoned the ironies and uncertainties of fantastic fiction for the specificity, the mathematical precision, the unrelenting historical accuracy of utopian planning.

The great thing about Wells is that he *never* did. Despite charges by his critics that he abandoned fiction for the shrill earnestness of mere "message," the reader of Wells will notice, even in the most unashamedly homiletic of his social prophecies, a concern for the *mode of presentation*, a subtle self-consciousness about the art, not just of persuasion but of fiction, that lifts his work above the normal range of economic and political utopia building.

By the end of his career, of course, Wells had come to a kind of defiant agreement with his critics. He had all the shyness, all the deep uncertainty about himself that usually goes with being a brilliant blusterer. And since his adversaries had been telling him, for years, that he had ceased being a storyteller and become a preacher, he naturally insisted that that was what he meant to do all along. But Wells talking about his work as a utopian writer is a very different character from Wells the utopian writer. He *was* a storyteller, and as soon as he began to tell a story, the diffidence and the sensitivity to attack vanished: he was H. G. Wells again.

Much of this complex self-consciousness about the invention of Utopias is evident in the first of his explicitly utopian fictions, *A Modern Utopia,* published in 1905 (the same year as the first of his explicitly realistic novels, *Kipps*). *A Modern Utopia* is usually regarded as the first assertion, by Wells, of economic and social theories which were to feature importantly throughout his later work. Utopian society, for one thing, could no longer be imagined simply as an ideal state, but rather has to be thought of as a whole system of planetary organization: for so complicated has become the interrelationship of human affairs that anything less than a worldwide transformation of life is bound to fail. On this utopian planet, furthermore, machines and technology will assume a primary role in the beautification of human life, so much so that the management and invention of new and more efficient machinery will become a new form of craftsmanship, a new and sublime art. Men and women in utopia will be as personally and publicly free as the society can make them, and the only laws they obey will be negative sanctions (thou shalt not) rather than restrictively positive sanctions (you will). Money will no longer be based upon the archaic standard of gold—a technologically useless, clumsy raw material—but upon units of *energy produced* by the individual citizen for the world state: a version of the Marxist ideal of industrial value, and of the older Gospel observation, "the laborer is worthy of his hire." A worldwide system of identification (by thumbprints) will ensure that every citizen, while enjoying his or her freedom of movement and self-determination, will be absolutely identifiable and absolutely traceable at all times for the sake of the larger public good. And, finally, although this utopian planet is kingless and even, to the naive eye, completely ungoverned, it will be managed, overseen, and guided by a special class of men. They are the Samurai: austere, physically perfect, philosophical technologues whose priestly task is to maintain the order and the rational direction of the planet-wide society, and also to serve as a model and a symbol of what mankind, at its very best, can become.

It is, in its way, a chillingly well-ordered world that Wells imagines, and it certainly seems a thumpingly unromantic one. There is no doubt that Wells really believed that such a triumph of bourgeois capitalism and industry (socialized and energized by a philosophy of absolute freedom) would be the best that could happen to mankind. He is quite clear, and quite unrelenting, in his insistence that this massively *willed* society is our only recourse against the principle of universal entropy, the tendency toward the ever-increasing chaos that is "nature." As the narrator observes midway through the book:

> The way of Nature in this process is to kill the weaker and the sillier, to crush them, to starve them, to overwhelm them, using the stronger and more cunning as her weapon. But man is the unnatural animal, the rebel child of Nature, and more and more does he turn himself against the harsh and fitful hand that reared him. He sees with a growing resentment the multitude of suffering ineffectual lives over which his species tramples in its ascent.

Wells's heritage from Darwin is, as ever, strong. But in a ringing passage like this one we see how far he has come from the mere assumption of universal struggle and universal violence as the way of the world. Man as "the rebel child of Nature" is, of course, also man as romantic hero—Faustian man wresting the universe of chance and change to the dimensions of his own imagination. Wells, more than almost any other writer of his age, helps us see how the romantic myth of the heroic rebel could become transformed into the myth of the engineer, the scientist who wages war against the cosmic machine that is trying to kill him. The alternative to the bloody struggle of the strong and the weak is, in the context of *A Modern Utopia*, an enlightened policy of birth control and rational eugenics that will simply eliminate the weak from the human stock (or that will, if some survive, allow them their own unendangered place). It is of course natural that arguments like this could seem, later in the twentieth century, grim anticipations of the nightmare of Nazi ideas about "eugenics" or of Lysenko's Marxist perversion of Darwinian theory (i.e., the assertion that socially inculcated characteristics might be transmitted). But such associations, though they have had their vogue, are finally silly. Wells does not really want to eliminate the weak: he wants to eliminate the situation that forces the weak, generation after generation, to be imposed upon and finally destroyed by the strong. And so he invents a world in which all are strong, with varying but respected degrees of strength, and where the natural brutality of class warfare is controlled and civilized out of existence.

We have come a long way, in other words, from the bully utopia of *When the Sleeper Wakes*. In the Samurai, the gangster ethics of Ostrog and his colleagues are transformed into something positive, noble. But to say this much about the book is to ignore the fact that *A Modern Utopia*, even more than *When the Sleeper Wakes*, also defines itself explicitly as fiction, and therefore as ironic, subtle, diffident about even its most ringing assertions.

In the preface to the novel, Wells insists that this is "the last book of its sort" he expects to write; the last book, that is, of social analysis and critique, for at the time he still feels his proper vocation to be that of romance and fiction, of "imaginative writing." And, although most of his later readers have not taken him at his word about this, he insists that none of the specific proposals he makes for an ideal society are meant all that seriously. They are only meant as signposts, intimations of what a truly successful society might look like. The novel, he says, is "the best way to a sort of lucid vagueness which has always been my intention in this matter."

"Lucid vagueness" is a fine construction for Wells's work as a social prophet and indeed for the art of fiction generally.

A Modern Utopia is not simply a projection into the future of the chances and rules of human survival, it is also a dream book, a book that explicitly describes itself as a dream. To read the book properly, Wells insists from the beginning, you must imagine an unseen voice reading a *manuscript* about possible utopian systems; and at times you must imagine a more personal, more immediate voice—that of the narrator— interrupting the public reading of the manuscript to inject personal comments and observations on the society the manuscript describes. In other words, before the book even begins, Wells locates his utopian fiction within a universe of performance and *fiction*. It is all a play, all a *show*. And, oddly enough, his honesty about the playfulness of the enterprise does not detract from as much as it underscores the urgency of the matters he addresses. For the "narrator" is Wells, magically transported to the planet of his best dreams—which is a planet exactly like ours in every respect, in every single human being, except that it is governed and organized according to truly human principles of civilization. In other words, this utopian fiction is not so much a fiction of an ideal society as it is a fiction of an ideal *self* for the narrator, and, implicitly, for every other inhabitant of the planet who reads the book. What might we all be like if we were really human, really good, really adequate to the nagging sense of our possibilities?

That is the question *A Modern Utopia* exists to answer, and the statecraft, economic theory, and social prophecy of the book are, finally, secondary to that major task. As the narrator observes, late in the book, "That I have come to Utopia is the lesser thing now; the greater is that I have come to meet myself." And this was to remain the bias of Wells's fictions, even at their most abstract and generalized: the invention of a world so that the world might make room for the self, but a larger, more generous, more fully humanized self. Wells's egotism and selfishness, in other words, were among his most important gifts as a writer, vices that became virtues as soon as he set himself to invent a story because, paradoxically enough, the story he most liked to tell was about a world where vices *could* become virtues, where little grasping men *could* become big men, Samurai or giants.

In *A Modern Utopia* the two voices of Wells we have previously noted are also present. The narrator is accompanied on his journey through utopia by a friend, the botanist, who is horrified and fearful whenever the narrator is exalted and invigorated. The botanist—whose vocation, of course, is the study of nature *independent* of human interference or rebellious organization—is that part of all of us (Wells included) who finds such ideal rationality, such transcendent organization, not an assertion but a threat. And the botanist is, throughout most of the book, treated as a butt for the narrator's growing excitement over the splendors of this newfound world. He is, of course, finally converted to the narrator's own enthusiasm for the new world. But in his initial fearful, even depressed response to the "modern Utopia" he is an important character in the book and in Wells's imagination. Like the narrator of *The Time Machine* or Dr. Kemp in *The Invisible Man,* he gives a presence and a voice to that part of human nature that will always resist the future, always resist change from the comfortable (even if the comfortable is also the intolerable), and that must also somehow be satisfied and appeased as we journey toward the future. For the botanist, no less than the narrator, is one of us.

As roundabout and suggestive as *A Modern Utopia* is in its presentation of the "lucid vagueness" of Wells's hopes for society, his next major book is even more so. In 1906 Wells published *In the Days of the Comet,* the book that finally established him as a scandalous writer, that alienated many of his closest friends, and that ensured his final break with the respectably revolutionary Fabian Society. For in *In the Days of the Comet* he took the implications of socialism to their extreme, and most intimate, reach, insisting that freedom of self-determination and freedom of choice must also include absolute freedom of sexual partnership (theme dear to his own heart).

It is for its loud and unequivocal assertion of "free love," that *In the Days of the Comet* was most celebrated or notorious at the time of its publication, and for which it is probably still best remembered. But, particularly in the context of Wells's own earlier work and his evolving ideas of the novelist's vocation as social analyst, it is a brilliant book in a

number of other ways. And not the least of its brilliancies is
its dreamlike beginning: "*I saw a grey-haired man, a figure of
hale age, sitting at a desk and writing.*"

Who is the "I" of this strange opening sentence? It is, of
course, the novelist, but the novelist imagined now not as the
wondering, enthusiastic explorer of *A Modern Utopia*, but
rather as the doubtful, diffident, everyday brother of the botanist of the earlier book—the novelist as one of us, in other
words, looking in puzzlement at the figure (as we learn) from
the remote perfected future. But the figure from the future is
also a writer, and he is writing, as the book will make clear,
the history of "the Change" (it is always capitalized), the astonishing and magical transformation that has turned the
world into a paradise.

That world appears at the beginning of the novel in a peculiarly deflected, fictive manner. As the narrator from the
present looks at the writer from the future, he notices a mirror
hung over the writer's head:

> I discovered that a concave speculum hung slantingly high
> over his head; a movement in this caught my attention
> sharply, and I looked up to see, distorted and made fantastic
> but bright and beautifully coloured, the magnified, reflected,
> evasive rendering of a palace, of a terrace, of the vista of a
> great roadway with many people, people exaggerated, impos-
> sible-looking because of the curvature of the mirror, going to
> and fro.

"Distorted and made fantastic but bright and beautifully
coloured": the city and the figures seen in the mirror are, of
course, deformed by the shape of the mirror. But the deformity
creates a greater brilliance, a nobler stature than the "real"
world enjoys. The people of this new world are "exaggerated,
impossible-looking because of the curvature of the mirror."
But perhaps the mirror tells a kind of truth about the real lives
of people that a less distorted glass could not. The mirror
hung over the head of the writer of the future is the lens of
utopian prophecy or, more simply, the lens of imagination
that allows Wells as fabulist to glimpse into a possible future
of the human race and as storyteller and mythmaker, to invent
a tale that shows us how we might be at our best.

If the mirror is a brilliant and complex image for the lens of utopian fiction, though, the writer is an even better one. We have seen in *A Modern Utopia* how the narrator is transported to utopia mainly to meet his double, to see what he would have been like in a perfectly organized, rationally administered society. In *In the Days of the Comet* that same confrontation occurs, only less schematically, and therefore with a greater force of poignancy.

The writer from the future, the aged man in the Tower, is Leadford, and the story he tells of the Change is also the story of his own awakening, his own Change from an undereducated, bitter young man of the working class into a free and wise citizen of a better world. Leadford, in other words—no less than Kipps, one of Wells's other "realistic" heroes—is a version, a projection, of what the young Wells had been. *In the Days of the Comet*, indeed, for most of its duration reads much more like a particularly grim realistic novel of Wells than one of his scientific romances or utopias. Leadford is disadvantaged by class, by economics, and by his own lack of formal education, and he is hopelessly in love with Nettie, a lovely young girl who spurns his affection for the love of Verrall, a wealthy and insufferably superior-seeming young man. As this ugly triangle of sexual warfare develops, there is also news of a strange comet approaching Earth on what seems to be a collision course. But though the green aura of the mysterious comet illuminates more and more of the sky each night, men still go about their petty concerns, their petty feuds and jealousies, as if it were not there.

Finally, when his jealousy and his sense of injured manhood have become unbearable, Leadford resolves to kill Verrall. But the night he chooses to track his enemy down is also the night on which the comet finally enters the atmosphere of Earth. In one of his most splendidly imagined and realized scenes, Wells tracks Leadford's path in murderous pursuit of the man who has stolen his lover, across the fields in which a rural celebration is taking place as the sky glows a sickly, ominous green from the comet's approach. The world is going mad. Leadford's jealousy is only a local outbreak of a murderous vindictiveness that is also impelling the nations toward a new and bloody, perhaps catastrophic war. The thousand little injustices and acts of selfishness of which "ordinary life" is composed are at last about to burgeon into one universal catastrophe of hatred that will consume the race who spawned it. And the approach of the comet, with its baleful green glow, seems to be the perfect apocalyptic symbol of that inevitable disaster.

But, as it turns out, the comet is precisely the reverse of what it seems. Leadford comes closer and closer to his prey: Verrall and Nettie are out, with the rest of the community, celebrating Beltane Eve (or Mayday—the traditional day for celebrating the fertility of the earth, its eternal potential for renewal and rebirth). This Beltane Eve satisfies all traditional expectations and pronouncements. For as the comet passes through Earth's atmosphere, it releases a gas that kills— literally kills—all the self-seeking, hateful, violent tendencies the human organism inherits from its biological past. Everyone on the planet falls asleep under the influence of the gas and awakens to a new, charitable, human world. As Leadford says:

> The intimate chemical processes of life were changed, its nervous metaboly. For the fluctuating, uncertain, passion-darkened thought and feeling of the old time came steady, full-bodied, wholesome processes. Touch was different, sight was different, sound and all the senses were subtler; had it not been that our thought was steadier and fuller, I believe great multitudes of men would have gone mad.

In the first awakening from the sleep of the comet, men and women are almost childlike in their delight at the change that has come over them. Suddenly, they need no longer lie or deceive, need no longer strive to best one another in social or economic competition, for they are all possessed of a new spirit of trust and honesty, mutually shared humanity, that makes the stresses and hatreds of the past seem foolish. But very soon they recover from their first unthinking enthusiasm for the new state of things, and begin to construct upon the basis of their newfound internal freedom a society and a culture adequate to be the external expression and form of that liberty.

It is a true apocalypse; it is a daydream. That "lucid vagueness" Wells wrote of in the preface to A Modern Utopia was never to be more fully, more convincingly realized. *In the Days of the Comet is* a daydream, and a daydream all the more compelling because it identifies itself as such. The comet, on at least one level of reading, is an absurd accident, an absurd intrusion into human life from the cosmos. And its effects—the chemical burning-out of the enzymes of hatred and selfishness—are equally absurd. Yet we believe it. Or, at least in the context of this book, we believe that it makes sense as an attitude toward human affairs and human fate. Wells here, unlike in *A Modern Utopia,* makes no specific proposals or formulations about the proper conduct of an ideal society, save that it be free, honest, and totally without the hypocrisies that determine ordinary human events as we know them. And yet that is enough. After the great Change, Leadford awakes to find that he is no longer jealous of Verrall. Joining a commune dedicated to organizing the new state, he finally marries Anna, a young women who for a while makes him forget all about his former agonies of passion. But, after a while, he meets Verrall and Nettie again. Under the new dispensation of universal charity and absolute honesty, however, he finds that nothing is left of his former hatred. And, most scandalously of all, he, Verrall, Nettie, and Anna soon form a ménage of lovers both sublimely unconscious of violating any moral norms and completely open—as is everyone else in the new world—to the possibility of new attachments, new lovers yet.

It was this aspect of *In the Days of the Comet*—especially in view of Wells's own life—that made the book so roundly condemned and widely read at the time. But the doctrine of "free love" is only a part, and perhaps only a minor part, of the tale's importance. For what the book is *really* about is the chances for change and the ways in which that saving change might manifest itself.

The epigraph to the novel is from that most beloved of poets for Wells, Shelley:

> The World's Great Age begins anew,
>   The Golden Years return,
> The Earth doth like a Snake renew
>   Her Winter Skin outworn:
> Heaven smiles, and Faiths and Empires gleam
> Like Wrecks of a Dissolving Dream.

Wells shares Shelley's infinite hopes for the apocalyptic future of mankind, and understands as well as his nineteenth-century precursor that those hopes are as much the stuff of poet's dreams—the "unacknowledged legislators" of the world, as Shelley calls them—as they are the stuff of the engineer's plans or designs. The Change in human nature, when it occurs, may well occur in a moment, in the twinkling of an eye: it does so in In the Days of the Comet, and it does so also in those early Christian visions of apocalypse upon which the young H. G. Wells was reared. This is not to say that Wells was hidebound or superstitious in his views of the future of the race, but rather to observe that he was, and remained, capable of grafting onto the new visions of technology and science a sensibility as old, and as profoundly religious, as the oldest imagination of his culture. The lens of apocalyptic fiction, in other words, was always a distorting one for Wells. But if he never forgot that it was distortive, he also never forgot that it was, in its very fictional nature, the best lens anyone had devised for peering into the future (and, more importantly, into the present).

Throughout this chapter we have been tracing fictions in which, in one way or the other, the author or the narrator dreams of what might be possible, desirable, or inevitable in human affairs. In the Days of the Comet, in that way as in many others, is the culminating book of Wells's career to its date. For it is the dream of a dream: the dream of waking to a reality that its narrator, Leadford, can only describe from the clarified vantage point of the dream world itself, and that we can only see through the distorting (but perhaps truth-telling) lens of the fiction. What would life really be like if none of us was selfish, none of us was grasping, none of us was dishonest or afraid? No one has ever, yet, been able to show us this impossible scene. But Wells, at least in In the Days of the Comet and the best of his later work, was canny and creative enough to show us the mirrors we might use, the lenses we might employ, to look for that lost, impossible, and devoutly-to-be-hoped world.

6

OUTLINES FOR HISTORY:
The Later Wells

In the Days of the Comet appeared in 1906. Wells's next scientific romance, The War in the Air, appeared only two years later in 1908, and it would be absurd to claim that any major change in the Wells psyche had occurred during the twenty-odd months between the two books. In some ways, The War in the Air, date notwithstanding, can seem the work of an "earlier" Wells than In the Days of the Comet. Its imagination of a world war fought by fantastic flying machines and giant bomber zeppelins is close in tone and technique to The War of the Worlds, and its reluctant hero, the humble Bert Small-ways, is eminently recognizable from the "realistic" novels.

Yet there is a difference, and an important one, in the spirit of the two novels. The simplest explanation, and a fairly common one even among admirers of the earlier Wells, is that at the end of his golden decade as a science-fiction writer, Wells began more and more to abandon the possibilities of pure fantasy, free imagination, for the strictures and the grey disciplines of social and economic preaching: he began turning his stage into a pulpit—and botched the carpentry of the thing.

I have mentioned this estimate of Wells's career and have suggested that it is deeply unfair to the later Wells at his best. But it is necessary, at this point, to admit that it is not entirely unfair to the later Wells in general. We cannot say that, for some odd reason or reasons, he stopped being a brilliant storyteller sometime soon after 1906. But we can say—Wells almost forces us to say—that at about this time, for a number of reasons, he stopped *wanting* to be a brilliant storyteller.

However complicated and personal were some of the reasons for this change, moreover, the most important was relatively simple, impersonal, and quite clearly implied in the books he had written up to that time. He became a prophet, sometimes to the detriment of his powers as a novelist, because his own best work as a novelist had been leading him, urging him, to the task of prophecy. We have examined, from *The Time Machine* to *In the Days of the Comet*, Wells's fantasias on the themes of evolution and human freedom, technology and morality, our bestial heritage and our possibly robotized future. And we have seen how those fantasias, from the internal momentum of their developing mythology, impelled him to invent more and more urgent threats to human existence and more and more radical, far-reaching solutions or responses to those threats. From the nightmare of human annihilation to the daydream of human survival to the dream of human transformation and triumph, Wells's first seven major scientific romances are an unbroken chain, a continuing process of imagination.

The key to that process, the indispensable link in the chain from book to book, dream to dream, is the concept of evolution. Man is doomed to extinction by every cosmic precedent, by all the accumulated evidence of the blind processes of nature that grind down even the mightiest and loveliest of species once they cease to adapt, cease to struggle efficiently against the environment that creates them as surely as it damns them. But man is also—through a cosmic accident or through a kind of divine grace—gifted with a power and a curse that sets him apart from the mechanisms that make and kill stars. He is conscious, and he is conscious of his consciousness. He has an edge; he holds a wild card. And while this may simply mean that he has the power to be more adept at his own destruction than other less intelligent forms of life, it can also mean that he is capable, through an exercise of will and intellect, of appealing and upsetting the verdict of universal history, of adapting himself to meet even the worst challenge of time.

But the value of a wild card depends upon how it is played. Wells had come, as a novelist, to assert that consciousness might be man's ultimate resource against the doom pronounced on him by evolutionary history. But this sheerly imaginative assertion was not enough; it was necessary not just to imagine the possibilities of consciousness for making a better world, but to *realize* those possibilities and to turn one's own consciousness, one's own intellect, toward the great business of constructing social bulwarks against the onset of entropy. One had, at whatever cost to the art of fiction, to awaken oneself from the dream of fiction.

There is something very Victorian about this turning in Wells's career; and it is important to remember that he was, however belatedly or complexly, a Victorian. Darwin had taught him, and his whole generation, a deep pessimism about the final fate of the human experiment. And that pessimism was to reassert itself, crushingly, in Wells's last books. But until the end of his career, he set his face resolutely against the full implications of doom with an energy even Tennyson might have approved of. Paradoxically, nothing is more "modern" about him than this very clinging to the bitter hopefulness he had inherited from the Victorian era. It underscores both his peculiar sensitivity and vulnerability to the uncertainties and doubts of the so-called "modern condition," and also, by contrast, the longing for certainty and for peace of mind against which that condition is defined.

We have examined at length the novels Wells wrote before he fully gave himself over to the self-appointed role of social critic and social prophet. They are the books through which he exercised, and continues to exercise, his strongest influence on science fiction, and perhaps also the books for which he is deservedly remembered and celebrated as a major writer. Nevertheless, if this were a book on Wells, rather than on Wells's science fiction, we should not yet have properly begun. We have examined only the novels of a decade, and Wells had nearly three decades as a writer ahead of him when *In the Days of the Comet* appeared.

But however disproportionate it may seem to treat all of Wells's later utopias in a single concluding chapter, there is some very real sense to it. After *In the Days of the Comet*,

Wells's practice as a storyteller and vision as a utopian prophet remains remarkably consistent—or, at least, developed only in points of specific policy, particular programs. In *Days of the Comet*, as we have seen, he indulges his apocalyptic imagination to its fullest and most powerful: the ordinary life of men on Earth has become an intolerable web of jealousies, hatreds, and class struggles, and the only thing that can save us from ourselves is a visitation from beyond, an atheist's *deus ex machina* that will purge the human chemistry of its competitive, murderous bacteria. It is a daydream, of course: a hope for deliverance that is hardly a program for social change (although it seemed enough of a program to get Wells expelled from the Fabian Society). And it is also the farthest reach of Wells's talent as a writer of scientific romances, the last "true" scientific romance he wrote.

He himself acceded to this estimate years later when, in 1934, Alfred A. Knopf published *Seven Famous Novels by H. G. Wells*. They were the seven major novels we have discussed so far, and Wells wrote for the collection a preface implicitly acknowledging that they were the main body of his work as a science-fiction writer (he suggested adding only *Men Like Gods*, 1923, as the last of his scientific romances).

If *In the Days of the Comet* is a dream of deliverance, though, *The War in the Air*, for all its resemblance to earlier Wells tales of disaster and chaos, is an attempt to awaken from that dream and face the implications and responsibility not of fiction but of history.

We have noted that by the late nineteenth century, all Europe was expecting the outbreak of a major bloody and technologically sophisticated world war. This cultural context made a book like *The War of the Worlds* as immediately successful as it was. And by 1908, the year of *The War in the Air*, that nagging sense of a catastrophe about to occur had grown, if anything, stronger and more oppressive. The secret of flight had been discovered only a few years before, in 1903 by the Wright brothers, and there was no real reason to suspect that airplanes might ever be used for any purposes other than exotic entertainment or travel—certainly not for so serious a business as warfare. In fact, the use of planes and balloons during the First World War was considerably more limited and tactical than the absolute determinative violence Wells imagines for them in The War in the Air. But if scenes like the aerial destruction of major cities were not an accurate forecast of the war immediately to come, they were to be all too well fulfilled in the war—World War II—that followed.

The interesting thing about The War in the Air, though, is not its relative success or failure as prophecy, but the way it turns itself, in the course of its narrative, into prophecy. We have spoken of the reorientation of Wells's talents at this stage of his career, and in The War in the Air it is possible to see that reorientation occurring in the course of a single narrative.

The book begins as the story of Bert Smallways, an unassuming, quite nonpolitical young man who hopes simply to make a go of his bicycle shop and win the hand of the young woman he loves. Through an absurd series of accidents, Smallways finds himself mistaken for the inventor of a flying war machine, abducted aboard a German zeppelin, and carried along on a massively destructive attack by the new German air force against the city of New York. His very name, "Smallways," suggests that he is a little man caught up in political and technological movements well beyond his understanding or interest. As the world war escalates in violence and waste, he finds himself less and less able to comprehend the shape of what is happening to him.

The war destroys civilization as we know it, casting mankind back into a semifeudal state of existence in which Bert, who has also survived the war, comically thrives and eventually even reunites with his lady love. This is, in its way, fairly predictable Wells. But toward the end of the novel there is a curious modulation in the tone of the narrative. In Chapter Eleven, which describes "The Great Collapse" of the world under the war, the heretofore conventional, omniscient narrator of the book suddenly becomes something—or someone— quite different:

> And now the whole fabric of civilisation was bending and giving, and dropping to pieces and melting in the furnace of the war. . . . To men living in our present world state, orderly, scientific and secured, nothing seems so precarious, so giddily dangerous, as the fabric of the social order with which the men of the opening of the twentieth century were content.

To us it seems that every institution and relationship was the fruit of haphazard and tradition and the manifest sport of chance, their laws each made for some separate occasion and having no relation to any future needs, their customs illogical, their education aimless and wasteful.

This is, as far as I can determine, the first full-scale appearance of the concept and phrase "world state" in Wells's fiction. It had been anticipated in the implicit arguments of *The Food of the Gods* and *In the Days of the Comet,* and even more strongly in the dream world of *A Modern Utopia.* Now, though, it is no longer a dream or an elegent (if serious) invention: it is a reality which the narrator wants desperately to bring into being, even at the price of shattering the tone of the fiction. *The War in the Air* begins as another Wellsian realistic fantasy. But *this* time the threat to ordinary human security is not from maddened scientists or extraterrestrial invaders, but from the all too immediate rapacity and senselessness of contemporary international politics. And, confronted with the terror of history, Wells is forced to devise a world in which possible disasters may be averted, not merely to imagine them.

Within a few pages of this announcement of the world state that succeeds upon the destruction of civilization by war, Wells—in his role as future historian—articulates another concept that will become gigantically important in his later work. What was the salient characteristic of early-twentieth-century man, he asks; what combination of blindness and bad thinking led him so inexorably into disaster?

For . . . three hundred years, indeed, the movement of the world seemed wholly beneficial to mankind. Men said, indeed, that moral organisation was not keeping pace with physical progress, but few attached any meaning to these phrases, the understanding of which lies at the basis of our present safety.

We can remember that Dr. Kemp in the *Invisible Man* and the narrator of *The War of the Worlds* both reflect upon the probable development of moral ideas with technological progress; and we can also remember that the apocalyptic situations of *The Food of the Gods* and *In the Days of the Comet* are really a playing-out of this crucial theme. Wells now makes it officially and permanently the central issue of his meditations on the fate of Homo sapiens. It was no longer enough to demonstrate fictively the murderous distance, the suicidal fissure, between moral ideas and technological development. The task at hand—a task, Wells passionately believed, upon which our survival depends—was to heal that fissure. How *should* moral ideas develop to keep pace with our vastly increased power, for both self-transformation and self-destruction? He was prepared to spend the rest of his life suggesting answers to the question.

As a novel, *The War in the Air* is tentative, confused: it does not know quite what to make of itself (though this very confusion makes it a wonderfully entertaining book to read). It is a comic presentation of a little fellow caught up in great affairs, an epic narrative of those great and destructive affairs—the world war—and, finally, a kind of blueprint for the future history of the world.

As future history the book is most important for Wells's later career. The rhythm of history established in *The War in the Air* was to become the *permanent* rhythm of his utopian histories of the future, the permanent situation he envisioned as necessary to the founding of a world state, the awakening of human beings to their endangered position and their only hope for survival. A massive, destructive, bloody, and universal war *must* occur, given the present conditions of human venality and shortsightedness—a war whose wholesale disaster is sufficient to return civilization to the primal sociological muck out of which all human communities have so arduously struggled. And after this war, shocked to their senses, the people of Earth might hope to invent a social system that avoids both the inhuman collectivism of communism and the unmuzzled competitiveness of capitalism, a new idea of the city that could give free rein to the human intelligence and the expansiveness of human enterprise, making possible a world of undreamed-of creativity, energy, and joy.

This is the plot—*the* plot—of the major exercises in scientific prediction Wells published after *The War in the Air: The World Set Free* (1914), *Men Like Gods* (1923), and *The Shape of Things To Come* (1933). And it is also, implicitly, the plot behind two of his most curious and richest later science-fiction novels. *Star Begotten* (1937) and *All Aboard for Ararat* (1940). It is also, of course, a very old plot, and one not at all original to Wells. For it is the plot of apocalyptic literature in general, particularly of that branch stemming from the Christian tradition of hope in the Second Coming of Christ or in the establishment of the New Jerusalem, the City of the Blessed, after the destruction of the corrupt Earth as we know it now. As we have had occasion to observe frequently throughout this study, Wells never quite outgrew his indoctrination, at his mother's knee, into the expectations of radical Christianity. But the "apocalyptic," at least as described by historians of the modern like Frank Kermode, is in many ways the definitive genre of twentieth-century writing. Classics of the modern sensibility like T. S. Eliot's *The Waste Land*, Ezra Pound's *Hugh Selwyn Mauberly*, Ernest Hemingway's *A Farewell to Arms*, and Graham Greene's *Brighton Rock* are all demonstrations, in varying degrees of urgency, that the apocalypse has, in fact, taken place. The final battle, in all these works, has been fought and lost by the forces of light, and there is nothing left to do except escape—escape into another aesthetic, religious, moral set of possibilities.

Wells was modern in his insistence, before any of these writers had published their most influential work, that the apocalytpic battle had been, or was about to be, fought and lost. He was, though, distinctively unmodern in his insistence, book after book, that there might be some hope for human survival or human triumph after this last of all battles. He never surrendered hope until the very end of his life, when he was sick and exhausted. This hope that men might make a better world, this faith in the power of will and will alone to transform the shabby spectacle of history into something noble and shining made him, during the thirties, a figure of some fun among intellectuals and, during the forties and fifties, a nearly inconsequential historical curio. What rational man could *really* believe such things?

No one, perhaps. But Wells's unflagging optimism—maintained with such energy, such grim force of will against his natural tendency to despair—seems less and less an accident of early-modern misdirected thought, and more and more a remarkably courageous, prescient anticipation (to use one of his favorite words) of the *fully* modern state of mind. For we now know that, if we do not *will* ourselves into civilization, we are surely doomed.

The particular shape of that doom—what a capitalist economy might expect if allowed to function uncontrolled and unexamined—is the subject of one of Wells's most curious novels, published in 1909, the year after *The War in the Air*. *Tono-Bungay* is not, strictly speaking, a scientific romance. By common critical consent, it is close to being Wells's best narrative performance, the semiautobiographical story of young George Ponderevo. The son of the housekeeper at the country estate of Bladesover (transparently the Uppark of Wells's youth), George tells how he tries to make his way in life, first as a baker's apprentice, then as an assistant to his uncle, and finally as an engineer experimenting with the possibilities of flying machines. In the course of his adventures George makes a bad marriage, separates from his wife, and finally enjoys a brief, liberated (and, by now, predictably Wellsian) love affair with the heiress of Bladesover, whom he has worshipped from childhood.

But *Tono-Bungay* is also the story of Edward Ponderevo, George's uncle, a sublimely amoral schemer and conman whose triumph is the invention of "Tono-Bungay," a worthless patent medicine that, for a while, makes him and his nephew very wealthy. So that, in a particularly interesting sense, *Tono-Bungay* is a science-fiction novel: and the "science" upon which it builds its baroque story is that most distinctively modern, and dangerously irresponsible, of sciences, advertising and marketing. Young George, to be sure, has moral qualms about the dispensing of Tono-Bungay, a cure-all that cures, in fact, nothing. But he is swept up in the enthusiasm and the wild profits of the enterprise. As he observes of the marketing of Tono-Bungay, it is really the marketing, to an undereducated and culturally disenfranchised populace, of that perishable commodity, hope:

> You perceive now, however, the nature of the services for which this fantastic community gave him [Edward] unmanageable wealth and power and real respect. It was all a monstrous payment for courageous fiction, a gratuity in return for the one reality of human life—illusion. We gave them a

feeling of hope and profit; we sent a tidal wave of water and confidence into their stranded affairs. "We mint Faith, George," said my uncle one day. "That's what we do. And by Jove we got to keep minting! We been making human con-fidence ever since I drove the first cork of Tono-Bungay."

In a world where moral perceptions have failed to keep pace with technological progress, it is inevitable that material goods, even the most worthless material goods, become a kind of debased sacrament, a shabby substitute for the human val-ues they have driven out. "We mint Faith," cries Edward, that genial monster of the power of advertising. And, tawdry as the whole enterprise is, it is the profits from Tono-Bungay that make possible George's first experiments with flying ma-chines—always, in Wells, an image of society's possibilities of self-transcendence.

For all its comic energy, *Tono-Bungay* is a very dark vision of the moral ambiguities of capitalist culture. Edward's decep-tion is unmasked and he dies a broken man; George's lover breaks off their affair to marry into her own class; and George is left, after the collapse of so many great expectations, with only a cosmic melancholy about the transience of all things human, and with his dedication to science and truth, to an al-most nameless ideal of intelligence, as the one thing that can hope to dignify life:

> Other men serve it, I know, in art, in literature, in social in-vention, and see it in a thousand different figures, under a hundred names. I see it always as austerity, as beauty. This thing we make clear is the heart of life. It is the one enduring thing. Men and nations, epochs and civilisations pass, each making its contribution. I do not know what it is, this some-thing, except that it is supreme.

These are grim, romantic, and, in their way, unsatisfying reflections with which to conclude a rich and intricate novel. They may even remind us of the Time Traveller's gloomy view of human progress; for what George comes to believe "is supreme" is austere, indeed, a standard of pure intelligence and abstract intellectual beauty that seems more a refuge from the chaos of history than a way of controlling or shaping that chaos. Beatrice Webb, who disapproved of Wells's tendencies to pessimism as detrimental to the cause of socialism, wrote in her diary that she found *Tono-Bungay* "a veritable carica-ture—and a bitter one . . . conveying an absurd impression of meaningless chaos." Concerned over Wells's apparent turn toward satire, she reflected, "It will be sad if he turns com-pletely sour."

He did not, of course, "turn completely sour." But *The War in the Air* and *Tono-Bungay* (both of which Beatrice Webb thought "amazingly clever") are necessary exercises in sourness, confrontations with the perils of history on both the international and the economic levels, and preparations for the next phase of Wells's writing career. Beatrice Webb could not, perhaps, understand how a mind and imagination like Wells's could function most insistently, optimistically, only after having explored fully the hopelessness of human affairs. But that is simply to restate why Wells was doomed, from the beginning, not to make a good Fabian: he was, and remained not a planner but a visionary.

Wells's next important work of social prophecy was to be unlike anything he had tried before. After the transitional books we have discussed, it was the first, and in many ways the definitive utopia of the "new" Wells, the Wells who was such an important and hotly debated presence in the intellec-tual life of the twenties and thirties.

Its full title indicates its novelty as well as its splendid ar-rogance: *The World Set Free: A Story of Mankind.* And it is startlingly ironic that it should appear in 1914, only a few months before the outbreak of the First World War, the night-mare that had brooded in the background of Wells's own imagination from the beginning. As the nightmare finally came to pass, Wells was turning to mythologies, fictions, vi-sionary programs for survival, ways of imagining the War as the prelude to civilization rather than its end.

The most memorable thing about *The World Set Free* is, of course, its prediction of the development of atomic power and the invention of the atomic bomb. Wells imagines this discov-ery occurring sometime in the thirties of the twentieth century (as, in fact, it did), and further imagines that atomic warfare will be the chief characteristic of the global war that—in good apocalyptic fashion—reduces humankind to a state of near savagery and forces men to reorganize the government of the world on a truly rational basis. Here again, as in his vision of the importance of aircraft in *The War in the Air,* he seems to have anticipated, not the First World War that was even then upon him and his countrymen but the Second.

More finally impressive than the "invention" of atomic weapons is the way in which *The World Set Free* maps out not only the only rational future development for mankind, but the only rational explanation, in terms of the good of society, of all mankind's past. After the global conflagration of the war, the nations of the Earth band together to form a new co-operative worldwide administration of life based upon the principles of common sense. And of this momentous event, the narrator writes:

> Sooner or later this choice [to create a world government or perish] would have confronted mankind. The sudden development of atomic science did but precipitate and render rapid and dramatic a clash between the new and the customary that had been gathering since the first flint was chipped or the first fire built together. From the day when man contrived himself a tool and suffered another male to draw near him, he ceased to be altogether a thing of instinct and untroubled convictions. From that day forth a widening breach can be traced between his egotistical passions and the social need.

The "widening breach" Wells here traces to the very inception of the use of tools is, of course, the gap between moral perceptions and technological progress which has, by now, become his overriding concern. And the formation of the world state, under the direction of a council of engineers and intellectuals who are, in effect, the world brain, is now seen as the indispensable shield against extinction, which all history has made necessary.

Indeed, "the world set free" is very largely the hero as well as the subject of the story. We have traced, with some attention, Wells's alternation between first- and third-person narrative, and noted the way in which this variation affects the overall tone of his stories. But *The World Set Free* cannot even be called, in the ordinary sense of the term, third-person or "omniscient" narrative. For its scope is not the experience of a single man, or even of a group of men, but the experience of the human race itself. Individual characters, some of them very important and even relatively "realistically" imagined, appear in the course of its tale. But these individuals finally do not matter except as the accidental agents of a course of development that is nothing less than cosmic. Before the outbreak of the great war, for example, Wells describes the journal of an intellectual, sensitive man, Barnet, who witnesses the worldwide economic depression that precedes the conflict and much of its bloodshed. Wandering among the out-of-work laborers of London, Barnet has a vision in which he *understands* where life is tending after all:

> I saw life plain. . . . I saw that we have still to discover government, that we have still to discover education, which is the necessary reciprocal of government, and that all this—in which my own little speck of a life was so manifestly overwhelmed—this and its yesterday in Greece and Rome and Egypt were nothing, the mere first dust swirls of the beginning, the movements and dim murmurings of a sleeper who will presently be awake. . . .

The image of the "sleeper who will presently be awake," of course, reminds us of Wells's earlier experiments in utopian fiction. But the important thing to notice here is not just the echo of another book, but rather the way in which, now, all the intelligent human beings on the planet seem aware of the great changes to come, and of the absolute necessity of those changes if the race itself is to survive. *The World Set Free* is written from the vantage point of a history text composed well after the advent of the war, the formation of the world state, and the consequent transformation of human life. It is, in other words, as impersonal a narrative as could be imagined: a historical survey *after* the great change has occurred in human affairs.

Issac Asimov, somewhere in his voluminous writing, defines science fiction as fiction whose hero is not an individual but the human race itself. It is a flattering definition of the genre, if not an entirely accurate one. But the work of Wells, at least after the publication of *The World Set Free*, satisfies that definition better than any other writer in the field (Asimov included). Far more energetically than in any of his previous books, Wells seeks here to insist upon a program that is not only possible but necessary, and to argue for its feasibility in the broadest terms imaginable.

Man, for Wells, is the tool-using animal—which is to say, the animal whose consciousness (and *self*-consciousness) both sets him apart from the unconscious circumambient universe and perhaps gives him a chance of surviving that universe's blind mechanism. What is novel for Wells by this time, and what becomes a permanent habit of narrative for him at his most visionary, is the insistence upon making this elementary and challenging fact the main point of his assertion. The "little fellows" of the earlier novels, the baffled ordinary men and the crazed scientists, the panic-stricken villagers and even the middle-class intellectuals and writers on philosophical subjects—all these characters matter less and less in the universal geological history against which Wells now poses the human drama.

This new narrative vantage point—a vantage point from the perspective of infinity—is made clear in the very first chapter of The World Set Free. For the book opens with the discovery of the very first human technology, storytelling:

> Man began to think. . . . And that first glimmering of speculation, that first story of achievement, that story-teller, bright-eyed and flushed under his matted hair, gesticulating to his gaping, incredulous listener, gripping his wrist to keep him attentive, was the most marvellous beginning this world has ever seen. It doomed the mammoths, and it began the setting of that snare that shall catch the sun.

"The setting of that snare that *shall* catch the sun": the narrator is unabashed in his confidence that the human enterprise, once fairly launched, must eventually succeed in the triumph of mind and imagination over matter. And the essential power behind the process is the power of mythmaking, the ability of humans to imagine for themselves a triumph, a victory which they do not yet have—and their consequent passion to make that imagined victory come true. Here, in the opening pages of his first real tract of social programming, Wells makes plainer than ever before or since the ideal relationship between the storyteller's art and the social scientist's

public duty. They are not, finally, in opposition to one another, but are rather successive moments in a single, and culturally crucial, process, the process of man's self-definition
and self-organization against chaos.

The meeting point of mythmaking or storytelling and social planning, then, is history: or is, at least, the understanding of history and its direction. Wells did not share
Marx's faith that history would, eventually, produce an ideal
society; nor did he share the faith of the Webbs that intelligent
and cultured people could, by the exercise of their intelligence and culture, direct history into the channels where
it belonged. He was too much a practical man to be a communist, and too much a visionary to be a member of the Fabian
Society. He did, though, believe in history, in his special way.
He believed in it as a road map into territory only partially
explored: a guide, but an uncertain one, whose directions and
lines have to be traced and sometimes filled out by the canny
observer. The brute force of historical process, the sheer iner-
tia of the past, may be driving us toward an unhappy meeting
with necessity; the workings of time and evolutionary biology
may be beyond our ken, and well beyond our control. But that
is not what Wells believed. Increasingly, during the years of
the First World War and afterward, he insisted that history
was not only comprehensible but malleable: and that men, if
only they could be made intelligent, might also be made powerful.

This is, surely, one of the reasons that Wells, at the end of
the First World War, took on the task of writing *The Outline
of History*: a job of writing that, for pure foolhardiness,
heartbreaking difficulty, and brilliance of execution, can only
be compared to Samuel Johnson's *Dictionary* at the end of the
eighteenth century. The *Outline*, published in 1920, is radically flawed, biased in its versions of crucial events, sometimes unreliable as an interpretative source. It is also one of
the stunning accomplishments of the twentieth century: a sus-
tained and wholly consistent act of imagination and intelligence, an attempt to grasp all of human history as a process
with a definite upward direction that, if only it can be
grasped, understood, and abetted, can yet save the race from
suicide. We have already remarked that the metaphysics of

history, the belief in historical process as concealing and progressively revealing a universal meaning, is one of the salient characteristics of nineteenth-century thought. And the complexities of Hegel and Marx as well as the simpler-minded optimism of the Victorian ideal of progress are all in the background of the *Outline*. But only in the background. Wells is too much a biologist, too much a skeptic—perhaps too much an Englishman—to trust abstract theories of historical change over the often unruly, contradictory plethora of facts. And he is too much a twentieth-century mind to trust in the optimistic view of history *except* as a tendency that can be nurtured, but can also be disastrously thwarted by human blindness and obstinacy.

In many ways the general argument of the *Outline* is the capstone of Wells's utopian theory, for he locates in the actual past arguments about human fate and human striving that are familiar, by now, from his visions of the future. Man is the unnatural animal: his duty, both to history and to his own intelligence, is to resist the inevitable entropy of natural selection, to create, as a kind of cosmic imperialist, an environment in which he can survive. The overall tendency of human history, as he describes it, is first a wide, wild, and often violent dispersion of cultures, beliefs, languages, tribes, and nations; a dispersion that for all its waste and carnage is nevertheless creative, the bloody struggle of intelligence out of the mire of superstition into the full light of reason. But that is only the diastole of history. Its systole, which, he argues passionately, is the phase of contemporary man, is the coming together of those disparate cultures, those antiphonal pieces of wisdom, into a unified, worldwide human culture. And the First World War may, indeed, have been the necessary if tragic disaster to shake the world awake to a sense of its desperate need for unification. This, of course, was uttered from the vantage point of 1920. But even in 1933, when belief in "the war that will end war" was only a sad memory, Wells would assert the same general tendency of history, the same desperate need for unification, in the opening chapter of his great history of the future, *The Shape of Things To Come*.

Throughout his "Plain History of Life and Mankind," furthermore, he locates essential tensions, epoch-making conflicts, which are familiar as the creative conflicts at the heart of his mythmaking almost from the beginning. He describes how as man is just in the process of becoming civilized, even before the founding of the first great city-states, a crucial dichotomy in types of cultures emerges: the dichotomy between the nomadic folk and the settled folk. The nomads are free-ranging, adventurous explorers of new places, herdsmen and hunters, while the settled folk are pacific farmers and builders, who are content with a single locale. In fact, this is largely the distinction between Paleolithic man and Neolithic man, and it is anthropologically rather more complicated than Wells makes it seem. He poses the two groups as opposites and insists that *in their very opposition* they form a larger unity: "It was inevitable that nomad folk and the settled folk should clash, that the nomads should seem hard barbarians to the settled peoples, and the settled peoples soft and effeminate and very good plunder to the nomad peoples."

They are, very simply, the Morlocks and Eloi of *The Time Machine*, located now not in an impossible future but in a remote past. And their opposition and complementarity are those of the "two voices" we have been tracing through Wells's fiction since *The Time Machine*. The sometimes disruptive, even "barbarian" energy of the nomad peoples is the necessary energy of a species that must remain alive (like the giants in *The Food of the Gods*). But the passivity, the concern for the common life of the settled folk is also necessary to the business of civilization, for it is they who build cities, and who at their best can make life not only bearable but pleasant (like the enlightened souls after the Change in *In the Days of the Comet*). Some hundred pages later in the *Outline*, as he describes the formation of royal and priestly castes at the time of the first city-states, Wells makes this fundamental tension even clearer. The conflict between priest and king, which is largely the conflict he will trace through the entire history of human struggle, is, he says, the conflict "between the made man and the born man, between learning and originality, between established knowledge and settled usage . . . and creative will and imagination. . . ." There is, of course, no doubt on which side of this ancient conflict Wells imagines himself to belong. But he also understands that, at best, the conflict is a creative one: not a war but that opposition which, as Blake said, is true friendship.

The shape Wells sees in history, that is, is inevitably the shape of his own mind, of his best hopes for the future of the race. His adversaries and critics, including vitriolic Catholic apologist Hilaire Belloc, were quick to observe this as soon as the book appeared. But, in a very important way, the *performance* which is *The Outline of History* is almost as much the "point" as are the details of the history it describes. *Of course* it is an individual, even an idiosyncratic act of imagination. But it is also the act of an imagination whose very idiosyncrasy is to insist upon itself as *commonplace*, as "a very ordinary brain"—and to insist that such personal vision, for the sake of the common good, is precisely the act of intelligence that can save mankind and redeem history. It has often been observed that Wells began his intellectual career as a teacher and that, with the *Outline* and the books that followed, he returned to that first profession as passionately as anyone could. But, like a great teacher, much of his lesson was in the example of his intelligence rather than its precise teachings. This is a way, and a useful humane way, to think about history, says the *Outline*: a way that orders not only the external history that produced you and that continues to affect your life, but also the internal history, the conflicts and contributions of your mind that you share with every other individual of the race. And, in an important passage we have already cited in Chapter One, he is splendidly clear about the correspondence between the individual mind and the cosmic shape of things, a correspondence the book exists not only to demonstrate but to create:

> The history of our race and personal religious experience run so closely parallel as to seem to a modern observer almost the same thing; both tell of a being at first scattered and blind and utterly confused, feeling its way slowly to the serenity and salvation of an ordered and coherent purpose. That, in the simplest, is the outline of history; whether one have a religious purpose or disavow a religious purpose altogether, the lines of the outline remain the same.

Wells had been a very successful, very influential writer for twenty years. With the *Outline*, he became a phenomenon.

The book was widely attacked for its partisanship, and even more widely praised for its scope, power, and eloquence: and both responses were the very best publicity. Wells's longtime friend, novelist Arnold Bennett, was one of many who was stunned. "It's a life work," he wrote to Jane Wells: and H. G. had written it in a little more than one year. Its eventual sales in England and America ran to well over two million copies, and it was translated into most major foreign languages. And in 1922 Wells published *A Short History of the World,* an abridgment of the original thousand-page *Outline* that sold, if anything, better.

The numbers, though, are only an indication of the book's success. It had been deliberately aimed at a wide readership—an intelligent, serious readership, to be sure, but an audience much broader than the normal group of intellectuals and academic specialists who might read such a book—and it fulfilled that aim brilliantly. If Wells had always been partly a frustrated teacher, partly a lay preacher, partly a prophet in search of listeners to whom to prophesy, with this book he satisfied those vocations (or that vocation) more fully than any writer has a right to hope. Throughout the twenties and thirties, the *Outline* was an important, almost an inevitable, piece of the intellectual furniture of any moderately well-trained English or American mind. Young men and women, future intellectuals and political theorists raised during those years would very likely have found it on their home bookshelves, and would have read, and at least subliminally remembered, parts of it. No study has yet been made of the probable or possible effect of this enormously popular book on the political thought and aspirations of the generations of the forties, fifties, and sixties, who would have been "raised" on the *Outline.* Such a study would be difficult, and necessarily tentative. But it is, nevertheless, probably the case that much of the liberal thought of the post-World War II years is in a tenuous—but serious—way traceable to the passionate rationalism and ardent internationalism of Wells's work.

And now, in fact, the role of social prophet *did* supervene over that of novelist, and particularly that of scientific romancer. The titles of Wells's major books of the twenties and early thirties indicate how deeply he had committed himself to discovering the shape of his vision in contemporary history: *The Salvaging of Civilization* (1921), *Washington and the Hope of Peace* (1922), *Democracy under Revision* (1927), *The Open Conspiracy: Blue Prints for a World Revolution* (1928), and—one of the most classically Wellsian of titles— *What Are We To Do with Our Lives?* (1931). He also published two volumes as massive and ambitious as the *Outline,* and intended to complete the arguments of that work in the spheres, respectively, of biology and technology: *The Science of Life* in 1930, and *The Work, Wealth and Happiness of Mankind* in 1932. The only scientific romance of these years—and the one he thought of as his last exercise in the form—was *Men Like Gods,* which appeared in 1923. And *Men Like Gods* is itself representative of the new politically engaged tone of Wells's writing.

Superficially, the book seems a version of *A Modern Utopia.* A group of characters from our world, through the sheerest magic, find themselves transported to an alternate Earth, one where men have solved the problem of self-control and intelligent world planning and have created a paradise that puts our chaos and confusion to shame. But in *A Modern Utopia* the travelers to this better world were simply the author and his companion (and double), the repressed, skeptical botanist. In *Men Like Gods* the earthlings who make the journey are a much broader, and deliberately more topically satirical, sampling of contemporary types. There is a movie magnate, his latest starlet, and a fine lady; and there are other characters who are quite broad caricatures of some of the day's most prominent political and intellectual figures. The judicious, apparently open-minded but actually indecisive liberal, Mr. Burleigh, is obviously meant to be Arthur Balfour; the bully imperialist, blustering Mr. Catskill, is the young Winston Churchill; the theology-obsessed, morally strident Father Amerton is probably Wells's none too kind version of his good friend G. K. Chesterton. And in the midst of these refugees from Earth is Mr. Barnstaple, a writer on political matters who has left his home for a vacation, weary with the stupidity and silliness of the contemporary scene, and finds himself, quite amazingly, in the utopia of his best dreams.

This mixed crew finds itself transported from a familiar

English countryside to the utopian counter-Earth through the experiments of two of the utopians who have been investigating the possibilities of travel across the dimensions. Surrounded by the kindly, telepathic, beautiful, and scantily clad utopians, they are at first dazzled and then rebellious at their fate. They learn that utopia, like Earth, had long ago passed through an "Age of Confusion"—a version of the twentieth century's special political and intellectual agony—and had experienced a disastrous, apocalyptic war that threatened to return civilization to a stone-age primitiveness. But the utopians survived this crisis and in their wisdom formed a world state, governed according to rational and generous principles, which is, of course, precisely the world state whose outlines Wells was drawing so devotedly in his historical and political writing.

But the Earthlings very soon have to be quarantined, for among the triumphs of utopia has been the elimination of harmful bacteria from their world; and the unwilling travelers carry within them diseases against which the citizens of paradise have no defenses.

The situation is a brilliant inversion of one of the most important metaphors of Wells's earlier work. In The War of the Worlds the alien, dehumanized future represented by the Martian invasion is defeated, finally, by the bacteria of the present Earth, the microbes which are our link to the elementary ecology of the planet as a living, vital, and indestructible whole. But here it is a ragtag army of present-day versions of ourselves who invade a future which is, not dehumanized, but superhuman. In the earlier novel, the presence of bacteria is a resonant symbol for the innate goodness of the Earth, the permanence of nature, and the hope of mankind as unity with the living world. But in Men Like Gods the basic meaning of the symbol has changed. The bacteria, the infection carried by the Earthlings is the disease (or the dis-ease) of our present confusion, our present acquisitiveness, violence, and hypocrisy in high places. It is precisely the "natural" to the degree that the "natural" is what damns mankind to a perpetual repetition of the blind and murderous processes of natural selection. As the narrator observes of these refugees from the present:

If making them obnoxious was being on their side then certainly Nature was on their side. By the evening of the second day after their arrival nearly everybody who had been in contact with the Earthlings . . . was in a fever with cough, sore throat, aching bones, headache and such physical depression and misery as Utopia had not known for twenty centuries. The first inhabitant of Utopia to die was that leopard which had sniffed at Mr. Rupert Catskill on his first arrival.

The detail of the leopard is important. The animal is one of the first sights that greets the Earthlings after they have arrived in utopia, a wild beast chastened to civilized behavior by the sheer force of the utopian reorganization of the planet. It is Dr. Moreau's experiment done *right* this time; but it is also an assertion that in the perfect world nature will survive, though chastened and controlled by intelligence.

The bacteria-laden Earthlings attempt a revolution or, better yet, a gangster-style takeover of the enlightened community into which they have been thrust. As their leader Catskill insists, their disease is their strength; they can threaten to pollute the entire perfect planet on which they find themselves—can use their own ugliness and uncleanness as a weapon against the inhabitants of an ideal world. The present may be shamed by the future into which it could evolve; but as a revenge against that impossible future, it may threaten infection.

Mr. Barnstaple of course rebels against this petty, reactionary rebellion. Entranced with the prospects offered by the utopian society, he deserts his Earthling compatriots—and thereby escapes the easy, almost offhanded way the utopians deal with the "threat" of the Earthling infection. Much of the rest of the novel Mr. Barnstaple spends being tutored by a fetching young utopian girl (Wells was still Wells) in the history, theory, and economic and social practice of the planet to which he has given his loyalty.

This instruction forms the body of the book and is also the least interesting part of the story, not because of the boredom inherent in its ideas, for the ideas themselves are both cogent and very advanced for 1923, but simply because they are the ideas—of a world brain, a rational dictatorship of the common people, a sexual and moral ethic based on principles of common sense—that Wells had articulated, and continued to articulate, throughout the decade in which the book appeared. They are ideas that have not yet been put into practice in any civilized country. And they are ideas that have been discussed since long before Wells and continue as some of the essential fulcrum points of contemporary debates about the nature and ends of politics.

When Barnstaple is returned, grudgingly, to the world from which he came, our earth, he carries back—in true Wellsian fashion—a sense of the littleness of contemporary human concerns, but also—in equally Wellsian fashion—a sense of their importance for the larger considerations of human fate, of species survival, which no one else in this world (according to Wells, at least) is willing to confront. "This world is really very childish," he observes to his wife on his return from his vacation, perusing a copy of the London *Times:*

> "Very. I had forgotten. Imaginary Bolshevik plots. Sinn Fein proclamations. The Prince. Poland. Obvious lies about the Chinese. Obvious lies about Egypt. People pulling Wickham Steed's leg. Sham-pious article about Trinity-Sunday. The Hitchin murder. . . . How silly it is—all of it! It's like coming back to the quarrels of servants and the chatter of children."

"Childish," of course, is an adjective that was often applied to Wells—and at no time in his career more frequently than during the twenties and thirties, the time of his maximum influence upon contemporary events and of his maximum production as a political/economic/social thinker and writer. And "childish" is an adjective he himself was fond of assigning to his critics. Indeed, in intellectual debate where maturity, reason, wit and self-consciousness are among the most highly valued of virtues, "childish" is in its way one of the terminal insults to be delivered against an adversary's program. But with Wells, the charge and the word itself take on a weight, a significance, that they sometimes lack in reference to other writers of his generation. Wells was childish, and remained childish to the end of his career, if by that word we mean, "vulnerable and open to the selfish, egocentric, irrational urgings of passion." But what makes his political and social thought, even at its most ponderous and doctrinaire, perennially fresh and humanizing, is that he *faced* that biological heritage, and thought of the business of politics not as the extirpation of childishness from human affairs (an impossible task), but as the integration of its disruptive promptings into a civilization which would be stronger, more finally mature, for that self-confrontation.

Short of changing man into something simultaneously more and less than human, there was no way Wells could see to eliminate the awesome, awful selfishness we carry with us from the cradle and, beyond that, from the savannas where our hunter-gatherer ancestors first banded together for the sake of a bigger kill. We are not bees, nor should we try for the perfect society of the hive. Wells was not willing to have man changed into something else for the sake of a perfectly balanced world. So he remained squarely in the line of classic liberal thought: a believer that man is more important than his institutions, even though those institutions largely form him, and that the optimal human institutions are those that make the most room for the elementary uncertainty of human needs—which is to say, make the most room for their own transformation. The dichotomy, first named in *The Outline of History* as the conflict between the nomad folk and the settled folk, remained profoundly descriptive of his own mind. We may mistrust or even smile at Wells when he is giving free rein to the "settled folk" side of himself, the urban planner, the builder of systems, the mapper-out of real programs for action. But we cannot smile at the imagination, the "nomadic" passion with which he continued to insist that the systems were *for man*, for the sake of the individual and the individual's peace with himself, and were to be abandoned the moment they began to impede rather than nurture that freedom.

This paradox, as we have been saying all along, is implicit in Wells's fiction from the beginning. But it is important to take note of it again, as a preface to the reading of Wells's last major prophecy, a book that for all its flaws is one of his most fascinating, most characteristic, and most stunning performances: *The Shape of Things To Come*, published in 1933.

Wells seems to have thought of *The Shape of Things To Come: The Ultimate Revolution* as a summary work. It was the first utopian novel he had written since *Men Like Gods*, ten years before, and after he completed it he began his autobiography.

And in this long, complex, valedictory projection of man's future, the essentially liberal tension between the order of the state and the freedom of individual passions remains strong. Near the end of this history of the future, the narrator surveys the history of society's liberation from the old social taboos, and acknowledges that the ideal world state (or the Modern State, as it is called) does not avoid but simply renders harmless and more free the exercise of desire:

> We cannot detail in this general review of history the reluctant lifting of one prohibition after another. We may now go naked, love as we like, eat, drink and amuse ourselves with our work or as we will, subject only to a proper respect for unformed minds. And no harm has been done at all. . . . Properly nourished people do not take to gluttony, properly interested people are not overwhelmed by sex. Instead of a tiger appeared a harmless, quiet, unobtrusive and not unpleasing pussy-cat, which declined to be in any way notable.

The "proper respect for unformed minds" that is the only sanction needed to preserve the decency of this ideal culture reminds us of the "proper respect for the opinions of mankind" invoked in the first paragraph of one of the classics of liberal thought, the American Declaration of Independence. The surprising thing is not to find Wells, in a vision of twenty-second-century society, alluding to Thomas Jefferson. The surprising thing is that anyone familiar with Wells should be surprised

The Shape of Things To Come, in fact, is a projection into the future of exactly those tensions Wells had, for the last decade, been locating in the shape of things as they were. But by 1933 it was obvious, as it had not been in 1920, that the First World War was not the final, apocalyptic battle which would finally shake Europe and, after Europe, the rest of the world awake to a sense of its responsibility before the tribunal of history. The worldwide economic collapse of the late twenties, the headlong development of larger and even more terrible machines of war than had been imagined in 1920, and above all the rise of fascism as a particularly virulent, particularly stupid form of the nationalism that had caused the tragedy of 1914–18: all these and other details indicated clearly that the world was in for another, and worse, bout with the powers of its own darkness. Wells had spent a decade arguing that something might, must, be made of the world after the First World War. And now, faced with the all but certainty of a second world war, he turned once again to fiction, to visionary prediction, to the art with which he had begun his career, to argue strenuously that something *had* to be made of the world as it was likely to become. *The Shape of Things To Come*, in other words, is an assertion of Wellsian liberal optimism on the basis of a very dark—and, as things turned out, accurate— pessimism about current trends. It is, as its title itself indicates, a version, a completion, a fictional twin of *The Outline of History*.

As in *The World Set Free,* the real "hero" of *The Shape of Things to Come* is not any single individual—although important and distinctive indivduals appear in the course of its tale—but rather is the human race. The story, beginning with the "Age of Frustration" immediately preceeding the First World War, tells how that war should have but failed to eliminate the poisonous elements of nationalism and greed from world affairs, and how, during the thirties, the world coasted toward a second and even more catastrophic conflict. Nearly a third of the book, that is, is not a "history of the future," but a history of recent, "real" events as seen from the vantage point of the future. It is a technique Wells had never before employed as fully or as energetically, and it allows him, with a minimum of journalistic argument, to impose his own vision upon the events of his world.

Once the Second War breaks out, however, the narrative becomes purely visionary—and, in some passages, almost Biblical in its apocalyptic urgency. The war to come is awful beyond all man's imagining, and over its protracted decades it reduces the human race—in by now familiar fashion—almost to the point of aboriginal savagery. But a saving remnant of engineers and airmen survives the general downward trend, keeping alive the twin lights of science and moral responsibility. In the years following the exhaustion of the war powers, they gradually—rather like the Samurai of *A Modern Utopia*—consolidate their control over world affairs. By controlling the power of flight they effectively control the means of world food supply and world communications. And they use this to establish the first truly rational society, the first organization of human beings designed to protect its members not only from the external threats of want and hunger, but from the internal threats of the human spirit itself.

The society they establish is a Puritan one, dedicated to self-denial, self-transcendence for the service of the state, the all but abolition of the individual in the name of the good of the social whole. This is an unpleasant aspect of the future for the modern reader, and even for the future historians who record it. But, argues the novel, it is a necessary stage in the formation of a truly organized sensibility, or a truly organized state:

> It needed the heroic "priggishness" of the Air Dictatorship, putting away the old literature and drama for a time, suppressing the suggestion systems of the old religions and superstitions, jailing and segregating men and women for "hate incitement," ruthlessly eliminating sexual incitation from the lives of the immature and insisting upon a universal frank sexual hygiene, to cleanse the human mind for good and all, to inaugurate the unconstrained civilisation of to-day. There was no other way to renaissance.

And "renaissance," the full exercise of unconstrained freedom following upon the lesson of restraint, is what history, in this lyrical prophecy, has to tend toward. After the Air Dictatorship and the Puritan Tyranny, the world is made safe for artists and lovers, and they return in force—but chastened, civilized, capable of integrating their privacy with a due consideration of the good of the whole. Science thrives along with the arts precisely because men have begun to understand that both fields are versions of the same, fundamental, eternally questing human impulse. Means of inducing genetic mutation are discovered, and new beasts and flowers are bred that fulfill man's destiny to rule the planet more efficiently than their "natural" ancestors. And the history of the future concludes with a rhapsody on the future *yet to be* of mankind that is deliberately, unmistakably, and shamelessly religious in its language.

Man has achieved much, but much remains to be achieved, perhaps even the transformation of the disparate members of the race into a single, quasi-divine being and will: "We in our time are still rising towards the crest of that transition. And when that crest is attained what grandeur of life may not open out to Man! Eye hath not seen, nor ear heard; nor hath it entered into the mind of man to conceive. . . . For now we see as in a glass darkly."

If it is no surprise to find Wells alluding to Thomas Jefferson in his description of the ideal future state, it is even less a surprise to find him quoting Saint Paul in his vision of what might lie beyond that ideal society. This passage is not quite the end of the text of *The Shape of Things To Come*, but it is the end of the "future history" of that book, and therefore, in its way, the end of Wells's major career as a utopian writer. And it is absolutely appropriate that, at this moment, he should give full expression to the ecstatic, mystical expectation which had always been so central to his measured hope for the future.

To read *The Shape of Things to Come* only in terms of its specific predictions, though, is to miss much of the point of the book. For it is also one of Wells's subtlest, most self-conscious performances in the genre of utopian prophecy, an outline of future history that manages to be not only broad, daring, sweeping, but also diffident and remarkably restrained. The last recorded date of the future history is 2106. But the book—unlike, say, *The World Set Free*, which pretends to be a history of the world being read at some undetermined date in our future—claims to be nothing more than a book published by H. G. Wells in the year 1933. And the narrative ploy through which Wells achieves this double "reality" for his book is one of his most clever inventions.

The history of the world to come, as the first chapter of the book announces, is actually "The Dream Book of Dr. Philip Raven." Philip Raven, the dreamer whose vision is the main text of the novel, is an official of the League of Nations, an elegant, intellectual, eccentric man who—as the first chapter tells us—befriends H. G. Wells, the "editor" of his dreams because

Wells is almost the anti-type of his own personality. On one of their first meetings, Raven describes Wells to himself. And the description is, perhaps, the best self-analysis Wells ever wrote:

> "You [says Raven to Wells] have defects that are almost gifts: a rapid but inexact memory for particulars, a quick grasp of proportions, and no patience with detail. You hurry on to wholes. You have to see things simply or you could not see them at all. Consequently you cannot endure any conventional elaborations, any side-shows. . . . It isn't, I think, that you have the power to take up all those things in your stride; I won't flatter you like that: no—but you have the intuitive sense to drop them in your stride. There's the secret of your simplicity; you come as near to stupidity as wisdom can."

It is not difficult to imagine, reading a passage like this one, that Wells was already thinking about his autobiography, the "discoveries of a very ordinary brain." It is a remarkably apt bit of self-portraiture, or self-caricature.

But it is because of the figure of Raven that Wells, in this novel, casts himself in this Watson-like pose of canny innocence. For, as Raven confides to his new friend, he has for some time been dreaming: dreaming of a book, a history of the world written in the twenty-second century, a book whose salient passages he remembers when he awakens, and writes down. Raven and Wells discuss the possibilities in some of his early stories—and when Raven suddenly dies, Wells takes it on himself to edit and publish the dream book, occasionally supplying comments or transitional paragraphs of his own where the manuscript is lacking.

It is a clever device, one that is maintained throughout the course of *The Shape of Things To Come*. For the book itself, the future history of the world written from the vantage point of a perfected society, is at times cold, unjust, or simply unfeelingly abstract in its presentation of some of the events. But Wells, as feeling man as well as thinking man, can at these junctures in the narrative interpose his own sympathies. One of the most melodramatic episodes in the story, for example, involves the airman Essenden, a noble intellect and the man who drafts the proclamation founding the Modern State. Essenden allows himself to desert his high public purpose for the love of a woman, Elizabeth Hortly, sacrificing his career and his influence over history for the sake of a private passion. The official history of the Modern State, naturally, judges him harshly for this abdication. But, of course, the tale of Essenden is in a touching way also the tale of H. G. Wells and his many, often disastrous, romances. And he is led to reflect on the "historian's callous and dispassionate narrative of the Essenden/Hortly affair, as only a blockage to World Order":

> Something in me rebels against that, just as it rebels against the assumption that the World War was a process of sheer waste, its heroisms and sacrifices blind blunderings, and its significance out of all proportion less than the social and economic dislocations that caused it.

The "something" that rebels is precisely Wells's instinct as a novelist rather than as a social planner. And the great accomplishment of *The Shape of Things To Come* is that, fully and for the last time, it allows him to give complete voice, complex play, to both those instincts.

But if the book is simultaneously an ecstatic vision of the possibilities of the future, a dire warning about its dangers, and a controlled self-conscious exercise in a narrative form Wells had employed for more than thirty years, it is also a document, paradoxically, of restraint. We have already observed that Wells was unwilling to argue that man's only hope lay in transforming himself into something *other* than man. And in this way, *The Shape of Things To Come* can almost be read as a deliberate critique of, and counterstatement to, one of the most important political and literary works of science fiction in the thirties, Olaf Stapledon's *Last and First Men*, published three years before *The Shape of Things To Come*, in 1930.

Stapledon was a disciple, an admirer, in some ways an idolater of Wells and Wells's proposals for the salvation of mankind. He was also a first-rate complex mind and a writer of great power, one of the unquestioned geniuses of science fiction. But in *Last and First Men*, Stapledon's first book, he goes beyond even his master's farthest imagination of the ultimate fate of the race. Mankind, in Stapledon's book, which carries history millions of years into the future, undergoes fully sixteen transformations into completely different *species* before it finally achieves the state of pure intellect and world-wide telepathic and spiritual unity which is our racial perfection. And while *Last and First Men* is one of the glories of the history of science fiction, executed with a power and an austerity totally unlike anything else in the field, it is finally too "Wellsian" even for Wells himself. In *The Shape of Things To Come* Wells is explicit about man's refusal to transform himself into a superspecies, explicit about the necessity of retaining the baggage of passion and raw emotional energy we bring with us from the caves. It is not exactly an "anti-Stapledon" position, though his foremost disciple was probably in Wells's mind during its writing (indeed, the dream-book device was probably partly inspired by the narrative technique of *Last and First Men*). The thirties were a decade of the wildest experimentation in political theories and the widest range of suggestions for the "final solution" to the human social dilemma, ranging from anarchism to the nightmares of fascism and the rhetoric of "racial purity." Stapledon's noble, if cold, attitude is only one of the more visionary. And in this context, Wells's book appears as, really a relatively conservative, traditional—and above all, humane—response to the apocalypse that was looming larger over Europe every year.

During 1935, Wells was to carry the warning vision of his last major prophecy into an art that had always fascinated him but for which he had never written: the film. For British producer Alexander Korda, he wrote a screenplay, *Things To Come*, which collapses the wide-ranging social and political theory of *The Shape of Things To Come* into a dramatic story that carries much of the original book's power. The major details of the book are recapitulated: the Second War breaks out and destroys civilization (with some startlingly prophetic scenes anticipating the carnage and destruction only four years off for Europe): the reign of the airmen brings order and civilization again to Earth and finally issues in an idyllic, scientifically administered world state. There are even some embellishments added to the story for the sake of dramatic interest. After the war has reached its nadir of brutality, for example, small towns revert to feudal dictatorships lorded over by absurdly self-important, blustering strongmen. The one whose career the film traces is the "Boss," an acid parody of a fascist dictator, complete with overdecorated uniform, and brilliantly played by Ralph Richardson. And, at the end of the film, mankind launches a rocket to the moon from a gigantic "space gun," against the violent protests of a reactionary crowd led by a crazed artist (Cedric Hardwicke); a broad but accurate allegory of Wells's hopes for the infinitely expansive future, and his suspicion of those whose "aesthetics" led them to undervalue the contributions of science. Directed by William Cameron Menzies, the film opened in 1936. It is a landmark in the history of science fiction in the cinema, both in intellectual content and in the dazzling achievement of its special effects, which defined the state of the art for many years to come.

Wells was pleased with his venture into film and contemplated a number of other projects to succeed it. As the twentieth century's most popular medium, with the power to reach and persuade a wider audience than the novel had ever attained, and as a medium with a natural affinity for the visionary as well as the visual, it seems the perfect vehicle for his self-appointed role. But the projects never materialized. Wells was growing old, and was ill. Furthermore, he felt—correctly—that the immense audience he had once addressed was in process of forgetting him, of turning to new pundits, newer (and in many cases less humane) analysts of the human condition. The work of his last decade is marked by a bitterness that at first seems only an appropriate gloom about the condition of the world, but that by the time of the last book he published during his lifetime, *Mind at the End of Its Tether* (1945) has grown all but unbearable.

But there was to be one more scientific romance: one of Well's least read and in its way one of his best. In 1937 he published *Star Begotten*; it is a sign of how radically history had altered that the book is dedicated to Winston Churchill, the bully imperialist whom Wells satirized in *Men Like Gods* and the statesman who was to become a national hero during the Battle of Britain. *Star Begotten* is a brief book, with nothing of the scope, the prophetic energy, or the grand ambitiousness of *Men Like Gods* or *The Shape of Things To Come*. In fact, it somewhat resembles the romances Wells wrote dur-

Wells near the end. This is one of the last photographs taken of Wells, and if it is self-consciously, melodramatically posed, it is also wonderfully expressive of his anger and his defiance of the world-suicide we seemed bent on committing during the last years of his life.

ing the 1890s and early years of this century. But it is characteristically a work of the late Wells. It is, in fact, *The War of the Worlds* rewritten from the vantage point of forty years later and with a startlingly different conclusion.

Star Begotten does not contain any of the scenes of violence or apocalypse that characterize the great novel of 1898. Its action is mainly conversation, argument, and speculation. It is about an invasion from outer space, but an invasion that takes place not with spaceships but through "Cosmic Rays," and whose effects are noticeable only to very few. Its hero, Joseph Davis, is a popular historian whose whole work has been devoted to glorifying the heroic accomplishments of great men, and who has just begun the book he considers the capstone of his career, The Pageant of Mankind. He has a wife, and a lovely, precocious son. His world is secure. And yet, as he begins his book, he finds himself obsessed with a strange idea. He learns from a scientific friend about the existence of Cosmic Rays continually bombarding Earth, and he has been thinking for some time about certain people of his acquaintance, his wife included, who seem different from ordinary humans, wiser, sharper, more observant, but also different. Slowly an awful thought begins to dawn on him. What if beings from some other world—Mars, say—were using Cosmic Rays to alter the genetic structure of babies in the womb? Suppose they were creating, at long range, a new race of beings who would be their children as well as children of Earth? It would be the perfect, the irresistible invasion. As he observes to his friends, in one of the funniest passages in Wells:

> "Mars, the planet which is being frozen out, exhausted, done for. Some of you may have read a book called The War of the Worlds—I forget who wrote it—Jules Verne, Conan Doyle, one of those fellows. But it told how the Martians invaded the world, wanted to colonize it, and exterminate mankind. Hopeless attempt! They couldn't stand the different atmospheric pressure, they couldn't stand the difference in gravitation; bacteria finished them up. Hopeless from the start. The only impossible thing in the story was to imagine that the Martians would be fools enough to try anything of the sort. But—"

But an invasion through Cosmic Rays, an invasion through our own children, would be the perfectly efficient strategy. It is one of the fine accomplishments of Star Begotten that though there is never a single shred of real evidence given for this theory, all the major characters in the book come to believe it irrefutably, and that it convinces the reader also, within the bounds of the fiction. Horrified at what he has "learned," Davis tears up his *Pageant of Mankind*, believing mankind doomed by the invasion of "Martians." He believes this until the final, wonderfully funny and wonderfully assertive chapter of the book, when he confronts his wife with the bitter knowledge that she is a Martian-tampered human being, as is their son. His wife, misunderstanding the drift of his explanation, concludes that he thinks himself to be one of the *different* people, the star-begotten. He is at first shocked that she would think so; and then shocked to discover that he probably *is:* "He too was star-born! He too was one of these invaders and strangers and innovators to our fantastic planet, who were crowding into life and making it over anew!"

The "invasion," finally, is a benevolent one. The star-born, the star-changed, are the "nomads" of Wells's outline of history, the innovators and creators whose difference, whose openness to change, is precisely the hope of the human race, the hope of making civilization anew. Like *The War of the Worlds*, *Star Begotten* is the story of a writer whose work is interrupted by an alien invasion and who survives the invasion to be reunited with his lost wife and to begin his work anew on a richer, wiser plane. But here the invasion succeeds; and the writer survives it precisely by comprehending that his fears have all been groundless. As Davis's wife says, on the last page of the book, after they have discovered the truth about themselves: "Why should one be afraid of change? All life is change. Why should we fear it?"

It is, of course, the fundamentally hopeful observation Wells had been making since *The Time Machine*. For only in resisting change do humans endanger their survival or their chances for true nobility. And the "new species" which Davis, his wife, and their compeers are becoming is not really a new species at all, but the *human* race, in process of becoming, exactly, human.

It is a graceful, immensely good-humored, and oddly moving little parable with which to have ended his career as a scientific romancer. The dark years of the Second World War, and the dark years of his long last illness were almost upon him, and his hopes for the race were darkening too. But Wells at his best, Wells as the first authentic genius of science fic-

An original illustration for *When the Sleeper Wakes*, the moment when Graham, the hero, makes his last, impassioned plea for sanity to the population of the world. In its way, this is a drawing of the archetypal Wellsian moment.

tion, had always been a man capable of, driven to, find assertions about life on the very edge of the abyss. And in the measured gaiety of this last romance it is possible to hear the voice of the narrator of *The Time Machine*, arguing still that, if the world *is* doomed, it remains for us to live as if it were not so. And it is possible to hear still in Wells's voice a special tone, a special human pathos, that he himself described most movingly in *When the Sleeper Wakes*. In that early book, Graham, the hero, attempts, in the midst of the world-destroying revolution he causes, to address the citizens of the future world through their massive, intricate radio-telegraph system, to talk them into reason for the sake of their own lives. And as he stands before the giant broadcasting system, Wells describes his frustration, his prophetic energy, and his common humanity in a brief passage:

> He found the thing in his mind too vague for words. He paused momentarily, and broke into vague exhortations, and then a rush of speech came to him. Much that he said was but the humanitarian commonplace of a vanished age, but the conviction of his voice touched it to vitality.

It might be the epigraph—and the epitaph—for all Wells's work. Few men could hope for a better one.

CHRONOLOGY

1866   Herbert George Wells, fourth and last child of Joseph and Sarah Wells, born September 21 in Bromley, Kent.

1881   Enters Midhurst Grammar School.

1880–83   Draper's apprentice in Southsea, with frequent visits to Uppark, Sussex, where his mother is housekeeper.

1883–84   Pupil-teacher at Midhurst Grammar School. In 1884 wins scholarship to the Normal School (later Royal College) of Science, South Kensington.

1884–87   Student at Normal School of Science. Studies under T. H. Huxley. Founds, edits, and writes sketches for the *Science Schools Journal*. Leaves without taking a degree.

1887–89   Begins teaching career, first in North Wales, then in London. Frequent and increasingly serious bouts of illness force him to return periodically to Uppark to recuperate.

1890   Serious hemorrhage and return to Uppark. While there, writes his first major scientific essay, "The Rediscovery of the Unique," which is accepted for publication by the prestigious *Fortnightly Review*.

1891   Marries Isabel Mary Wells, his cousin.

1894   Elopes with his student, Amy Catherine Robbins ("Jane"). By now a popular journalist, he is, in his own words, "writing away for dear life."

1895   *The Time Machine* published, his fame as a writer consolidated. During the next five years he will publish thirteen books, mostly "scientific romances."

1900   Builds Spade House, Folkestone, Kent, where he and Jane live until 1909. Both legitimate sons, George Philip (1901) and Frank Richard (1903) born there.

1903   Joins the Fabian Society, where he almost immediately becomes an obstreperous and divisive presence.

1906   First visit to America. Publication of In the Days of the Comet, with its advocacy of free love, scandalizes many readers and further alienates his Fabian colleagues.

1908   Resigns from the Fabian Society after a bitter feud with its leaders.

1911   Moves to Easton Glebe, Essex, where he will live until 1929.

1912   Meets novelist and critic Rebecca West, with whom he will have an eleven-year liaison.

1914   Outbreak of World War I. Wells, at first a rabid anti-German, later regrets his war fever. Son, Anthony West, born.

1915   Quarrel with Henry James over the nature and use of fiction. Wells increasingly dedicated to writing as social prophecy.

1920   Publication of The Outline of History. Visits Lenin in Russia.

1922–23 Twice stands for House of Commons as Labour Party candidate, and is twice roundly defeated. Disillusionment with Labour Party.

1923   End of affair with Rebecca West. Beginning of affair with Odette Keun, with whom he will live frequently in France until 1933, when the affair ends with great rancor on both sides.

1927   Death of Amy Catherine Wells.

1933   The Shape of Things To Come, his last major science-fiction prophecy, published.

1934   Experiment in Autobiography published. Meets with Josef Stalin and Franklin Delano Roosevelt.

1936   Moves to 13 Hanover Terrace, Regent's Park, London, where he will live until his death. Things To Come, with screenplay by Wells, premieres.

1939   Britain declares war on Germany. Wells near despair at what he sees as the world-suicide of civilization.

1942   Gains his Doctorate in Science.

1945   After use of atomic bomb against Japan, makes plans for a film on dangers of atomic warfare.

1946   H. G. Wells dies August 13. Following his instructions, sons G. P. Wells and Anthony West scatter his ashes over the sea.

CHECKLIST OF WORKS
BY H. G. WELLS

There is no complete edition of Wells's fiction, although there exist two important editions of the work of his early and middle years: *The Atlantic Edition of the Works of H. G. Wells* (London, 1924–28) in twenty-eight volumes, and *The Essex Edition of the Works of H. G. Wells* (London, 1926–27) in twenty-four volumes. The *Atlantic Edition* was a limited printing (1670 copies); Wells himself approved all the texts and contributed new prefaces to the works.

Wells published so much, with so many different publishers, and often (especially in the early years) in such variant versions, that a bibliography of his works can sometimes appear an impossibly tangled thicket. *H. G. Wells: A Comprehensive Bibliography*, published by the H. G. Wells Society (London, 1968), is so far the best guide through the undergrowth. In general, Wells's major science fiction has remained steadily available in any number of low-priced, reliable editions; his best "realistic" novels are somewhat less available, depending on the caprices of publishing; and the rest—including many of the books he took most seriously—are long out of print, available, however, in any reasonably good library.

What follows is a checklist of Wells's works most relevant to his influence on science fiction. It is highly selective, particularly after 1920, just as for Wells himself "scientific romance" became a comparatively secondary outlet for his creative energy after that date. The dates are those of first publication in book form.

1895

The Time Machine: An Invention
The Wonderful Visit
The Stolen Bacillus, and Other Incidents

1896

The Island of Doctor Moreau
The Wheels of Chance: A Cycling Holiday Adventure

1897

The Platter Story, and Others
The Invisible Man, a Grotesque Romance

1898

The War of the Worlds

1899

When the Sleeper Wakes: A Story of Years To Come
Tales of Space and Time

1900

Love and Mr. Lewisham

1901

The First Men in the Moon
*Anticipations of the Reaction of Mechanical and Scientific Progress
    upon Human Life and Thought*

1902

The Discovery of the Future
The Sea Lady: A Tissue of Moonshine

1903

Twelve Stories and a Dream

1904

The Food of the Gods, and How It Came to Earth

1905

A Modern Utopia
Kipps: The Story of a Simple Soul

1906

In the Days of the Comet

1908

New Worlds for Old

The War in the Air, and Particularly How Mr. Bert Smallways Fared
   While It Lasted

1909

Tono-Bungay
Ann Veronica

1910

The History of Mr. Polly

1911

The New Machiavelli
The Country of the Blind and Other Stories

1912

Marriage

1914

The World Set Free: A Story of Mankind

1915

The Research Magnificent
Boon

1916

What Is Coming: A Forecast of Things after the War

1917

War and the Future

1920

The Outline of History

1921

The Salvaging of Civilization

1922

Washington and the Hope of Peace
A Short History of the World

1923

Men Like Gods

1924

The Dream

1926

The World of William Clissold

1927

Democracy Under Revision

1928

The Way the World Is Going
The Open Conspiracy: Blue Prints for a World Revolution

1929

The King Who Was a King: The Book of a Film
The Common Sense of World Peace

1930

The Science of Life: A Summary of Contemporary Knowledge about
    Life and Its Possibilities

1931

What Are We To Do with Our Lives?

1932

The Work, Wealth and Happiness of Mankind

1933

The Shape of Things To Come: The Ultimate Revolution

1934

Experiment in Autobiography: Discoveries and Conclusions of a
    Very Ordinary Brain–Since 1866

1936

Things To Come (screenplay)
The Idea of a World Encyclopaedia

1937

Star Begotten: A Biological Fantasia

1939

The Holy Terror
The Fate of Homo Sapiens

1940

The Common Sense of War and Peace: World Revolution or War
    Unending
All Aboard for Ararat

1941

Guide to the New World: A Handbook of Constructive Revolution

1942

Science and the World-Mind
A Thesis on the Quality of Illusion in the Continuity of the Individ-
    ual Life in the Higher Metazoa, with Particular Reference to the
    Species Homo Sapiens

1945

The Happy Turning: A Dream of Life
Mind at the End of Its Tether

SELECT LIST OF WORKS
ABOUT H. G. WELLS

Aldiss, Brian, *Billion Year Spree* (New York: Shocken Books, 1973). An admirable critical history of science fiction, from Mary Shelley to the present, by a distinguished practitioner and historian of the field. The chapter on Wells is one of the best short essays on the quality of his work and its lasting influence.

Amis, Kingsley, *New Maps of Hell* (London: Victor Gollancz, Ltd., 1961). Amis's book was a milestone in the serious recognition of science fiction. Though his concern is mainly with the sociological implications of science fiction of the 1940s and 1950s, he makes frequent and illuminating reference to the early work of Wells in relation to these later developments.

Bellamy, William, *The Novels of Wells, Bennett, and Galsworthy* (London: Routledge & Kegan Paul, 1971). Bellamy's primary interest is the relationship of Wells's realistic fiction to the work of his two Edwardian contemporaries. But as he analyzes the "Edwardian" quality of Wells's novels, Bellamy also reveals important historical and cultural contexts for the science fiction.

Bergonzi, Bernard, *The Early H. G. Wells* (Manchester: Manchester University Press, 1961). A very important historical and critical study. Bergonzi identifies the debt of Wells to the *fin de siècle* mood of late-nineteenth-century art, and discusses his early science fiction, in that context, with real perceptiveness and authority. A valuable appendix to the book is the complete tale of "The Chronic Argonauts"—the earliest version of what became *The Time Machine*.

————, *H. G. Wells: A Collection of Critical Essays* (Englewood Cliffs, N.J.: Prentice-Hall, Inc., 1976). A very well-chosen collection of essays, most of them recent, on the whole range of Wells's work.

Brooks, Van Wyck, *The World of H. G. Wells* (St. Clair Shores, Mich.: Scholarly Press, 1970). First published in 1915, this is a sympathetic but tough-minded and acute essay on Wells as social analyst and utopian planner. It is valuable as a contemporary response to Wells in one of his most creative phases; and, moreover, many of its perceptions still ring true.

Caudwell, Christopher, *Studies and Further Studies in a Dying Culture* (New York: Monthly Review Press, 1971). "Christopher Caudwell" (Christopher St. John Sprigg) was a brilliant young English Marxist who died in 1937 in the Spanish Civil War. His essay on Wells in *Studies in a Dying Culture* (published in 1938) is a bitter indictment of what he saw as the reactionary, bourgeois sentimentalism of Wells's utopias.

Chesterton, G. K., *Heretics* (New York: John Lane, 1909). Chesterton, the Roman Catholic apologist, was a close friend and friendly adversary of Wells. His essay on *The Food of the Gods* in *Heretics* is a witty and suggestive critique of Wells's utopianism from a conservative, theological point of view—and an interesting counterpoint to Christopher Caudwell's Marxist attack.

Clarke, I. F., *Voices Prophesying War 1763–1984* (New York: Oxford University Press, 1966). An exhaustive survey of European and American fiction about "future war" from the eighteenth century to science fiction of the late fifties. Clarke concentrates particularly on writings preceding the First World War: essential historical and literary background for *The War of the Worlds, The War in the Air*, etcetera.

Dickson, Lovat, *H. G. Wells: His Turbulent Life and Times* (New York: Atheneum, 1969). An affectionate and readable biography, especially good on Wells's often intricate dealings with his publishers, and on the day-to-day business of being a successful writer.

Edel, Leon, and Gordon N. Ray, editors, *Henry James and H. G. Wells* (Urbana: University of Illinois Press, 1958). This is an edition of the letters of James and Wells, largely culled from the massive collection of Wells manuscripts owned by the University of Illinois. It is fascinating reading, since both James and Wells were accomplished and brilliant letter writers; and it is crucial documentation of one of the most significant literary quarrels of the twentieth century.

Gunn, James, *Alternate Worlds: The Illustrated History of Science Fiction* (Englewood Cliffs, N.J.: Prentice-Hall, Inc., 1975). Gunn is a professor of English and a respected scholar and science-fiction writer. But this book, unlike Aldiss's *Billion Year Spree*, is only partially a work of criticism and analysis. It is a lavishly illustrated history of the careers of major science-fiction authors, and of the growth and development of the science-fiction "industry." The chapter on Wells is a fine short summary of his life and career, with some perceptive observations about his importance for the science-fiction genre.

Hillegas, Mark R., *The Future as Nightmare: H. G. Wells and the Anti-Utopians* (New York: Oxford University Press, 1967). A careful and sound academic study that insists that Wells's early work, as distinguished from his later books, *was* anti-utopian: and that it was this Wells who most deeply influenced the mainstream of intellectual science fiction. Most of the book consists in valuable analyses of writers in the "Wells line" like Karel Čapek, Yevgeny Zamiatin, Aldous Huxley, and George Orwell.

Hynes, Samuel, *The Edwardian Turn of Mind* (Princeton: Princeton University Press, 1968). A central, celebrated work of literary, intellectual, and social history. Hynes traces, skillfully and concisely, the main currents of Edwardian thought, and locates Wells—among many other figures—within those currents.

Kagarlitski, J., *The Life and Thought of H. G. Wells* (London: Sidgwick and Jackson, 1966). Kagarlitski is the leading Soviet scholar of Wells, and this critical biography is a sensitive reading of the man from a socialist viewpoint.

MacKenzie, Norman and Jeanne, *The Time Traveller: The Life of H. G. Wells* (London: Weidenfeld and Nicolson, 1973). The definitive biography of Wells. Meticulously researched, detailed, and gracefully written, it is satisfyingly complete both as to the personal details of Wells's life and as to the evolution of his ideas and career as a writer. Essential reading for anyone interested in Wells or in the art of biography.

Parrinder, Patrick, *H. G. Wells* (Edinburgh: Oliver and Boyd, 1970). An informed and articulate study of Wells as novelist.

———, editor, *H. G. Wells: The Critical Heritage* (London: Routledge & Kegan Paul, 1972). An immensely valuable collection of reviews and responses to Wells by his contemporaries, from 1895 to after his death. Many of the pieces Parrinder has assembled here are almost unavailable anywhere else, and they are a fascinating record of the ongoing response to Wells's changing ideas and styles.

Philmus, Robert M., *Into the Unknown: The Evolution of Science Fiction from Francis Godwin to H. G. Wells* (Berkeley: University of California Press, 1970). The derivation of modern science fiction from nineteenth-century romantic traditions of thought has long been a cliché. But Philmus, in this careful work of scholarship, traces that process completely and articulately for almost the first time—and, in doing so, provides crucial background to Wells's early work.

———, and David Y. Hughes, *H. G. Wells: Early Writings in Science and Science Fiction* (Berkeley: University of California Press, 1975). Philmus and Hughes have collected and reprinted a number of Wells's very early scientific sketches and fantasies, and have prefaced them with important essays of their own summarizing his early thought. The book also includes a complete, meticulously catalogued bibliography of all the early journalism, the complete 1894 *National Observer* version of *The Time Machine,* and chapters from the 1895 *New Review* version of the novel.

Pritchett, V. S., *The Living Novel* (New York: Reynal & Hitchcock, 1947). The distinguished English critic and novelist includes, among these brief essays, one on Wells's fiction that remains among the wittiest and fairest estimates of his performance as an artist.

Ray, Gordon N., *H. G. Wells and Rebecca West* (New Haven: Yale University Press, 1974). Dame Rebecca West assisted Ray in this biographical study, allowing him access to her and Wells's letters. It is a sensitive account of their relationship, and of its effect upon Wells's own work.

Scholes, Robert, and Eric S. Rabkin. *Science Fiction: History, Science, Vision* (New York: Oxford University Press, 1977). The best short guide to the genre as a whole, with a brief history of the form, essays on individual classics in the field, and a valuable section on key scientific concepts as they are used by science-fiction writers. The historical section on Wells is yet another acute and resonant estimate of his central and influential position, and there is a good short exegesis of *The Time Machine*.

Suvin, Darko, and Robert M. Philmus, editors, *H. G. Wells and Modern Science Fiction* (Lewisburg, Penn.: Bucknell University Press, 1977). The outgrowth of a 1971 scholarly symposium on Wells, this is a collection of original essays dealing with his central metaphors, his structural influence on later writers, and his bibliography.

West, Anthony, *Principles and Persuasions* (New York: Harcourt Brace, 1957). Novelist and critic West is Wells's son by Rebecca West. This collection of essays includes a touching and revealing personal reminiscence of his father.

West, Geoffrey, *H. G. Wells: A Sketch for a Portrait* (London: Howe, 1930). An early critical biography, written by an unabashed admirer of Wells, and with Wells's assistance.

Williamson, Jack, *H. G. Wells: Critic of Progress* (Baltimore: Mirage Press, 1973). Williamson is a prolific, influential science-fiction writer, with a Ph.D. in English literature. This book is a series of convincing close readings of Wells's major science-fiction novels as cautionary tales about the unbridled growth of technology and technological social control.

INDEX